W9-BBP-224

DATE DUE			

WRITERS AND POLITICS IN WEST GERMANY

K. Stuart Parkes

ST. MARTIN'S PRESS
New York

©K.S. Parkes, 1986
All rights reserved. For information, write:
Scholarly & Reference Division,
St. Martin's Press, Inc., 175 Fifth Avenue, New York, NY 10010
First published in the United States of America in 1986
Printed in Great Britain

Library of Congress Cataloging-in-Publication Data

Parkes, K. Stuart, 1943-
Writers and politics in West Germany.

Bibliography: p.
Includes index.
1. Authors, German – 20th century – Political and
social views. 2. Authors, German – Germany (West) –
Political and social views. 3. German literature –
Germany (West) – History and criticism. 4. German
literature – 20th century – History and criticism.
5. Germany (West) – Politics and government. I. Title.
PT405.P34   1986   830'.9'358   86-13900
ISBN 0-312-89347-7

CONTENTS

ACKNOWLEDGEMENTS

I should like to thank the following people and institutions for their help:

- for financial assistance: The German Academic Exchange Service, The British Academy;
- for assistance with facilities and materials: The National Literary Archive of the Federal Republic in Marbach, The Friedrich Ebert Foundation (particularly for permission to refer to archive material), The Social Democratic Party of Germany, The Christian Democratic Union;
- for information and comment: Professor Walter Jens (University of Tübingen), Professor Kurt Sontheimer (University of Munich), Frau Heinke Jaedicke of the Sozialdemokratische Wählerinitiative, Dr Martin Walser;
- for support and advice in Sheffield: Professor J. M. Ritchie (University of Sheffield), Dr Ian King of my own institution, who undertook the important task of reading and commenting on drafts, Miss Barbara Russell, who typed the manuscript, Miss Nikki Walters, who saved the author time by helping with secretarial tasks.

The support of my family goes without saying.

Stuart Parkes
Sheffield City Polytechnic

INTRODUCTION

Why writers and politics? Would it not be equally legitimate to investigate 'writers and cooking' or 'writers and gardening', as both these might well be areas in which many writers take an interest? The shortest answer would be to quote George Orwell, who in his essay 'Why I Write' sees politics as anything but peripheral to the task of the writer. His simple claim is that 'no book is genuinely free from political bias. The opinion that art should have nothing to do with politics is itself a political attitude.'[1] It is also generally held that writers belong to the social group known as intellectuals, who in turn are frequently identified by their concern for social and political questions. Whilst it hardly needs saying that not everybody who writes is an intellectual, this book on German writers and politics will be concerned with those authors whose stance can generally be associated with that of the intellectual.

This last statement begs at least two questions: 'What is an intellectual?' and 'What is his or her situation in society?' Both questions have attracted considerable attention, particularly among American social scientists. It is generally accepted that an intellectual is not simply someone who has attained a certain level of academic achievement. For Seymour Martin Lipset intellectuals are 'all those who create, distribute and apply *culture*, that is, the symbolic world of man, including art, science and religion.'[2] The common denominator in all attempts at definition is that intellectuals are characterised by a certain detached, critical position in the society in which they live. Lewis A. Coser writes: 'Intellect . . . presumes a capacity for detachment from immediate experience, a moving beyond pragmatic tasks of the moment, a commitment to comprehensive values transcending professional or occupational involvement.'[3] A non-American reinforcement of this claim is Ortega y Gasset's statement: 'The world the intellectual finds seems to him to exist for the very purpose of being questioned.'[4] The concept of detachment does not of course answer the question of what it means if intellectuals involve themselves directly in society, as a certain Henry A. Kissinger did, or if a writer accepts a political appointment, as André Malraux did under de Gaulle. Indeed, for Noam Chomsky at the time of the Vietnam War intellectuals were

1

not so much detached but rather part of established American society, with the result that they could not fulfil their proper function, namely 'to speak the truth and to expose lies'.[5] Suffice it to say that the question of how far intellectuals occupy or should occupy the position of 'insider' or 'outsider' in society remains a major issue in the debate.

If it is assumed for the moment that the intellectual occupies some position of critical detachment *vis-à-vis* society, the question then arises of what his or her exact role is. That there is a gap between, for example, the world of the intellectual and that of the practising politician is generally taken for granted. It is not always, however, seen as a source of tension. Professor Max Beloff, whilst admitting of a potential gap between the practical world of the politician and that of intellectual utopias, sees the possibility of co-operation between intellectuals and politicians. It is the task of the intellectual to 'make himself the voice of the inchoate and confused and complex aspirations of the society of which he forms part',[6] a voice that the politician should then heed in his legislative task. The ultimate policy that will arise according to Beloff from this kind of divided labour will be characterised by compromise, something that is inevitable given the nature of human society. This model rather leaves out the question of how far the intellectual will or should accept compromises. Mutual suspicion between politician and intellectual, with the one stressing the moral and the utopian and the other restricting himself to purely pragmatic considerations, would seem to be just as likely an outcome as an acceptance of complementary roles. In short, Beloff's ideal of compromise seems utopian iself.

One solution to this problem is to accept that the gap between intellectual and politician is inevitable and even welcome. This is more or less the position of Theodor Geiger in his book *Aufgaben und Stellung der Intelligenz in der Gesellschaft* (Tasks and position of the intelligentsia in society) and of the more well-known *La Trahison des clercs* (The betrayal of the intellectuals) by Julien Benda. Geiger believes that the intellectual should stick to a critical stance rather than seeking alignment with any political force:

> The intelligentsia cannot structure political activity and in this way help direct the course of events, because power will always follow the goals of its own will. The intelligentsia must not within its own sphere of professional activity submit to political

power, because in this way it would offend against intellectual substance and betray its profession.[7]

The betrayal Benda refers to is the intellectual attaching himself to a particular cause or ideology, be it of the left or the right. He should rather be concerned with the universal and theoretical, performing almost the function of society's conscience. More concretely, Geiger speaks of the intellectual restraining the misuse of political power by awakening general suspicion towards power, which is seen, not surprisingly given the time the book was written, as essentially corrupting. The major objection to the theses of Geiger and Benda must be that they rest on the assumption that those criticised will allow their intellectual antagonists to pursue their task without interference. It is one thing to say, as Professor Ralf Dahrendorf did in 1963, that it is the job of the intellectual as a modern court-jester to doubt and call into question traditional beliefs and authorities;[8] another to ensure that conditions prevail in which this is possible. History suggests that the stances of Geiger and Benda are somewhat over-idealistic. The other extreme, which might well be more undesirable, would be for intellectuals to be mere apologists for a particular political faction or ideology. There is much to be said for the alternative suggested by Anthony Arblaster that intellectuals should combine 'detachment and commitment',[9] although this may well be easier in theory than in practice.

Whatever the differences of emphasis, most of the discussion relating to the role and status of intellectuals summarised above implies to some degree a positive attitude towards them, a standpoint exemplified in Coser's claim that through their questioning intellectuals preserve a culture from dying. Equally affirmative are the comments by Karl Mannheim in his book *Ideology and Utopia*. This introduction to the 'Sociology of Knowledge' centres especially around the proposition that knowledge is not absolute and that the world is in constant need of re-interpretation. It is the function of the intellectuals to fulfil this need; they are described in such glowing terms as the 'watchmen in what otherwise would be a pitch-black night',[10] as the group 'in which the perspective and interest of the whole is safeguarded'.[11] By contrast, Joseph A. Schumpeter in his *Capitalism, Socialism and Democracy*, appears to see them, despite his claim to be only analysing objective social processes, in an almost wholly negative light. He speaks of 'the absence of direct responsibility for practical affairs'[12] and of intellectuals being a growing force for the subversion of bourgeois society which, because of its liberal nature, is powerless against them. Because of their marginal status they must 'flatter, promise and incite',[13] in short be generally disagreeable.

Schumpeter's negative vision is of a growing left-wing academic proletariat in the vanguard of a march into socialism. What Schumpeter ignores is that many intellectuals have taken up and continue to take up stances that are far from left-wing; as for the concept of an academic proletariat, it is worth pointing out that when intellectuals did apparently indulge in revolutionary activity in the 1960s, it was at a time of prosperity and full employment, not least for them. He also assumes that intellectuals enjoy if not an influence to create events, at least the ability to mould them, a proposition that is difficult to prove.

It is not the intention now to provide a single synthesis of truth out of all the views referred to above. The intention was to show some of the parameters of the task this book on German writers sets itself, particularly to point to the range of discussion on such subjects as the relationship between intellectual activity and the world of official politics. The general conclusion that can be drawn is that it is not only a legitimate activity for writers and intellectuals to concern themselves with politics, but also that the relationship is subject to particular tensions because of their essentially critical role. Such a conclusion does not include the view that they should embrace a particular political standpoint. Again, Orwell is very direct:

> Today, for example, one can imagine a good book being written by a Catholic, a Communist, a Fascist, a pacifist, an anarchist, perhaps by an old-style Liberal or an ordinary Conservative: one cannot imagine a good book being written by a spiritualist, a Buchmanite or a member of the Ku-Klux-Klan. The views that a writer holds must be compatible with sanity, in the medical sense, and with the power of continuous thought.[14]

It might well be possible to argue with Orwell over where to draw the line; nevertheless, it is intended here to follow him in the general point about plurality. Emphasis will be put on what writers say, what they intend by their political comment — something easier to discern than any influence they subsequently had — and how and in what context they make their remarks, which means not just an examination of style but the measuring of their views against political reality.

There remains the German context. It may well be that the subject of writers and politics can be justified in relation to any culture but, in the case of Germany, it has a particular piquancy. It is not too much of a generalisation to say that the relationships between writers and the world of politics in Germany have traditionally been extremely bad. Before the creation of a unified German state in 1871, writers were frequently at the mercy of brutish princelings whose desire to emulate Versailles did not extend to the cultural sphere. That celebrated 'enlightened' despot of the eighteenth century, Frederick the Great of Prussia, had no time for either the German language or German culture. In the same century it was not uncommon for critical writers to end up in prison, as Christian Dietrich Schubart did for ten years in the State of Württemberg after expressing his sympathy for the American Revolution. Even being in the service of a ruler, as Lessing discovered as a librarian in Wolfenbüttel, was often only one step up from prison. Despite Goethe's ministerial career in Weimar, a relatively enlightened dukedom, it is difficult to disagree with the claim made by the writer Hans Christoph Buch in 1978: 'Goethe and Beethoven became classical artists not because of but in spite of Germany. Other less fortunate spirits were destroyed by conditions in Germany.'[15] Two writers of the early nineteenth century, the poet Hölderlin and the dramatist Kleist, come immediately to mind as examples of Buch's second category. In the light of these tensions, it became commonplace in Germany to speak of a dichotomy between the world of the intellect *Geist* and that of politics or power *Macht*. The two terms have remained opposites until today in many people's perception of the relationship between writers and politics in Germany. By contrast, whether rightly or wrongly need not concern us here, France is regarded by many Germans, not least by many writers, as the country where rulers have generally respected men of letters and taken notice of intellectual opinion on political issues.

Given that German writers were largely excluded from politics, it is not surprising that many developed what may be regarded as essentially non-political attitudes. It is true that many writers in Germany welcomed the French Revolution, but the major literary movements of the following two decades owed little to its ideals.

Both the Weimar Classicism of Goethe and Schiller, which propagated 'aesthetic education' and moral utopias, and German
Romanticism, whose revolutionary zeal was restricted to the cultural sphere and which in part aligned itself to the nationalistic
cause of the Wars of Liberation against Napoleon, failed to put
democracy high on their agenda. Later in the nineteenth century
writers like Georg Büchner and Heinrich Heine, who supported the
demands for freedom that culminated in the abortive 1848 revolution and suffered for their beliefs, tended to be exceptions. Many
Germans preferred to take comfort in Madame de Staël's flattering
view that Germany was 'the land of poets and thinkers'. At the end
of the century too, Gerhart Hauptmann, whose early dramas show
the sufferings created by the Industrial Revolution, soon turned to
writing plays that transcended naturalism in favour of neo-
romantic mysticism. Germany did not produce a counterpart to
Emile Zola, whose involvement in the Dreyfus Affair set a new
standard of intellectual commitment.

   The dual tradition among German writers in their attitudes to
politics was no more apparent than in the differing attitudes of the
Mann brothers, Heinrich and Thomas, at the time of the First
World War. Whereas the democrat Heinrich found himself at odds
with his country, Thomas rallied to the German cause, invoking
Frederick the Great and saying that it was necessary to defend
German 'culture' against the mere 'civilisation' of the French. It is
significant that his rejection of Western democratic values is found
in a series of political writings of this time with the title *Betrach-
tungen eines Unpolitischen* (Reflections of a Non-political Man).
By contrast, in 1910, Heinrich had favourably contrasted Voltaire
with Goethe. Whilst showing some sympathy for Goethe's predicament in the Germany of his day, he concludes: 'His work, his
memory, his name have changed nothing in Germany, not eradicated any inhumanity, not paved an inch of way towards a better
time.'[16]

   When democracy finally arrived with the Weimar Republic
Thomas Mann changed his political stance. The strength of his new
democratic convictions has been disputed; nevertheless, they
earned him in certain quarters the title of *praeceptor Germaniae*
(teacher of Germany). Other writers on the left of the political spectrum, however, were less than happy with the democracy of
Weimar. Brother Heinrich too saw no reason to believe that *Geist*
and *Macht* in the form of the state were anything other than

opposites. In his speech at the opening of the Prussian Academy of Arts in 1928, he said:

> We call intellect the human ability to pursue truth regardless of weal or woe and to strive for justice even against the dictates of practical reason. The state, on the other hand, represents human nature just to that extent that it seeks advantage and for its sake also accepts what is bad.[17]

Whether this distinction was justified even in the admittedly flawed democracy of Weimar could be open to question. What is beyond dispute is that the next German state totally abused power, dealing with its opponents from the world of the intellect — and not just them — with unsurpassed brutality.

Given this period of barbarity and the besmirching of the German name, it was only to be expected that once the nightmare ended many writers would begin to rethink their position in society, to decide that it was impossible to ignore the world of politics. As Dieter Lattmann, a writer who became a member of parliament in the 1970s, puts it in the form of a rhetorical question: 'For where were the German writers who after the thousand-year *Reich* could still afford to say that politics did not concern them?'[18] Conversely, the politicians could not entirely ignore writers. Literature was prospectively a means through which the German name, sullied by National Socialism, could be dragged out of the mud. It is the intention of this book to examine how writers reacted in this challenging situation, in particular to look at those writers, probably the majority and certainly the most famous, who have broken with the non-political German tradition to reassert the notion of the political being an integral part of literary life.

Finally, a few words on more technical aspects of the project are needed. Its shape is visible from the list of contents and does not need further explanation. What does need to be explained is the question of who is to be understood under the term 'writer'. In general, I have concentrated on writers whose fame is based on their achievements in the sphere of literary fiction. At the same time, it has been impossible to exclude people who might more accurately be called primarily academics, journalists or, to use a term common in Germany, publicists. In other words, the term 'writer' is flexible. The same is true of the kinds of writings that form so to speak the raw materials used. Because they are more overtly political, manifestos, speeches, essays and the like have provided the major source material. Nevertheless, to omit all reference to fictional works and to the development of literature in the period covered would have been unduly restrictive and made the treatment of the topic excessively one-sided. There is one further area where it has proved impossible to be clear cut. In general, I am writing about West Germany, not least because the nature of that state, the organisation of the literary market and with it the mass media, make possible the open intervention of writers — and others — in political discussion. To have extended the inquiry to the German Democratic Republic would have meant examining a very different social order, where the role of the writer and intellectual is played out under different rules. At the same time, writers have moved from one German state to the other, there have been areas of common concern which cannot be overlooked, hence the need to refer to East German writers. A more detailed study of their part in political processes would, however, require another work of no doubt similar proportions to the present one. A final word on translations. Where possible I have used existing English translations, as the footnotes will make clear. Otherwise, translations are my own, and in the case of titles, mine have small letters.

Notes

1. G. Orwell, *Collected Essays* (Secker & Warburg, London, 1961), p. 438.
2. S. M. Lipset, *Political Man* (Mercury Books, London, 1963), p. 311.
3. L. A. Coser, *Men of Ideas* (The Free Press, New York and London, 1965), p. viii.
4. Ortega y Gasset, 'Der Intellektuelle und der Andere' in W. Bergsdorf (ed.), *Die Intellektuellen* (Neske, Pfullingen, 1982), p. 23.
5. N. Chomsky, *American Power and the New Mandarins* (Chatto & Windus, London, 1969), p. 257.
6. M. Beloff, *The Intellectual in Politics and Other Essays* (Weidenfeld & Nicolson, London, 1970), p. 13.
7. T. Geiger, *Aufgaben und Stellung der Intelligenz in der Gesellschaft* (Ferdinand Enke Verlag, Stuttgart, 1949), p. 71.
8. R. Dahrendorf, 'Der Intellektuelle und die Gesellschaft', *Die Zeit*, no. 13, 29 Mar. 63.
9. A. Arblaster, 'Ideology and Intellectuals' in R. Benewick, R. N. Berki, B. Parekh (eds), *Knowledge and Belief in Politics* (George Allen & Unwin, London, 1973), p. 128.
10. K. Mannheim, *Ideology and Utopia* (Routledge & Kegan Paul, London, 1968), p. 143.
11. Ibid., p. 144.
12. J. A. Schumpeter, *Capitalism, Socialism and Democracy* (Unwin University

Books, London, 1970), p. 147.
  13. Ibid., p. 154.
  14. Orwell, *Collected Essays*, p. 414.
  15. H. C., Buch, 'Deutschland, eine Winterreise', *Der Spiegel*, no. 11, 13 Mar. 78, 142.
  16. H. Mann, *Essays* (Claasen, Hamburg, 1960), p. 20.
  17. Ibid., p. 299.
  18. D. Lattmann, 'Schriftsteller in der Wohlstandsgesellschaft' in W. Kuttenkeuler (ed.), *Poesie und Politik* (Kohlhammer, Stuttgart, 1973), p. 395.

PART ONE:
CAUSES

1 MANY CALL BUT NONE ARE CHOSEN — THE POST-WAR YEARS

Nowadays it is only with a certain degree of embarrassment that one can commence any investigation of recent developments in Germany at the seemingly appropriate date of 1945, as it has frequently been shown that any talk of 'year zero', be it in economics, politics or literature, is ultimately impossible. What is more, the choice of such a starting-point might seem a contribution to the myth, already implied by the word 'zero', that everything and everybody started anew from the same line in 1945 and that the road to achievement was equally open to all. In reality, there was no economic equality, with much of the burden falling on those who saw their money rendered worthless after the war. As for politics, it was the politicians of the Weimar era, seen by a younger generation as the tired failures of a bygone era, that were to assume prominence in the Federal Republic, whilst in the arts and literature, the careers of many of those who had published before 1945, be it in exile or within Germany, did not come to a close — not even those who had compromised with Nazi ideology.

Nevertheless, starting this study at 1945 can be justified if the above is borne in mind, and if it is remembered that many younger writers and intellectuals did themselves believe that there was a possibility for a radical new beginning once the tyranny of National Socialism had been thrown off. It is now clear that no such change occurred, as many writers realised by the end of the decade. In the 1950s, the pejoratively used term 'restoration' became current to describe what happened; whatever its objective merits, it clearly reflects the frustrations of post-war reformers. It is the intention of this chapter to show the aspirations of the younger generation of writers and to suggest reasons why they were not fulfilled. Again, an introductory note of caution would seem appropriate. It is wrong to believe that great numbers of mainly young people, stung by the betrayal of their youth by the lies of National Socialism, launched into a frenzy of radical political and literary activity. Such people did exist, but met with much passivity among their fellow citizens. What is more, their activities did not reflect any single ideology or purpose. Both coming to terms with the past and plotting a future for Germany provided significant subjects for debate.

An early controversy was that between those who had emigrated in the face of the Nazi dictatorship and those who had remained in Germany, many of whom claimed to have lived in 'inner emigration', that is to say a state of mental and moral alienation from the horrific events taking place around them. How far such an existence can have been possible remains even now a matter of controversy, which cannot be resolved here. Suffice it to say that Alfred Andersch, one of the editors of the periodical *Der Ruf* (The call), wrote in 1947 that the only German literature worthy of the name written between 1933 and 1945 was that of the emigration.[1] Nevertheless, those writers who had gone into emigration were unable after the war to re-establish themselves as the representatives of a better Germany — at least in the Western zones. The situation was very different in the Soviet zone, where former émigrés were encouraged to return and, given the right political credentials, achieve positions of prominence. The poet Johannes R. Becher, for instance, became the Minister of Culture in the German Democratic Republic, whilst Brecht was able to found his Berliner Ensemble. Heinrich Mann too was about to return to the East to become president of the Academy of Arts when he died. However fraught the relationships of Brecht and some other émigré figures may have been at times with Stalinist bureaucracy, they remained the dominant figures on the literary scene of the eastern part of Germany.

In the west, émigrés did not enjoy a similar status. This was not only the case with writers. Well into the 1960s a politician like Willy Brandt had to suffer the jibe that by leaving his country, he had somehow betrayed it in its hour of need; presumably, he should have stayed to be executed. In the literary field much of the controversy surrounded Thomas Mann, who had been a regular broadcaster against National Socialism and whose novel *Doktor Faustus*, published in 1947, was at least in part a critical evaluation of the unhappy and problematical course of German history and culture. It was as early as the first months after the war that Mann especially, and émigrés in general, found themselves the object of hostile criticism.

The essence of this criticism is contained in a juxtaposition of inner emigration and geographical emigration by the novelist Frank Thiess, who had remained in Germany and lived between conflict and compromise with the Nazis. In August 1945 he spoke of émigrés viewing the German tragedy 'from the vantage point of abroad, in the pit seats and boxes'.[2] In as far as this implies that émigrés generally enjoyed material comforts, it contrasts sharply with the picture of emigration in Paris and its financial uncertainties, as portrayed by Lion Feuchtwanger in his novel *Exil*. Moreover, the abstract idealistic language used by Thiess raises doubts about his arguments:

> I, too, have been often asked why I did not emigrate and could only always give the same answer: that if I were to succeed in surviving this dreadful epoch . . . I would have gained thereby so much for my mental and human development that I would emerge from it richer in knowledge and experience.[3]

Thiess's comments followed an open letter from another writer, Walter von Molo, urging Thomas Mann to return to Germany. When Mann refused, and added that all books published in Germany between 1933 and 1945 carried the stench of blood and shame, the stage was set for a vitriolic exchange, with Mann being accused by Thiess of hatred of Germany. This criticism was repeated by the critic Friedrich Sieburg in 1949 in an article entitled 'Frieden mit Thomas Mann' (Peace with Thomas Mann).[4] To be fair, the article is not entirely hostile to Mann but seeks rather to separate Mann the artist, whose genius is acknowledged, from the political writer, whose comments are condemned out of hand. This is possibly the major interest in the article, the clear separation of the literary and the political that was to be typical for the 1950s in conservative literary circles. Sieburg became a leading critic of this era, generally viewing the emergence of post-war writers like Günter Grass and Martin Walser with little sympathy. It is also significant that Sieburg, a man who had compromised with the Nazis, could regain a position of prominence.[5]

As to the specific argument surrounding Thomas Mann and the whole question of emigration, what matters here is less the rights and wrongs of the case than the fact that public consciousness turned against the émigrés, so that by the end of the 1940s few publishers were willing to consider their works for the simple reason that there was no longer a market. Those whom tyranny had forced to leave the country were unable to establish themselves as the leaders of a new Germany. The same also became true of the young writers whose careers generally began after the war and who form the main subject of this chapter. That the two developments are linked can be seen from the way they saw themselves as the potential allies of the exiles. Their appeals are framed very differently from those of Thiess and von Molo. When Alfred Andersch appealed in *Der Ruf* in 1947 to university teachers to return, it was to help with the task of making education more democratic and ending middle-class privilege, not to do with sharing some existential German destiny of suffering, as Thiess and von Molo had in mind for Thomas Mann.

When talking of the new generation of writers after the war, it is normal to claim that the political and moral bankruptcy of Nazi Germany in 1945 led such people to proclaim that a new kind of literature and a new kind of writer were required. Given the fate of Germany and the frequently non-political tradition of German literature, it was now necessary for writers to involve themselves directly with politics and to help forge a new democratic Germany. In this context it is usual to cite the number of new political and literary magazines that came into being and mention particularly *Der Ruf*, the publication of young writers and intellectuals whose aggressively radical stance caused it to fall foul of the American occupation authorities. Then, out of the death of *Der Ruf*, there arose the literary group of generally non-conformist writers, the Gruppe 47, whose members were to dominate West German literary life for the next twenty years, and whose general stance made it into a kind of, at least, cultural opposition against the conservative Christian Democrat government of Dr Adenauer. Such a conception of post-war developments whilst not incorrect, is, as one might expect, an over-simplification. It does not take into account that the various publications, even if they did talk of the necessity of a new beginning in Germany, reflected various opinions about what form it should take, some of which differed considerably from the democratic socialism propounded by the authors of *Der Ruf*. What is more, it was not only a new generation that raised its voice, but also older writers who had stayed in Germany in some degree of opposition to the Nazi regime. Whilst in no sense fascistoid — it was too early immediately after the war for former Nazis or sympathisers, either writers or members of any other profession, to start making loud excuses — some of these writers represented anything but a radical or socialist tradition.

One member of such an older generation of writers was Ernst

Wiechert. He had in fact spent two months in Buchenwald because of his support for Pastor Niemöller, an experience reflected in his book *Der Totenwald* (The Forest of the Dead) that appeared in 1945. His hope for the future lay in a moral regeneration of German youth based on the humanistic values of Goethe and Weimar Classicism. He rejected any idea of a new start, claiming that cultures, religions and languages were like slowly growing trees that could only provide shade after centuries had elapsed. He wished rather to regenerate what he saw as the traditional German qualities of kindness, wisdom, tolerance and humanity as a counterbalance to a world increasingly enveloped in darkness.[6] However worthy such sentiments were, it is not surprising to find a parody of them in *Der Ruf* with the title '500 Rede an die deutsche Jugend. Eine Parodie frei nach Ernst Wiechert' (500th speech to German youth. A parody in the style of Ernst Wiechert).[7] Similarly idealistic are the views of Marie Luise Kaschnitz, whose literary career like that of Wiechert dated back to the Weimar Republic. She too stressed the positive qualities of nature and love, and urged men to abandon the search for power.[8]

Just as it is impossible to report all the views expressed in the aftermath of the war, it is equally impossible to refer to all the political and literary magazines that came into being at that time. A look into the catalogue of the exhibition Als der Krieg zu Ende war (When the war was over), held at the Federal Republic's National Literature Archive in Marbach in the early 1970s shows that these appeared literally in dozens, especially if all the zones of occupation and publications produced by the Allies themselves are taken into account. Their titles reveal something of the mood of the time, for example *Neues Europa* (New Europe), *Die Wandlung* (Transformation) and *Die Besinnung* (Reflection). However ephemeral some of them were, others survived to become an integral part of the political and cultural scene of the Federal Republic, for example *Merkur* and *Frankfurter Hefte* (Mercury, Frankfurt Journal).

Nearly all the magazines show the desire for changes after the horrors of the immediate past, but at the same time reflect the considerable differences of emphasis already referred to. *Die Gegenwart* (The present), which started publication in Freiburg in the French zone, sought to continue the traditions of the originally liberal *Frankfurter Zeitung*, the forerunner of today's *Frankfurter Allgemeine Zeitung*, often considered as the nearest equivalent

Germany's regional-based press allows to *The Times*. The *Frankfurter Zeitung* had continued publication with a limited degree of independence after 1933, but had ceased to appear during the war. The word that seems to characterise the early editions of *Die Gegenwart* is *wahrhaftig* (truthful). It seeks to look at the contemporary world from such a standpoint, whilst in its discussion of the concept of the 'collective guilt' of the German people for the atrocities of National Socialism, as propounded by the Allies at the end of the war, it rejects a crude external condemnation of all things German in favour of a collective and individual examination of conscience by the German people themselves, as the basis of a new beginning based on a spirit of 'absolute truthfulness'. In common with other periodicals of the time, it is sceptical about all political ideologies. This is apparent from a report on East Berlin, dating from the autumn of 1949.[9] Commenting on propaganda demanding the 'ruthless extermination of all agents and spies', it notes that extermination is the method used by all systems that cannot convert everyone to their point of view. The views expressed are a forerunner of the totalitarianism theories of the 1950s and 60s, which equated Nazi and communist tyranny. The economic views of *Die Gegenwart* — the need to reconcile true personal freedom with the well-being of the community — seem a forerunner of the concept of the 'social market economy', as propounded and practised in the 1950s and 60s in the era of the 'economic miracle'. In its beginnings, however, *Die Gegenwart* is primarily concerned with moral renewal: thus Ernst Wiechert is said to have saved his soul by writing *Der Totenwald*, part of which is reprinted in an early edition of the magazine. *Merkur* — subtitled a 'German Periodical for European Thought' — is similar in tone to *Die Gegenwart*. There is again the rejection of all one-sided ideology and stress on the need to preserve the lasting values of the past in any new political order.

Frankfurter Hefte, which first appeared in April 1946, sought to come to terms with the past and influence the future from a Christian or, to be more exact, a radical Catholic standpoint. One of its editors, Eugen Kogon, had been a prisoner in Buchenwald; his book *Der SS-Staat* (The SS-State), which was first published in 1946, remains a classic. The first number of *Frankfurter Hefte* states that its viewpoint is to be determined by Christian conscience, although this should not be taken to mean in any sense withdrawal from the real world. In political terms this meant the reconciliation of Christianity and socialism. In the third edition of the magazine, K. H. Knappstein begins his leading article:

> The Christians of this age are called to participate actively in the realisation of the almost a century old longing of the workers' movement for a humane social order and thus make good the failure of earlier generations of Christians . . . The historical goal of the workers' movement remains today what it has always been: socialism.[10]

Similarly, in the same year, Kogon's co-editor Walter Dirks seeks to reconcile the two concepts 'right' and 'left' and sees Christian attitudes combining both poles.[11] The Christian is of the right in that he owes much to tradition but is left-wing in his desire to change the world and work towards a condition of harmony and happiness. *Frankfurter Hefte* in its early numbers reflects prevalent Christian attitudes of the time, which also motivated some of the early statements of the new Christian Democratic Union (CDU), in particular the Ahlen Programme, which speaks of the party being anti-capitalist and anti-Marxist. It was not, however, this strain of CDU thinking that came into power with the first Chancellor Konrad Adenauer and his Economics Minister Ludwig Erhard. Hence, it is not surprising that the radical Catholics associated with *Frankfurter Hefte* began to look more towards the Social Democratic Party (SPD) in the 1960s and 70s. Another major theme of the magazine in its early years, not surprisingly, is the recent past, in any case a major topic for Christians at the time. In the first edition, Kogon, whilst recognising that the 'collective guilt' theory and the idea of re-education as practised by the Allies have not achieved their aims of changing the consciousness of the Germans, asks individuals to look at their own consciences. Taking the anti-Hitler conspirators of 20 July 1944 as models, he wants the Germans to judge themselves so that they need not fear any other judge. Only in this way does he see the possibility of renewal in Germany.

Frankfurter Hefte followed its original principles for nigh on forty years, remarkably under the same editors. In 1951 Karl Wilhelm Böttcher was noting with regret that the young West German State was pursuing other goals than those of equality and justice, and that the differences between rich and poor were increasing.[12] Some thirty years later, in the first edition of 1984, the magazine was considering the question of the relationship between the Sermon on the Mount and practical politics, a topic raised by the Peace Movement. In Walter Dirks' view the Sermon was not just a set of absolute demands, but rather could help point the way, provided political realities were taken into account, towards a reduction in armaments and towards peace. Unfortunately, the magazine was forced to cease independent publication later in the same year for financial reasons, with Dirks and Kogon sadly reflecting that from the beginning they had under-estimated the forces resisting change.

It is now time to turn to *Der Ruf*, the most celebrated of the post-war magazines. Although a periodical of the same name had first been produced by largely the same people when they were American prisoners of war, the real history of *Der Ruf* begins with the first independent edition of 15 August 1946. It comes to an end after sixteen issues following the intervention of the American zonal authorities in April 1947, even though the magazine lived on in name under new editors until 1949. The importance of *Der Ruf* is not based solely on the subsequent fame of Alfred Andersch and Hans Werner Richter, from edition number four named as its editors, who both became leading writers in the Federal Republic and, in the case of Richter, the convenor of the Gruppe 47. *Der Ruf* is significant because of its circulation, which reached 100,000, and because of the ideas put forward in the magazine. These, at least in the area of politics, were to remain dominant among radical intellectuals, in many cases for over a decade.

In a nutshell, the political aspirations of most of the writers of *Der Ruf* can be summed up as a free socialist Germany and Europe. Free implies not only the rejection of Nazism but also dislike of the Soviet model of socialism. In the first issue, in one of the magazine's most celebrated articles, 'Das junge Europa formt sein Gesicht' (Young Europe takes on its complexion) Alfred Andersch says that if there ever were to be a choice between socialism and freedom, freedom would have to take precedence. It is less easy to categorise what the writers of *Der Ruf* meant by socialism, given their rejection of Marxist-Leninist ideology. In the same article Andersch differentiates between socialism and social reform, and speaks of a planned economy and the acceptance of technology. In general, however, there is little in *Der Ruf* about the organisation of the economy. What there is often seems abstract and idealistic. Walter Manzen, in an article based on the Marxist concept of

alienation 'Die Selbstentfremdung des Menschen' (The self-aliena-
tion of man) rejects the market and the criterion of profit in favour
of planning, but also sees dangers in a centralised planned
economy. He asks that every economic policy should be judged by
whether it contributes to human fulfilment. As for the idea of
Europe, this is made clear in an article by Richter: 'Churchill und
die europäische Einheit' (Churchill and European Unity). Richter
rejects what he sees as the Churchillian concept of Europe, based
on a capitalist system and having the role of a bulwark against the
Soviet Union. Instead, he claims that the new Europe will have to
be socialist. 'This new Europe, however, will be socialist or it will
not be.'[13] Nor does he accept the need for defence based on nuclear
weapons, but sees political friendship as the means to combat
uncertainty. Furthermore, Richter sees the policy of splitting and
dividing Germany back to something like the pre-1871 position as
incompatible with European unity. This raises the question of the
future shape of Germany, something that was vital to the writers of
Der Ruf. The ideal was a single German state that should act as a
bridge between East and West. In an article with this title,
'Deutschland — Brücke zwischen Ost und West', Richter states
that Germany — in 1946 without a state or an economic system —
can begin anew and, by observing both the Eastern and Western
systems on its territory in the shape of the occupying powers, can
avoid the mistakes of both and create a kind of synthesis. In this
way Germany's geographical position between East and West
would be complemented in the political sphere. Such hopes, it
hardly needs saying, were doomed to be dashed.

The sub-title of *Der Ruf* was 'Unabhängige Blätter für die junge
Generation' (Independent writings for the young generation). This
sub-title not only reflects the illusory belief that the post-war years
presented the opportunity for a new generation to rebuild Germany
from the beginning, it also implies a certain political attitude, along
with a concern for the affairs of youth. The political attitude, as
has been implied already, is one of hostility towards all political
ideologies. This lack of theory has been criticised subsequently, but
is easily explained by the contributors' personal experience of
fascism and the similarly unacceptable face of Stalinism. In fact,
the rejection of ideology was to remain a constant feature of
West German intellectual life until the student movement of the
1960s and the re-birth of interest in Marx. In the post-war period
this standpoint was reflected in the sceptical view taken of the

re-emerging political parties, which were seen as too bound by ideology. This distance from the parties, which as institutions were to have a central role in the re-creation of political life in the Western zones, can legitimately be seen as misguided and unrealistic. For the writers of *Der Ruf*, however, the parties were in the hands of an old generation who had learned nothing from the past. Richter's 'Parteipolitik und Weltanschauung' (Party politics and world view) sees German politics as traditionally motivated by parties' desires to impose their own particular world view, which in turn has led to tragedy. He fears that the post-war parties are about to make the same mistake. Elsewhere, he says that rather than such parties, what is required is 'the creation of a large community of practical socialists, who join together in a climate of intellectual tolerance'.[14] In a similar vein, Andersch speaks of leadership being assumed by a ' "heimatlosen" Linken' (a homeless left) outside the parties. This term, particularly in the 1950s, came to be used pejoratively by right-wing critics of those intellectuals who were at odds with developments in the Federal Republic. Here though, it refers to a hope for the future which was and could not be realised.

The problems of a youth at odds with all political ideologies form a major concern of *Der Ruf*. As early as the second issue Richter asks: 'Warum schweigt die junge Generation?' (Why is the young generation silent?) The reason advanced is that young people, because of their previous experiences, are immune to all propaganda of the type still being employed by conventional ideology-bound politicians. Of particular concern to *Der Ruf*, too, is the situation at the universities. In his article 'Professoren und Studenten' (Professors and students), Carl-Hermann Ebbinghaus is worried about the lack of contact between the two groups; he also criticises the attitudes of professors who are frightened to express an opinion because it might be politically inopportune. The poet Walter Bauer, who was to leave Germany disillusioned by the course of events, asks in verse for the professors to give a lead. Nicolaus Sombart views the students as the future elite. Although he supports equality of opportunity, he does not believe that society can do without an elite. He therefore feels it important that courses of study go beyond the narrow concern with a single discipline and incorporate sociological, historical and economic questions. This stress on the need for an elite, which is prevalent in *Der Ruf*, stems from suspicion of the mass of the people created by the knowledge that so many had succumbed to the propaganda of the Nazis. By contrast, youth generally represents hope for the writers of *Der Ruf*. It is not tainted by any kind of 'collective guilt', as Andersch points out in his remarks on the Nuremberg trials, 'Notwendige Aussage zum Nürnberger Prozess' (Necessary statement on the Nuremberg trial); it, too, has been the victim of its former leaders, towards whom it can only feel hatred and anger. Thus, according to Andersch, a great gap differentiates the ordinary soldier from the war criminal. This feeling explains why it is felt that the new Germany should be an equal partner. It is in keeping with the tone of *Der Ruf* that Dietrich Warnesius can confess his love of the German people, even though he rejects nationalism and accepts that German crimes must be atoned for.

That the leading figures associated with *Der Ruf*, once they could no longer work on the magazine, became so important in the primarily literary Gruppe 47 should not be thought of as some kind of second-best escape route. Literature and political commitment were inseparable for them; hence cultural matters too were a major theme of *Der Ruf*. The most significant literary article of the magazine was by Gustav René Hocke and entitled 'Deutsche Kalligraphie' (German calligraphy). Just as many political articles in *Der Ruf* look for a new beginning, Hocke hopes for a radical change in German literature. In particular, he sees all stylistic effects which may have been appropriate as a contrast to the brutal reality of dictatorship, as no longer in order. What he prefers is a simple realistic style, which reflects the deprivations of post-war life. He gives as an example of such writing the many descriptions of life in various areas of the country that were published at the time. According to Hocke, these seek to describe reality as it is, that is to say what life is like among the ruins. The term usually associated with this kind of literature is *Kahlschlag*, a word taken from forestry and meaning deforestation. In other words, the landscape of literature was to be rid of the overgrown trees of rhetoric. Rhetoric was associated with propaganda; it is clear, therefore, that scepticism about certain kinds of language was connected with the rejection of ideology. In fact, the articles in *Der Ruf* itself are not free of rhetorical devices, but be that as it may, Hocke's ideal inspired a whole school of writing. The most famous example is probably the poem by Günter Eich 'Inventur' (Inventory), which at first sight consists of a simple listing of a prisoner of war's belongings:

Dies ist meine Mütze
dies ist mein Mantel,
hier mein Rasierzeug
im Beutel aus Leinen.

(This is my cap/this is my coat/here's my shaving kit/in the canvas bag.)

The early stories of the Berlin writer Wolfdietrich Schnurre and those of Heinrich Böll also come largely into the same category, although in the case of Böll especially, the term *Trümmerliteratur* (ruins literature) is also used. It is fair to say that the attempted break with a compromised literary tradition runs parallel to the break hoped for in the field of politics.

Nevertheless, it must not be thought that this was the only direction taken by post-war literature, any more than the political views of *Der Ruf* enjoyed any kind of monopoly position. Nor was the Gruppe 47 at its inception a kind of literary court that only tolerated *Kahlschlagliteratur* in the way that the authorities in the East soon only tolerated socialist realism. Literature and literary life showed considerable variety in the early post-war years. The whole of modernism, which had been suppressed in the Nazi period, had to be absorbed, most especially the works of Kafka, which were to be of profound influence for the whole of German literature until well into the 1950s. Some works which took as their theme the totalitarian past or the threat of a totalitarian future, used anything but a realistic technique. Hermann Kasack's *Die Stadt hinter dem Strom* (The City beyond the River), which appeared in 1947, describes a city where the same processes of destruction and rebuilding alternate. This can be taken as either an allegory of fascism or of a senseless world threatened with destruction. That elsewhere not even political themes, let alone social realism, were dominant can be seen from the rapid re-emergence of nature poetry after the war.

Whether or not this diversification of literary forms in any way reflected social developments, it certainly can be concluded that the political aspirations of the young radical writers, in particular those of the contributors to *Der Ruf*, were not realised. They had hoped for a united socialist Germany; with the emergence of the Federal Republic they had to live in a capitalist state covering only part of German territory. Nor did the democratic elements of the new state, dominated as they were by political parties, coincide with what had been hoped for. The same was true of writers' European aspirations. In this way the stage was set for their alienation throughout much of the next decade. There remains to be considered only the question of why all the hopes of 1945 were dashed.

Symptomatic of the end of these post-war hopes is the early death of so many of the periodicals that had apparently hailed in a new era. The Marbach catalogue already referred to notes the end of approximately a dozen magazines in 1949 and 1950 alone. At one level this process had to do with economic changes. With the currency reform in the Western zones in 1948, goods began to appear again on the market quite freely. Consumers had the choice whether to buy a magazine or something else. Previously, there had been little to buy with the devalued currency — with the exception of the printed word. This is one reason advanced by Alfred Kantorowicz for the decline in circulation of his magazine *Ost und West* (East and West) from its peak of 70,000 to, at its end, about five or six thousand. Yet this kind of collapse has to do with more than technical readjustments of currencies. The fate of the magazine *Ost und West* provides a good example of how the aspirations of many writers and intellectuals became increasingly out of step with political reality.

With his magazine, Kantorowicz, who had returned from exile in America to East Berlin, hoped to build up a publication for all the zones of occupation and incorporating a variety of views. As the circulation figures show, he did have some initial success despite difficulties with distribution caused largely by the attitude of the American authorities. Furthermore, his intention of preventing the different zones of occupation from drifting apart reflected the views of a majority of writers. This can be seen by the stress on German unity in the manifestos issued by the First German Writers' Congress held in Berlin in 1947 — in fact the only gathering of writers from all four zones, with the exception of a celebration in Frankfurt a year later, to commemorate the centenary of the 1848 revolution. In particular, the second manifesto speaks of the danger that Germany might cease to exist as a whole. This, it was claimed, would especially have devastating effects for German culture. Quoting Heine's phrase 'Germany enjoys eternal existence' the manifesto says that the writers will do all in their power to preserve Germany: 'And therefore we promise that Germany will be our conscience'.[15] Even if one leaves aside the question of whether there has been more than one German literature following the division of the country, the relative lack of success of the writers' efforts to preserve unity can be seen from the way more than thirty years were to elapse before a similar large-scale gathering of writers from East and West took place again, this time occasioned by worries about peace. In fact, the bourgeoning Cold War left its mark on the relationships between writers in the two parts of Germany. In June 1950 a congress attended by West German authors took place in West Berlin, producing a manifesto which contained the statement 'No political ideology, no economic theory can usurp the general right to determine the concept of freedom.' Ideological differences became more overt the following year when the German branch of the international PEN club split between East and West. Against such developments, the attempt of Thomas Mann in 1949, the bi-centenary of Goethe's birth, to bridge the ideological divide by attending the celebrations in both Frankfurt and Weimar was bound to fail. However much writers might have desired unity, they were powerless before the pressures of political events.

This powerlessness, underlined by the way that the future of Germany lay in the hands of foreign occupiers, is ultimately the main reason why the aspirations of writers were thwarted in so many areas. In the first edition of *Ost und West* in 1948, Kantorowicz noted that Germany was destined to be more the 'object' than the 'subject' of world politics; in other words, outsiders were to determine its destiny. With hindsight it seems surprising that this was not more fully realised by others, for example the writers of *Der Ruf*. Introducing the selection of articles from the magazine published thirty years later, Richter admits that this naïveté can only be understood in terms of the atmosphere of the time, when hope predominated in spite of the appalling physical conditions.

Even if, in the end, the imposition of the Allies' various wills thwarted the aspirations of intellectuals, it would also seem an over-simplification to claim that this was achieved against the express wishes of the majority. The school of thought that claims that the majority of the German population wanted radical changes in the direction of some kind of socialism can only provide indications of this mood, for instance the referendum in Hesse in 1946 which supported the taking of key industries into public ownership. Rather than pursuing actively the aim of a united socialist Germany, the great mass of the population appears to have been passive, as the articles in *Der Ruf* about the silence of the young generation imply. Moreover, the Allies' doctrines of 'collective guilt' and 're-education' did not help, as no differentiations were made and superficial lip-service to Western democratic ideals encouraged. Whether or not any other nation, say the French or the British, would have allowed itself to be divided remains speculation — thankfully there has been no occasion for this to be put to the test. Nevertheless, that it did occur in Germany with relatively little resistance implies that there was no mass active support for at least one goal of writers and intellectuals. What is more, however large the circulations of many magazines may have been, a glance at some of the readers' letters they received does suggest that they faced difficulties in communicating their views to a populace still affected by the experiences of the recent past.

A correspondent to the second edition of *Die Gegenwart*, for example, blames the victors of the First World War for the rise of Nazism, which served as a kind of 'safety-valve' for the frustrated Germans. Furthermore, he expresses doubts, which he claims all his friends and acquaintances share, about the veracity of Allied reports on concentration camps, saying that very few people know anyone who had been in one. This neatly overlooks the point that the inmates were hardly sent forth to broadcast their experiences but rarely left alive. In reply, the editors see the letter as typical of the attitudes of many Germans. Specifically they recommend reading Wiechert's *Der Totenwald*. That neither the Allies nor the intellectuals with their desire for moral renewal changed these attitudes is suggested by the subsequent reluctance to confront the past on the part of many Germans. In the case of *Frankfurter Hefte*, Walter Dirks felt obliged at the beginning of the second year of the magazine's publication to justify its aims in the face of readers' letters. He is particularly concerned that criticism is not accepted by those who feel directly touched by it. He asks to be spared insults and insinuations, adding that the magazine's criticism is motivated by the desire to help the country and its people. That such justification was felt necessary shows the task that, not surprisingly, faced a democratic press so soon after the end of dictatorship. As for the situation of the young, letters to *Ost und West* from young people themselves give some indication of general states of mind. The nineteen-year-old Gerhart Baumert credibly attributes the disorientation of the young to the destruction of their false idol of National Socialism.[16] He sees as characteristic an uncertainty towards themselves and towards life. He calls upon the older generation, especially writers, to act as teachers to show them the way towards humanity and freedom. By contrast, the Marburg student Käte Fuchs says that the young only require leadership to a certain degree: they must take decisions themselves.[17] She sees as the main characteristic of young Germans the desire to escape from reality into a variety of worlds ranging from Rilke's mysticism to escapist cinema. Suffice it to say that these letters indicate further the ultimately insuperable difficulties faced by the young writers and intellectuals who hoped for a 'new' Germany in the face of the wishes of the Allies and the 're-established' German politicians. However one regards these hopes — as naïve illusions or indications of a better way — their confounding could only have one consequence, the feeling of alienation that became so prevalent in the early years of the Federal Republic.

Notes

1. A. Andersch, *Deutsche Literatur in der Entscheidung* (Verlag Volk und Zeit, Karlsruhe, [1947]), p. 7.
2. F. Thiess quoted in *Vaterland, Muttersprache* (Verlag Klaus Wagenbach, Berlin, 1979), p. 47.
3. Ibid., p. 47.
4. F. Sieburg, 'Frieden mit Thomas Mann', *Die Gegenwart*, vol. 4, no. 14 (1949), 14–16.
5. Sieburg worked in the German Embassy in Paris during the occupation. He never sought to deny charges of complicity with the Nazis.
6. These metaphors were used in a 1946 essay, reprinted as follows: E. Wiechert, 'Über Kunst und Künstler' in B. Schmidt, H. Schwenger (eds), *Die Stunde Eins* (DTV, München, 1982), pp. 47–56.
7. There have been two major publications of collections of articles from *Der Ruf*. All articles referred to in this chapter are to be found in one or both collections. These are:

H. Schwab-Felisch (ed.), *Der Ruf. Eine deutsche Nachkriegszeitschrift* (DTV, München, 1962).
H. A. Neunzig (ed.), *Der Ruf. Unabhängige Blätter für die junge Generation. Eine Auswahl* (Nymphenburger Verlagshandlung, München, 1976).

8. M. L. Kaschnitz, 'Von der Verwandlung' in Schmidt, Schwenger, *Die Stunde Eins*, pp. 42–6.
9. Anon. 'Alltag der Ostzone', *Die Gegenwart*, vol. 4, no. 24 (1949), 6–7.
10. K. H. Knappstein, 'Die Stunde der Sozialreform', *Frankfurter Hefte*, vol. 1, no. 3 (1946), 1–3.
11. W. Dirks, 'Rechts und links', *Frankfurter Hefte*, vol. 1, no. 6 (1946), 24–37.
12. K. W. Böttcher, 'Die neuen Reichen und die Neureichen in Deutschland', *Frankfurter Hefte*, vol. 6, no. 5 (1951), 331–8.

13. H. W. Richter, 'Churchill und die europäische Einheit' in Schwab-Felisch, *Der Ruf*, 156.
14. H. W. Richter, 'Die Chance der SPD' in Neunzig, *Der Ruf*, 155.
15. Quoted in *Vaterland, Muttersprache*, p. 74f.
16. G. Baumert — letter to *Ost und West*, vol. 1, no. 4, (1947), 85–7.
17. K. Fuchs — letter to *Ost und West*, vol. 2, no. 2 (1948), 85–7.

2 RESTORATION TRAGEDY — THE 1950s

The distance between official political life in West Germany and the majority of writers that emerged so soon after the war continued apace throughout the 1950s. It is fair to speak of two largely separate worlds existing for most of the decade, each viewing the other with suspicion and distrust. This dichotomy is particularly visible in the two novels of political life, Wolfgang Koeppen's *Das Treibhaus* (1953) (The hothouse) and Günther Weisenborn's *Auf Sand gebaut* (1956) (Built on sand), whose critical tone epitomises the relationship. As for the politicians, in particular the CDU under the leadership of Konrad Adenauer, they largely ignored writers and did not assign them any role in the construction of the new West German State.

With the foundation of the Federal Republic as a capitalist state which encompassed only a part of the German nation, many writers began, as has been noted, to speak of 'restoration', the term being used negatively as the antithesis of their hopes for a new united socialist Germany. What did they mean specifically by this expression? First, it signified the preservation of an economic order based on private ownership of the means of production, despite the active support sections of private industry had given to the Nazi party and the general post-war feeling, expressed in the CDU's first Ahlen Programme, that capitalism had not served the interests of the German people. Secondly, in the realm of party politics, it referred to the phenomenon already noted of political life being in the hands of parties and, specifically, politicians who had been involved in the failure of Weimar democracy. Thirdly, and more ominously, restoration meant the return to prominence of individuals whose past, at least for many writers, was tarnished by their activities during the Third Reich. The most notorious example of this was the civil servant Dr Hans Globke, who had written the commentary to the Nuremberg Race Laws that had marked one step on the road from the discrimination to the extermination of Germany's Jewish population, and who subsequently became a close and powerful adviser to Adenauer in the Federal Chancellory. With the foundation of the West German army (*Bundeswehr*) in the mid-1950s, many active officers from its precursor, Hitler's

Wehrmacht, also returned to important positions of command.

It is of course possible to produce counter-arguments against the blanket term 'restoration' to describe the first years of the Federal Republic. In the economic area, apologists of *Soziale Marktwirtschaft* (social market economy) can point to the wide prosperity achieved through the 'economic miracle', to the system of social security that prosperity made possible and to the elements of co-determination, that is to say the power of workers to influence their companies' development, that became part of the economic system in the 1950s. In foreign policy there were the compensation agreements with Israel as an attempt to atone for the crimes of the past. Moreover, the major plank of the new state's foreign policy, its integration into the Western system, and most particularly the reconciliation with the old enemy France, was a radical new departure. Thus, it could be claimed that the Bonn system was in no way a repeat of Weimar with its dreadful economic problems, and even less a continuation of the Third Reich. Defenders of the new Federal Republic accused the intellectual critics of ignoring all the changes that had taken place. Whatever the merits of the different cases, it is sufficient at this stage to point out the divide between the world of the politicians and that of the writers.

The change in atmosphere from that of the post-war years can be seen if one looks at the literature and literary life of the 1950s. The term Kahlschlag ceases to be in any sense appropriate, even if a writer like Heinrich Böll continued to use realistic techniques to chronicle the early years of the Federal Republic. Formal experiment, modernism, existentialism became increasingly dominant influences with Kafka continuing to be a major inspiration. What is more, the changed atmosphere from the radicalism of the immediate post-war period allowed a re-awakening of interest in writers like Gottfried Benn and Ernst Jünger, who at least in some of their ideas had been less than implacable opponents of National Socialism. The atmosphere of the 1950s can to some extent be deduced if one looks at the winners of the Peace Prize of the German Book Trade in that decade, and specifically at the reasons given for the award of the prize. In 1951 it was awarded to Albert Schweitzer, because he 'was active to promote a more noble human kind'; in 1953 to Martin Buber as 'philosopher and creator of an idea of humanity that pervades all life'; in 1954 to the critic Carl Jakob Burckhardt because of 'unwavering western philosophy'; and in 1956 to Reinhold Schneider, because he 'fights for a new

moral order'.[1] To refer to these awards is not to belittle those
gaining them; it is simply to show how they reveal an attitude to
writing far different from that based on direct political involvement, as favoured by so many immediately after the war. In 1962,
in an essay entitled 'Literaturkritik und Restauration' (Literary
criticism and restoration), Franz Schonauer spoke of most criticism
requiring writers to present eternal values in a maɪ.ɪer that allowed
no direct reference to contemporary reality.[2]

It is now necessary to look at the Gruppe 47, founded, it will be
remembered, by radical publicists and writers after the demise of
Der Ruf, in the changed world of the 1950s. It must first be stressed
that, despite its political origins, it had become primarily a literary
institution. It did not though, as has been seen, propagate a particular type of literature. Moreover, as an organisation it lacked
structure and statutes, not least because its originators continued to
view anything that might smack of regimentation with suspicion
because of their experiences under the Nazis. It met twice a year for
three days, writers coming solely at the personal invitation of Hans
Werner Richter. The principal activity was the reading of literary
texts which were subjected to instant criticism. The group also
awarded a prize, which in the course of the 1950s went to such — at
the time — promising writers as Heinrich Böll, Martin Walser and
Günter Grass. It acted when in session as a kind of literary salon or
café, even perhaps, as is sometimes claimed, as a temporary capital
in a country without a literary metropolis. In view of all this, it is
wrong to see the writers who attended the meetings of the Gruppe
47 as distinct within the literature of the time. They were part of
literary life, albeit a significant part, but as the group had no real
organisation or membership as such (how is one to view the status
of those who only attended once or twice and had no desire to
repeat the experience?), they cannot be classified neatly.

The writers of the Gruppe 47 contributed to a literature generally
far removed from that propagated at the end of the war. Lyric
poetry was possibly the dominant genre, a poetry seen by the poet
and critic Peter Rühmkorf in 1960 as characterised by 'unthinking
flight from time and reality'.[3] Helmut Koopmann notes that the
new West German State hardly existed in the literature of the day,
and sees a dominating autobiographical element in prose writing.[4]
This lack of any clear political commitment in literature has sometimes been seen as a result of the atmosphere of the age: 'an
inevitable reaction . . . to the increasing hardness of society', as a

book on the Gruppe 47 puts it.⁵

As for dominant literary forms, the critic Walter Jens uses the term 'reduction' to describe the kind of literature that came to the fore under the influence of modernism and whose appearance he links with the spring 1952 gathering of the Gruppe 47.⁶ By this term he means a movement away from realism and psychology towards concentration on detail, repetition and non-epic forms. It is worth noting that Wolfgang Hildesheimer, creator of 'absurd' plays and Helmut Heissenbüttel, whose poetry is marked by linguistic experiment, both attended the gatherings of the Gruppe 47. It was only in the late 1950s that a new generation of writers turned to overt social and political themes, Hans Magnus Enzensberger in poetry and Grass and Walser in the novel, although they did not generally revert to simple realistic forms.

Despite the apparently non-political nature of much of the literature of the 1950s, including that of many associated with the Gruppe 47, it should not be assumed that writers had abandoned their concern for political matters. Their approaches to literature did not preclude an interest in politics. In itself, Richter's conception of the Gruppe 47 as a forum for 'creation of a democratic elite in the field of literature and higher journalism'⁷ and for the practice of democracy within a circle of individualists is a direct descendant from the ideas of *Der Ruf*. Equally, many writers viewed formal experiment as such as in some way an expression of opposition to the regressive tendencies of the age, as exemplified by the Adenauer administration. This was, for instance, the position of the philosopher of the Frankfurt school, Theodor W. Adorno. Pointing out that undemocratic systems generally require affirmative realism from writers, he saw formal experiment as a more valid expression of opposition than realistic writing based on a traditional concept of political commitment, a viewpoint totally at odds with that of dogmatic Marxists, who demand realism and scorn writers like Kafka as unpolitical. Thus, it is not too surprising that many writers, whatever modes of specifically literary expression they used elsewhere and despite the generally hostile atmosphere of the time, expressed their views on a number of areas of political concern.

The area that was of prime concern to writers for most of the 1950s was that of the military, initially the creation of a West German army and subsequently the possibility that it might be equipped with atomic weapons. Following the defeat of 1945, a wave of anti-militarism had swept through Germany; on its inception, the new West German State did not possess an army, indeed the very idea appeared anathema. Very shortly all that changed as the new state moved towards becoming a member of the Western bloc. As early as 1950, the CDU Minister of the Interior Gustav Heinemann, subsequently to become Federal President as a member of the SPD, resigned from the cabinet over the question of rearmament. By 1955, after the failure of attempts to set up some kind of European defence force, the Federal Republic had an army and was a member of NATO. Conscription followed a year later. These rapid changes in attitudes towards the military are satirised in Martin Walser's play of the early 1960s *Eiche und Angora* (The Rabbit Race). A pacifistic memorial put up in 1950 with the approbation of all is removed some ten years later at the height of the Cold War as 'the plaque of shame'.

That German rearmament should provoke great hostility among writers is not surprising. The German military tradition had proved itself morally bankrupt — despite acts of resistance by certain officers — long before the collapse of 1945, with the army's acquiescence in Hitler's aggressive plans. Now, less than a decade after this collapse, a new army was to be created. Opposition was by no means confined to writers associated with the Gruppe 47 or who might be deemed leftist. The resignation of the Protestant Gustav Heinemann was the result of Christian conscience; a similar motive inspired the Catholic writers Reinhold Schneider and Stefan Andres to oppose rearmament and nuclear weapons. In 1949 Schneider spoke of the individual's responsibility for peace:

> Everything depends on this: that we make peace a matter of our conscience and that we do not cease to ask ourselves before our conscience whether it is possible to place any hope in war or the maintenance of circumstances akin to war.[8]

In 1951, Schneider rejected war as a means to preserve freedom: 'Freedom can only be founded on poverty, on the power of personality and the spirit, on radical social justice.'[9] Not least because some of his comments appeared in East Germany, Schneider found himself the object of harsh attacks in the West. His comments on the issue of war and armaments, motivated by a radical Christianity, were an unacceptable challenge to those willing to accept an army as the price for material prosperity.

In addition to this kind of individual protest, attempts were made to mobilise a broad opposition to rearmament. Gustav Heinemann was the chairman of the Notgemeinschaft für den Frieden Europas (Emergency Campaign for European Peace) founded in 1951, out of which grew the Gesamtdeutsche Volkspartei (All-German People's Party) that contested the 1953 Federal elections without gaining the 5 per cent of the vote needed to gain seats in parliament. In keeping with their suspicions of party politics, writers were primarily involved with mass movements that sought to prevent rearmament like the Paulskirchenbewegung (St Paul's Church movement) of 1954–5. At a meeting in early 1955 at this famous church in Frankfurt, the scene of the deliberations to create a united democratic Germany in the aftermath of the 1848 revolutions, it issued a manifesto warning that the creation of a West German army within the framework of the Western alliance would inevitably extinguish hopes for German reunification. All individual and collective protests, whether based on moral considerations or political ones like the question of reunification, failed, however, to change the government's resolve, even if opinion polls too had initially suggested general hostility to its military policy. Nevertheless, the opposition to this policy was not silenced, as the next conflict, over atomic weapons for the Bundeswehr, was to show.

In 1956 Franz Josef Strauss became the Federal Minister of Defence. This ebullient right-winger from the Bavarian sister party of the CDU, the Christian Social Union (CSU), whose rhetoric alone was enough to strike fear in many hearts, became the *bête noire* of most critical intellectuals, a state of affairs that has continued until the present. Shortly after his appointment the question of atomic weapons for the Bundeswehr became acute, with the Federal Government and Strauss in particular not averse to any largesse on the part of the United States. This not only mobilised the official SPD opposition into protest but also large numbers of writers and intellectuals. Stefan Andres was horrified that certain theologians could contemplate nuclear war with apparent equanimity as a way of confirming to God that atheistic communism would be resisted. For Andres, this was 'theology without morality'.[10] The novelist Hans Henny Jahnn too rejected 'all better dead than red' ideology: 'The individualists — I count myself as one of them — do not have the right to demand the death of millions because their own particular desired kind of freedom might possibly not be recognised in future.'[11] Again, writers' individual voices were reinforced by organisations seeking to rally what again, according to polls, was mass opposition to atomic weapons. The most important of these, suported by the SPD, was Kampf dem Atomtod (Fight Atomic Death). This name came from the group's declaration, issued in 1958 and signed by Andres, Böll, Jahnn, Kogon, Dirks and others, which pointed to the certain annihilation of the German nation in the event of nuclear war. Hans Werner Richter formed a parallel Komitee gegen Atomrüstung (Committee against Atomic Weapons) in April 1958 which also attracted support among many writers, especially those associated with the Gruppe 47 like Günter Eich, Walter Jens, Helmut Heissenbüttel and Wolfgang Hildesheimer. Although on occasions the anti-nuclear protesters were able to mobilise large numbers of followers at their rallies, over 100,000 in Hamburg in April 1958, for instance, and connections were established with parallel groups in other countries, in particular CND in Britain, it is again impossible to speak of their achieving much success. Even if West Germany did not become a nuclear power — because of other nations' sensitivity towards there being German fingers on the trigger — the build-up of atomic weapons in Western Europe continued. By the middle of the 1960s, these particular anti-nuclear movements along with the Easter marches of the beginning of the decade had largely run out of steam.

Throughout the 1950s the political interests of writers were not limited to possible threats to the future; they were equally concerned about the Nazi past, which, in the official terminology of the time, remained 'unbewältigt' (not overcome). Many attempts by writers to make their fellow citizens confront the phenomenon of National Socialism took the form of fiction, for instance Wolfgang Koeppen's novel *Der Tod in Rom* (Death in Rome) of 1954 and Heinrich Böll's *Haus ohne Hüter* (The Unguarded House) of the same year. In the 1960s too the theme of National Socialism remained, with, for instance, the Auschwitz trial of 1965 providing the background for Peter Weiss' 'documentary' play *Die Ermittlung* (The Investigation). Even in the 1980s the topic remains relevant, as is shown by the novel *Saumlos* by Peter O. Chotjewitz about a village, which formerly had a large Jewish community, and by Heinar Kipphardt's play *Bruder Eichmann* (Brother Eichmann). In the 1950s the major concern of writers was that the direction the new West German State was taking did not favour a genuine confrontation of the past. In particular, rearmament and Cold War propaganda against the Soviet Union, felt by many to be almost a continuation of Goebbels' tirades against 'sub-human Bolsheviks', favoured convenient amnesia about the past. By the early 1950s memoires of Nazi officers were beginning to appear, and the producer of the anti-semitic film *Jud Süss* (Jew Süss), Veit Harlan, was back in business by 1952 after he had been acquitted by a Hamburg court. When demonstrations against his first post-war film took place in several towns, the police reacted strongly. This provoked Erich Kästner, whose writing is frequently humorous, to the following bitter comment on the basis of the court's verdict:

Thus the police is acting legally in moving against demonstrators. Thus the only people acting illegally are those called by their conscience to protest in the name of humanity against such justice and its visible as well as its incalculable consequences.[12]

For many writers, the consequences of such attitudes were visible for all to see after the desecration of a Jewish cemetery in Cologne on Christmas Eve 1959. They bemoaned the total failure of the government to combat the re-emergence of nationalism and anti-Semitism. Walter Jens connected the events in Cologne with official policy: 'Whoever requests missile bases 15 years after Hitler cannot be surprised if not only sabre-rattling occurs but also paint smearing.'[13] Stefan Andres pointed to the number of former Nazis in prominent positions, adding that such an example was hardly likely to change the unpolitical German *Spiessbürger* into a committed democrat. The term Spiessbürger, literally 'spear bourgeois', refers to an unimaginative, authoritarian and authority-loving person of the kind who helped Hitler to power. Andres' words are: 'The *Spiesser* is, however, well known: he is the opposite of the citizen and ethical person. He lives exclusively for his own interests and is politically dead.'[14] For the Austrian writer Robert Neumann, the only answer was for parents to tell the truth about the Third Reich and force teachers to do so too.[15]

How far writers have helped the German people to confront the past and how far such a confrontation has ever taken place remains a moot point some forty years after the war. For Walter Jens in 1984, in an interview with the present writer, the year 1945 in the sense of a liberation from the past was still awaited. Despite the massive popularity of Anne Frank's diary and the reverberations caused by the television series *Holocaust*, such an attitude is justified. Suspicions are roused not just by the overt neo-Nazism of certain extremist newspapers — it was specifically against such pernicious influences that Hans Werner Richter formed the Grunwälder Kreis (Grunwäld circle) in 1956 — but by the continuing insensitivity of those who should know better. When the dramatist Rolf Hochhuth unearthed the past of the then prime minister of Baden-Württemberg, Hans Filbinger, in the late 1970s, discoveries which finally forced his resignation (this was, incidentally, one of the few occasions when a writer could be said to have directly influenced the course of events), the reactions of the former military judge showed little moral awareness. The positivistic claim that what was legal then could not be wrong afterwards betrayed no sense that the Third Reich was anything other than a normal state based on the rule of law. Problematical too was the attitude expressed by Chancellor Kohl in 1984 on his visit to Israel. Seeing himself as the representative of a post-war generation that had no connection with the past, as if the date on one's birth-certificate had some kind of intrinsic value, he spoke of crimes committed 'im deutschen Namen' (in the name of Germany) rather than of crimes by Germans. The efforts of writers to help in the process of 'overcoming the past' cannot be said to have been universally successful; on the other hand, they have been by and large the only group of society to have paid more than lip-service to this significant task.

In general, the 1950s did not favour the raising of awkward questions. People wished to enjoy the new-found prosperity and forget anything that might be thought distasteful. The government too preferred the appearance of harmony at the expense of controversy and conflict. That the official ideals of the time were often in stark contrast to reality is shown in Fassbinder's film of post-war life *Die Ehe der Maria Braun* (The marriage of Maria Braun) where the ideal of marriage, as propagated at the time, is set against the world of the 'economic miracle' in which, rather than love, a ruthless competitive struggle for success dominates. At a time when criticism and the presentation of darker sides of reality were not favoured, it is not surprising that writers at times felt that the freedom of expression was endangered. In the early 1950s the government sought to introduce a law against what it considered pornography, which was eventually passed in 1952 under the name *Gesetz über den Vertrieb jugendgefährdender Schriften* (Law against the dissemination of literature that endangers the young). Erich Kästner protested that a similar law in the Weimar Republic had lowered the public esteem of literature, with the result that Hitler's subsequent persecution of the arts met with little resistance. Other writers too saw the legislation as a potential threat to freedom, and pointed out that it was impossible to make a direct connection between the written word and criminality, which was one of the pretexts for the new law. Even if the government on this occasion did seek to consult authors in the persons of Kästner and Stefan Andres, it was impossible for them to save the writers' case.

Some years later, on two occasions where freedom of expression appeared endangered, writers were on the side that prevailed, although it might be exaggerated to claim that they alone were responsible for what was achieved. First, there was the case of the second television channel. Since the war all broadcasting had been in the hands of the Federal States rather than of the central government, to prevent any repetition of a centralised system of propaganda as had existed under the Nazis. In 1959, however, the government put forward a plan for a new Federal television channel. Many of the writers associated with the Gruppe 47, including Böll, Hans Werner Richter, Grass and Walser, protested that the new station would be an instrument of the government and powerful interests, and announced their intention to boycott it. In the end the Federal Constitutional Court pronounced the planned second channel unconstitutional, in the projected form. Secondly, in 1962 there was the Spiegel Affair, an event that showed that the Adenauer government, so dominant in the 1950s, was losing its grip.

Under the pretext of having betrayed military secrets in an article about NATO, the editor of the news magazine *Der Spiegel*, Rudolf Augstein, and one of the journalists, Conrad Ahlers, who was at the time in Spain, were arrested. Suspicions were quickly aroused that the executive, in particular Defence Minister Strauss, were involved in the action against a publication that was a trenchant critic of the government in general and Strauss in particular. For some, the magazine constituted the only effective opposition of the time. When the affair broke, the writers of the Gruppe 47, which happened to be meeting in Berlin, expressed their solidarity and called for the resignation of Strauss. This, in fact, occurred when the coalition partner of the Christian Democrats, the liberal Free Democratic Party (FDP) left the government, and only returned with the additional assurance that the octogenarian Chancellor would retire in a year's time. The Adenauer era was drawing to a close; what is more, freedom of expression had been safely defended. The way was open to challenge the society created by the CDU until success was achieved at the end of the decade.

Another event that damaged the reputation of Konrad Adenauer as a successful politician who had brought economic success and returned (West) Germany to a respected place within the family of nations, was the building of the Berlin Wall in August 1961. Adenauer had always contended that integration into the Western alliance and a policy of strength towards the Soviet Union would force concessions and finally German reunification. The building of the Wall was literally concrete proof that this policy was not realistic and, equally importantly, could no longer be presented as such. The division of Germany now appeared fixed for the foreseeable future. Up to the building of the Wall, many writers had continued to express their concern about the division of Germany and had seen, as already noted, a connection between rearmament and division. This, incidentally, was the view of the Social Democrat opposition in the 1950s. The primacy of the need to prevent division had also been stressed by East German writers, who were in this in no sense out of step with the officially presented party policy of the time. In 1952 Anna Seghers stressed that a united, democratic Germany was a prerequisite for peace,[16] a sentiment echoed by Brecht four years later when he said there were peaceful opportunities for reunification.[17] In the 1950s some West German writers still propagated the idea that Germany should mediate between East and West, Roland Schneider for instance in 1951.[18] The original declaration of the Kampf dem Atomtod movement uses the word *Entspannung* (détente), whilst Stefan Andres in his speech during the Easter march of 1960 spoke of the need for negotiations. Some contact between East and West German writers, although difficult, had never stopped entirely, as a discussion in Hamburg on the role of the writer in society as late as the spring of 1961 showed.

After the erection of the Berlin Wall, writers who had not followed the government's line towards the East, were taken massively to task. Even if their hopes for reunification were illusory, it does appear strange that an event proving the failure of one policy propagated as the path to reunification — namely that of the government — should have been used for attacking a different one

— that of many writers. For Wolf Jobst Siedler, for instance, writers who spoke of the need for dialogue suffered from foolish delusions: 'Talking, it is said on both sides, is better than shooting; in this the somewhat touching assumption is made that there is some kind of relationship between one's own loquaciousness and world peace.'[19] Moreover, according to Siedler, West German writers had ignored the fact that their East German counterparts were nothing more than the loyal servants of their government. Heinrich Böll's comment that negotiations with the Soviet Union, under less favourable conditions than previously, were now rendered even more necessary, seems an adequate reply to Siedler and one which the détente process of the 1960s showed to be correct. The other major criticism that was directed at West German writers was that, despite their willingness to criticise their own society, they did not make adequate protests against the Wall. The rightist author Rudolf Krämer-Badoni did not mince words when he accused many of his colleagues of being *Dummköpfe* (fools) and *Feiglinge* (cowards). Again, Heinrich Böll found a rejoinder to this hysteria: he saw it as ironic that support was now being sought from those whose views had previously been scorned.

In reality, there was plenty of reflection from West German writers of all political persuasions. It was two writers associated with the Gruppe 47, Wolfdietrich Schnurre and Günter Grass, both residents of West Berlin, who reacted as forcefully as anybody. In an open letter to Anna Seghers, Grass compared East Germany to a concentration camp and the Communist Party leader Walter Ulbricht to a camp commandant. In a letter to the East German Writers Association, dated 16 August 1961, Grass and Schnurre called on their counterparts either to express their condemnation of their government's measures or to condone them. Not surprisingly, the latter course was taken by Stephan Hermlin in a reply. Schnurre's concern continued over the following months. He spoke in September 1961 of the writer as the 'conscience of the nation' — a title generally rejected as too vague and idealistic by his colleagues — and called on East German writers to follow their consciences. A month later, he resigned from the PEN club, because of what he saw as the lethargy of the West German section and the inhumanity of the East German one. Other writers reacted less emotionally than Schnurre. Twenty-three, mainly associated with the Gruppe 47 and, it must be said, including Grass and Schnurre, deferentially called on the United Nations to turn their attention to the situation in Germany. Hans Werner Richter, believing that Schnurre's moral stance was not sufficient, called for an active policy towards the East in order to alleviate the position of the East German population, something that was only fully attempted with the change of government in 1969. Other comments were less concerned with direct political steps; after all, the Wall was a *fait accompli*. Given the nature of the debate, it is not surprising that both Böll and Hans Magnus Enzensberger pointed to the similarities in tone adopted by the West German Right and the hard-line East German authorities. Enzensberger speaks of statements on both sides that are 'blackmailing, stupid and crude'.[20] It is hard to disagree.

Before concluding this survey of the 1950s, it is worthwhile to look first at some of the publications available to writers in this decade, and secondly at an author whose essays embody many of the concerns of the time. With the demise of so many magazines in the late 1940s and early 50s, opportunities for the publication of critical comment became limited. One important new magazine, however, appeared in the shape of *Die Kultur* (Culture), founded in Munich in 1953 and announcing itself for a time as Germany's only independent cultural newspaper. It appeared fortnightly with comment on both cultural and political matters, often providing a forum for such critical writers as Erich Kästner and Stefan Andres. For example, in 1958 it reprinted a controversial address by Andres to the Kuratorium unteilbares Deutschland (Committee for an Indivisible Germany), a body closely associated with the government of the day, in which he called for discussions between the two German governments. This was at a time when the West German government regarded its Eastern counterpart as a pariah. Andres presented his argument in moral terms, saying that such dialogue would reflect 'the moral law, the life-preserving principle'.[21] The tone of this article is typical of *Die Kultur*; it seldom concerned itself with everyday aspects of political life.

Very different were the publications of the then Hamburg students Klaus Rainer Röhl, for a time the husband of Ulrike Meinhof, and Peter Rühmkorf. In 1955 they founded *Das Plädoyer* (Plea), which in turn became *Der Studentenkurier* (Student courier) and *Konkret*, this last title being an important voice of the extra-parliamentary Left during the student movement of the 1960s. At that period it was characterised by a mixture of radical political comment, epitomised in the columns of Ulrike Meinhof, and words and pictures that can only be summed up under the general rubric 'sex'. In the 1950s it stuck more exclusively to radical politics, something rare enough at the time, announcing itself in 1958 rather grandiosely as 'Published under the auspices of the Working Party for Progressive Art at the University of Hamburg'. It is possible to gain insight into the nature of the journal and the general atmosphere of the time by reading Rühmkorf's recollections *Die Jahre die Ihr kennt* (The years you know). Copies of the magazine itself reveal an unconventional layout remarkable given the sobriety of the time and no doubt a reflection of the magazine's Bohemian aspirations. They occasionally give rise to a wry smile, as when the then less celebrated Hans Magnus Enzensberger is given the forename Ernst, and when the young Helmut Schmidt in a 1958 interview speaks of a general strike as a legitimate weapon in the struggle against nuclear weapons. Some twenty years later his different attitude as Chancellor to nuclear weapons did not endear him to the radical writers associated with the peace movement. Nuclear weapons, in fact, along with Algeria and the continuing presence of former National Socialists in leading positions, were major topics for *Konkret*, at the end of the 1950s. For Krämer-Badoni in 1961 *Konkret* represented an ignoble fifth column. That, along with other publications like *Frankfurter Hefte*, *Der Spiegel* and *Die Kultur*, it existed at all shows that there were exceptions to the general picture of a tame press generally supportive of the Adenauer government.

The essays of Paul Schallück remain an interesting document of the Adenauer era. Schallück, born in 1922, was associated with the Gruppe 47 and wrote a series of novels in the late 1940s and 50s about the war and post-war developments in West Germany. In 1962 he published a volume of collected essays *Zum Beispiel* (For example), which contains a section on political topics of the day. The first three essays, from the mid-50s, deal with qualities that are seen as marking the Germans at the time, hence the use of the word *deutsch* in the titles. In 'Von deutscher Tüchtigkeit' (On German efficiency) he warns his countrymen against solely directing their attention to economic matters, a propensity that arouses justifiable suspicion among Germany's neighbours. The essentially moral basis of Schallück's criticism can be seen in the following comment:

> When life becomes only economically quantifiable, as is becoming more and more common, if everything is given an economic denominator and, what is more, one of achievement, success,

unrestrained desire to be ahead of all others, then, along with individuality, inner freedom, too, is endangered and with it kindness, mercy, solidarity, neighbourly love, including that neighbourly love which one people should show to another one.[22]

As a corollary to this economistic thinking, Schallück sees a desire to suppress all thoughts of the past, which is the topic of the second essay: 'Von deutscher Vergesslichkeit' (On German forgetfulness). Here, he speaks of the hopes of the post-war era having been replaced by a 'condition of emptiness, of coldness of heart, of purely material well-being'.[23] According to Schallück, this is an injustice to all the victims of the war, from those who died in bombing raids to the victims in concentration camps. Not only does Schallück see moral dangers in this, he also fears that what has been suppressed about the past could return in a virulent and dangerous form. In the third essay, 'Von deutscher Resignation' (On German resignation), Schallück links the unwillingness to talk about the past with a passive, resigned state of mind that ignores anything that might be potentially controversial. This, in turn, is harmful to democracy: 'The active presence of the citizen in all questions, at least in as many questions as possible, is an essential precondition for a democracy and moreover adds a piquancy to life that makes living it worthwhile.'[24] In 1960, in the essay 'Gedanken über den Pazifismus' (Thoughts on pacifism), Schallück turns to the dangers of war. He distinguishes between morality, which is concerned with ends, and politics, which has to do with means and purpose. He rejects as insufficient a purely moral or ideological attitude to peace, as in the nuclear age it is insufficient merely to be against war, and demands knowledge from all those concerned about peace. In his view the way to peace consists of a series of small steps in a particular situation. This essay in particular shows that Schallück goes beyond abstract moralism, although at the same time his social concern would carry much less conviction without its moral foundation. It is also important to note that this concern does not express itself in a hectoring dismissal of his fellow Germans for their failings. Schallück seeks rather to educate in a quiet, almost gentle tone. There are no extravagant metaphors; the Germans avoid the past 'like a student a feared examination'. He stresses that his comments are based on worry and not the desire to be aggressive. Although it is impossible to speculate on whether this approach had any success, there would appear to be much in its favour, given the general reluctance towards controversial political debate in the 1950s.

All in all, it has to be concluded that the political commitment of writers had little effect in that decade, except possibly in the area that was closest to their own professional activity, namely that of freedom of expression. The clearest area of failure, by contrast, was on the question of rearmament. In conclusion to this chapter, it is necessary to ask why this was so, despite the justification for their moral outrage so soon after the war and, at a more practical level, the proximity of their views to those of the major opposition party. One major factor to bear in mind is the effectiveness of the Christian Democrat government and particularly of Chancellor Adenauer, who did not mince words when clashing with opponents. In 1951 he is reputed to have said of the opposition to rearmament that anybody opposing the government's policy was either 'a fool of the very first order or a traitor'. This was taken as a reference to Reinhold Schneider in particular. When eighteen atomic scientists warned of the danger of nuclear weapons in 1957 in what is known as the Göttingen Declaration, Adenauer simply dismissed their views saying: 'To judge this declaration one must have knowledge these gentlemen do not possess — because they did not come to me.' Given such attitudes, it is not surprising that Pastor Niemöller, probably the leading figure in church resistance to Hitler, maintained that the early 1950s were even harder to bear for him as a pacifist than the Third Reich. Nevertheless, however detrimental Adenauer's authoritarian pronouncements must have been to the advancement of democratic debate in the new West German State, their efficacity, at least in electoral terms, cannot be denied, particularly when seen in connection with the anti-communism of the day. This, as already has been noted, was morally suspect as a continuation of Goebbels's propaganda, however many reasons there may have been for viewing developments in the East with suspicion, but once again its political success is apparent. The malevolent depths of the anti-communist crusade of the Adenauer era can be seen in the publication in 1960 of a so-called *Rotbuch* (Red Book) by an officially backed group called Rettet die Freiheit (Save Freedom), in which the opponents of atomic weapons, including such writers as Kästner and Koeppen, were accused of communist subversion. This nefarious publication led to an indignant complaint from Enzensberger that he was not featured among the subversives. Such propaganda helps to explain the electoral triumphs gained by the Christian Democrats at Federal level in 1957 and at state level in 1958, when it appeared that the anti-nuclear protesters enjoyed majority popular support. It was only necessary for them to connect opponents with the 'ogre' Walter Ulbricht to mobilise the electorate. For the Social Democrats, in opposition to the government's nuclear policy, defeat in the state elections of 1958 in North Rhine Westphalia, which contains the industrial centre of the Ruhr, must have come as a bitter blow.

It must then be asked why intellectual protest and the Social Democratic Party failed to form any kind of effective alliance. It must be remembered that many writers retained their suspicion towards political parties as manifested in *Der Ruf*. With hindsight this attitude must be regarded as wrong, as Hans Werner Richter has subsequently admitted, saying that it is only explicable in terms of the belief of the time that literature was an equally valid medium to change the world.[25] At the same time, certain comments made in the 1950s reveal doubts about the SPD, in particular the fear that the party was willing to sacrifice principle for expediency, a fear that has never been far from writers' minds throughout the history of the Federal Republic. Thus, Kästner in 1954 saw the party as having abandoned the role of opposition in favour of preparing itself for governmental responsibility.[26] There is a similar complaint from Rühmkorf a year later.[27] It is true that the party's opposition to rearmament was not total, whilst at the end of the decade in its Godesberg Programme it consciously changed itself from being a working-class party into a *Volkspartei*, a term that sounds more positive in German than the English equivalent 'catch-all party'. In this process it abandoned many leftist positions, including its support for the Kampf dem Atomtod movement. Regardless of whether this change in the party's nature is seen as a 'betrayal' or as necessary 'modernisation' on the road to the assumption of power, it certainly helped in the decline of the anti-nuclear campaign of the 1950s.

As a final reason for writers' failure in this decade, it must again be suggested as with the 1940s that they themselves made mistakes. In a volume issued to mark the first twenty years of the Federal Republic's existence, Krämer-Badoni, whilst agreeing that the Nazi past was in no sense ever overcome and finding 'terrifying political and moral indolence'[28] in large sections of the bourgeoisie, blames the excessive criticism of left-wing writers for this state of affairs.

He asks: 'Does a person examine himself if he is insulted?'[29] Ultimately the criticism is untenable — it is akin to blaming the Versailles treaty exclusively for the rise of Hitler — but it is arguable that derogatory comments about Spiessbürger of the type made in the 1950s were counter-productive. Shortly before his suicide, in a curiously entitled volume to which Böll also contributed, *Die zornigen alten Männer* (The angry old men), the writer Jean Améry mocked his own and fellow writers' previous attitudes in an essay 'In den Wind gesprochen' (Spoken into the wind). He says that in the first years of the Federal Republic the Left lived in a dream world on many issues, whilst the ordinary people had a much better grasp of reality on such questions as Berlin. He speaks of unforgivable arrogance and 'an even more unforgivable blindness towards the longings, hopes and fears of our fellow-men'.[30] This was seen as particularly true in the economic sphere: 'People ate their fill, had rebuilt their houses, lived decently, were well-dressed. What did it matter? They were "alienated" — clearly so much so that they did not feel how unhappy they were whilst feeling happy.'[31]

One example of this kind of arrogance is an article by the poet and novelist Rudolf Hagelstange which appeared in *Die Kultur* in 1958 under a title which invokes Tennessee Williams: 'Endstation Kühlschrank. Mass und Vernunft frieren ein' (A desire named fridge. Restraint and sense congeal). Rather than from a leftist standpoint, Hagelstange attacks the mentality of the 'economic miracle' from a standpoint akin to the cultural pessimism of Oswald Spengler, proclaiming despair at the attitudes of a majority whose ultimate aspiration is the possession of a refrigerator. He complains:

> It would be a worthless delusion to appeal to the intellect, to preach morality. A generation . . . cannot be enticed away from the fire at which it warms itself and cultivates tranquillity in enjoyment and self-satisfaction with responsibility, intellect and moral demands. Its battlefield is the economy, its heroic death, the heart attack. It fights for refrigerators, for Volkswagens and more expensive vehicles, for summer residences and foreign orders.[32]

However elegant the prose, this passage reveals a most questionable attitude, not least in the way it implies a preference for traditional heroics.

At the end of the 1950s, therefore, it is not surprising that, given their failures, many writers began to search for different approaches in their political commitment. It seemed that their generally unsystematic reactions to events, however well motivated by justifiable moral concerns, were bound to fail. The 'homelessness' that had been defiantly proclaimed in the 1940s had become not only the derisive taunt of opponents but also an inadequate stance. The slogan *ohne mich* (count me out) coined in connection with the opposition to rearmament appeared equally dubious. In the search for allies that now seemed necessary, there was, however, not much alternative to nailing their colours more closely to the Social Democratic mast, a process that will be examined in Chapter 3.

Notes

1. Quotations from K. Fohrbeck, A. J. Wiesand, *Der Autorenreport* (Rowohlt, Reinbek bei Hamburg, 1972), p. 354.
2. F. Schonauer, 'Literaturkritik und Restauration' in H. W. Richter (ed.), *Bestandsaufnahme* (Kurt Desch, München, Wien, Basel, 1962), pp. 477–93.
3. P. Rühmkorf, *Die Jahre die Ihr kennt* (Rowohlt, Reinbek bei Hamburg, 1972), p. 96.
4. H. Koopmann, 'Die Bundesrepublik Deutschland in der Literatur', *Zeitschrift für Politik*, vol. 26, no. 2 (1979), 164.
5. H. L. Arnold (ed.), *Die Gruppe 47* (Text und Kritik, München, 1980), p. 94.
6. W. Jens, *Deutsche Literatur der Gegenwart* (DTV, München, 1964), p. 129f.
7. H. W. Richter (ed.), *Almanach der Gruppe 47* (Rowohlt, Reinbek bei Hamburg, 1962), p. 11.
8. R. Schneider, 'Verantwortung für den Frieden' in *Vaterland, Muttersprache*, p. 87,
9. R. Schneider, 'In Freiheit und Verantwortung' in ibid., p. 107.
10. S. Andres, 'Rede zum Ostermarsch 1960' in ibid., p. 157.
11. H. H. Jahnn, 'Am Abgrund' in ibid., p. 147.
12. E. Kästner, 'Offener Brief an Freiburger Studenten', in ibid., p. 111.
13. W. Jens quoted in ibid., p. 180.
14. S. Andres quoted in ibid., p. 179.
15. R. Neumann, 'Noch geschieht es bei Nacht und Nebel' in ibid., p. 179.
16. A. Seghers, 'Rede auf dem Völkerkongress in Wien' in ibid., pp. 114–16.
17. B. Brecht, 'Offener Brief an den Deutschen Bundestag Bonn' in ibid., pp. 135–6.
18. Schneider, 'In Freiheit und Verantwortung' in ibid., pp. 106–7.
19. W. J. Siedler, 'Die Linke stirbt, doch sie ergibt sich nicht' in H. W. Richter (ed.), *Die Mauer oder Der 13. August* (Rowohlt, Reinbek bei Hamburg, 1961), p. 111. This volume is a compilation of articles, letters, etc. reflecting the debate that followed the construction of the Berlin Wall. It contains the material referred to at this point in the chapter.
20. H. M. Enzensberger, 'Bürgerkrieg im Briefkasten' in Richter, *Die Mauer*, p. 175.

21. S. Andres, 'Um die Freiheit unseres Handelns', *Die Kultur*, vol. 6, no. 113 (1958), 1.
22. P. Schallück, *Zum Beispiel* (Europäische Verlagsanstalt, Frankfurt am Main, 1962), p. 9.
23. Ibid., p. 14.
24. Ibid., p. 19.
25. H. W. Richter, *Briefe an einen jungen Sozialisten* (Hoffmann und Campe, Hamburg, 1974), p. 113.
26. E. Kästner, 'Ein politischer Eilbrief' in *Vaterland, Muttersprache*, p. 124.
27. Rühmkorf, *Die Jahre*, pp. 58–60.
28. R. Krämer-Badoni, 'Zwanzig Jahre Bundesrepublik' in *Zensuren nach 20 Jahren Bundesrepublik* (Verlag Wissenschaft und Politik, Köln, 1969), p. 108.
29. Ibid., p. 109.
30. J. Améry, 'In den Wind gesprochen' in A. Eggebrecht (ed.), *Die zornigen alten Männer* (Rowohlt, Reinbek bei Hamburg, 1979), p. 226.
31. Ibid., p. 265.
32. R. Hagelstange, 'Endstation Kühlschrank. Mass und Vernunft frieren ein', *Die Kultur*, vol. 6, no. 112 (1958), 2.

3 PARTY TALK — THE 1960s

The developments to be described in this chapter, namely the increasingly close relationships between a significant number of writers and the Social Democratic Party, may seem at first sight paradoxical in that they occurred at a time when that party, through its new Godesberg Programme, was abandoning positions that were dear to many writers. Rather than demanding socialism in the traditional economic sense, the party was now accepting the market economy with planning reduced to a subsidiary 'where necessary' role; what is more, it had also come to terms with the Federal Republic's membership of the Western alliance. Was it then only some kind of despair born out of an increasing feeling of impotence that now led previously 'homeless' writers towards the Social Democrats? In fact, paradoxically enough, it was partly the Godesberg Programme itself that made the rapprochement possible. By declaring itself a *Volkspartei*, the Social Democratic Party was opening itself to middle-class influence, writers being one largely middle-class grouping with a potential part to play within or at the fringes of the now non-ideological party. Secondly, from the early 1960s, the figure of Willy Brandt begins to assume considerable importance in the relationship between writers and the Social Democrats, a state of affairs that has continued until the present. Not only was Brandt a former journalist with insights into the world of writing, he also possessed one supreme attribute that made him acceptable to critical intellectuals. Because of his emigration from Germany during the Third Reich and his anti-fascist past, he was totally untainted by Nazism, something that was very important to writers. Here, then, was a man trusted by writers, who in turn took them seriously. It seems more than a coincidence that the first major public endorsement of the Social Democrats by appreciable numbers of writers during the Federal election campaign of 1961 should coincide with Brandt's first candidature for the office of Federal Chancellor.

That writers and Social Democrats came together in the 1960s was not an overnight development. As early as 1956 writers and Social Democrat politicians, including the subsequent minister and SPD chancellor candidate Hans-Jochen Vogel, had met together in Hans Werner Richter's Grünwalder Kreis, mainly, as already mentioned, to combat the re-emergence of any kind of National Socialism. Following a series of public gatherings, however, Richter had allowed the circle to lapse after only two years. In his *Briefe an einen jungen Sozialisten* (Letters to a young socialist), he says this was because a more structured organisation was becoming necessary.[1] The idea of an organisation with clearly defined procedures clearly remained anathema to the generation of Richter, whose Gruppe 47 was deliberately run on very loose lines. Nevertheless, the existence of the Grünwalder Kreis, although brief, does appear to be a precursor of the events of the 1960s.

Another indication of a change in attitude from the 1950s is the volume of essays *Ich lebe in der Bundesrepublik. Fünfzehn Deutsche über Deutschland* (I live in the Federal Republic. Fifteen Germans on Germany) which appeared at the beginning of the new decade. The title in itself implies a greater degree of identification with the Bonn State than had been apparent before. That is not to say, however, that the essays do not contain many of the persistent criticisms that characterised intellectual comment in the 1950s. There remains the general unease about the mindless materialism engendered by the 'economic miracle'. The novelist Martin Beheim-Schwarzbach states simply: 'Everything, simply everything is geared to material expansion, to earning money';[2] whilst his fellow novelist Wolfgang Koeppen conjures up an apocalyptic vision of the end of the good times: 'I do not think that I shall continue to live like this for long. Miracles do not last. Close seasons come to an end at a fixed date'.[3] Geno Hartlaub implies that the material prosperity of the Federal Republic is akin to a kind of dance on the edge of a volcano:

> Only on the horizon of the days stands the atomic cloud as a warning, and if we were not constantly reminded of its existence by the cross-fire of press, radio and television we could almost forget it, so securely and cosily have we settled ourselves in our shells.[4]

Other themes that recur are the re-emergence of former National Socialists and the disregard of the Germans in the East, who in practice have been abandoned to their fate under communism. One of the most vituperative comments comes, somewhat surprisingly, from Paul Schallück. In reply to his own question about the kind of spirit pervading the Federal Republic, he answers that it is the 'spirit of mediocrity and restoration, marked by a lack of ideas, symbols and trust in one's fellow-men'.[5]

As opposed to this, there are comments that reflect a different attitude from that of the 1950s. In his initial comments the editor of the volume, Wolfgang Weyrauch, says of his motives: 'I love my home. Because I love it, I worry about it. Because I worry about it, I have compiled and edited this small and incomplete volume.'[6] Even Wolfgang Koeppen, despite his presentiments, admits to living well and being basically satisfied with his lot: 'I am a writer. A German writer. I would not like to be anything else.'[7] This statement moreover implies some sort of identification with the idea of Germany at least. The volume also contains in a long article by Johannes Gaitanides a strong condemnation of the attitudes prevalent among intellectuals in the 1950s. Entitled 'Von der Ohnmacht unserer Literatur' (On the powerlessness of our literature), it castigates writers for their blanket condemnation of all aspects of the Federal Republic, their total lack of self-criticism and their ignoring of such achievements as increased social security, the integration of so many refugees into society and the reconciliation with the Western powers. Given that this contribution is written from a clearly conservative standpoint, as is indicated by the contention that history consists of a fabric, 'at which the timeless, constant laws *and* the laws of change incessantly weave',[8] these criticisms are not particularly surprising. What is more remarkable is that the leftist writer Martin Walser should combine the criticisms of society manifest in his article 'Skizze zu einem Vorwurf' (Sketch of a reproach) with a critique of writers and intellectuals for remaining at the fringes of political and social life. He concludes his essay by stating:

> How embarrassed we should be by a state, a society that invited our co-operation. Our present democracy could do with our help, it is true, more than any other, but as it neither wants us nor does not want us, it allows us to conceal that each one of us wants nothing more than himself.[9]

All in all, *Ich lebe in der Bundesrepublik* represents some kind of watershed. Many of the criticisms of the Federal Republic reflect the mood of the 1950s, others look forward to the attitudes of the next decade, in particular the willingness to work within existing institutions. Given this mixture, the claim by Helmut Koopmann in an essay that appeared in 1979 after the Federal Republic had existed for thirty years, that this volume marked the zenith of writers' identification with the state appears exaggerated.[10] It is one stage along a road marked next by the role of writers in the Federal elections of 1961.

Martin Walser's unease, as expressed in 'Skizze zu einem Vorwurf', about the attitudes of intellectuals in the Federal Republic prefigures his activities in election year. Largely on his own initiative, he compiled a book in which twenty writers endorsed the Social Democratic Party. This volume entitled *Die Alternative oder Brauchen wir eine neue Regierung?* (The alternative or do we need a new government?) embodies the new wish to sustain the democracy of the Federal Republic. It is true that Willy Brandt invited the contributors to a meeting in Bonn, but in essence *Die Alternative* is probably the first example of writers taking of themselves a new kind of initiative. The 'homelessness' of the 1950s is replaced by a degree of identification with the SPD at least great enough to advocate that a vote for the Social Democrats is preferable to one for the ruling Christian Democrats of Chancellor Adenauer.

This is not to say that the book consists of a eulogy of the SPD of the kind that is normally found in political parties' election literature. In fact, the general impression conveyed is one of considerable scepticism towards the post-Godesberg SPD, as it sought to move towards the middle ground of West German politics. How much such scepticism was justified from a left-wing standpoint can be seen from the party's willingness after the election to offer a coalition to the Christian Democrats when the strengthened Free Democrats, the CDU's coalition partner until 1957, started imposing conditions for a new coalition, particularly about the future of the octogenarian Adenauer. The doubts about the SPD are even visible in the editor's contribution, Walser speaking of the party having made sacrifices to the most vulgar anti-communism. Comparable doubts are to be found in many more of the contributions. Peter Rühmkorf says he is loaning his vote to the SPD 'with the greatest misgivings',[11] whilst the novelist and librettist Heinz von Cramer reproaches the party, even in opposition, of having taken the path 'of least resistance, of conformity, of popularity at any price'.[12]

In the case of Hans Magnus Enzensberger, the reader is left

wondering how the writer of the following comments can recommend the SPD at all:

> There is in our country a party that is called democratic and social and is in opposition. It ingratiates itself with its enemies, it is tame, it retrieves and begs like a dog. A sight that admittedly is not what might be called elevating, a sight that is unsavoury, boring, mediocre.[13]

The only reason that Enzensberger can advance for voting for the SPD is that is is the lesser of two evils. This is, in fact, quite a common refrain throughout the book. Equally unreflective of great conviction about the merits of the alternative government is the argument put forward by the novelist Siegfried Lenz and the journalist Erich Kuby: namely 'it is time for a change'. Claiming that changes of government are the lifeblood of democracy, Kuby even says that he would probably be saying the same thing if the SPD had been in office for twelve years. In general, it is hard to find much positive endorsement of the SPD in *Die Alternative*. Gerhard Schoenberner praises its plans for a more democratic society and for a more flexible foreign policy, whilst Siegfried Lenz congratulates some of its leading figures for not separating politics from the idea of justice. Indeed, it is in terms of personalities that much of the support is given, the sympathy towards the figure of Brandt being particularly noticeable. Hans Werner Richter, for instance, states baldly that, just as he prefers Kennedy to Eisenhower: 'similarly the young, democratic Willy Brandt is more sympathetic to me as chancellor of the Federal Republic than the autocratic great-grandfather Konrad Adenauer.'[14] It must be admitted that the level of argument employed by Richter here is not convincing. Whatever the degree of correctness in the assertions about the attitudes to democracy of the two candidates, the stress on age is a red herring in political terms.

Rather than committed support for the Social Democrats, it is the condemnation of the Christian Democrat Government of Konrad Adenauer and the kind of society it has engendered that is the most marked feature of Walser's volume. Here again, personalities loom large, not just Adenauer himself but the up-and-coming Franz Josef Strauss. In 1961, a good year before his fall over the 'Spiegel Affair', many of the contributors to *Die Alternative* saw the then Minister of Defence with his strongly pro-nuclear policy as the natural successor to Adenauer. Such a contingency made them fear not just for the survival of democracy in the Federal Republic but also for peace itself, an over-statement given the limited freedom of action of the Federal Republic. The literary critic Franz Schonauer sees Strauss as 'bursting with hunger for power',[15] whilst Walser, after referring to his scenarios for nuclear war, calls him the 'nightmare from Bavaria, who can defend us against anything — except himself.'[16] Beyond the question of personalities, the criticisms directed against the CDU are to some extent familiar ones from the 1950s, for example the failure to confront the Nazi past and the blind anti-communism encouraged by the government. The most repeated complaint is probably that the CDU has created a society concerned only with material well-being and whose atrophied authoritarianism, symbolised by the slogan 'no experiments', represents a threat to democracy. Particularly singled out for comment also is the phenomenon of 'clericalism'.

This term refers to the power of the church, the Catholic Church specifically, to impose its conservative tenets on society through the ruling Christian Democrats. The radical Catholic writer, Carl Amery, in his essay 'Eine kleine Utopie' (A small utopia) calls for a separation of church and state, whilst Heinz von Cramer attacks the Catholic Church for supporting dictatorships and the CDU government for being an 'instrument of church power'.[17] The writer on religious matters Gerhard Szczesny attacks the hypocrisy bred by advancement in society being dependent on paying lip-service to Christianity. His essay is a plea for the establishment of a Humanist Union to preserve the rights of all citizens regardless of their religious convictions.

One of the criticisms made in *Die Alternative* became more and more prevalent throughout the 1960s, namely that because society had become so stagnant, the Federal Republic was in danger of becoming a backwater. What was proclaimed was the need for 'modernisation' in all areas of society. As part of this process, the 'taboos' which prevented progress had to be overcome. One of these, as referred to by Axel Eggebrecht in *Die Alternative*, was the refusal to have anything to do with communist countries. Gerhard Szczesny comes up with a whole range of areas where he considers radical change to be necessary:

> The release of thought from the tutelage of theology, the libera-
> tion of people from the bonds of authoritarian and clerical ties,

the proclamation of human rights and duties, the expansion of educational, technical and caring institutions which are open to all, the development of academic freedom, a free press, literature and art.[18]

Specifically, Inge Aicher-Scholl, sister of the Munich students Hans and Sophie Scholl martyred by the Nazis, expresses her fear that the Federal Republic is falling behind because the education system is neglected in favour of private affluence and consumption. As a whole, *Die Alternative* contrasts a backward-looking society embodied by the CDU with the ideal of dynamic development, which requires a change of government if it is to be achieved.

It is hard to believe that *Die Alternative* played a great part in the increase of the popular vote achieved by the Social Democrats in 1961. Its lukewarm support for the party would no doubt have professional campaign managers running for the smelling salts. Some contributors even wrote that they did not believe in an SPD election victory, hoping only that they would gain the third of the vote necessary to block constitutional changes that might threaten the democratic substance of the state. At least this hope was fulfilled. Nevertheless, for all its amateurishness, *Die Alternative* is a likeable collection. The contributions are marked by an honesty and openness that one would expect from critical writers. Historically, it is interesting as the first example of systematic support to be given to a party by a significant number of authors.

Between the appearance of *Die Alternative* and the next Federal election in 1965, in addition to reacting to specific events like the Berlin Wall and the Spiegel Affair, intellectuals appear to have indulged in a period of reflection. This mood is summed up in the title of a volume edited by Hans Werner Richter that appeared in 1962: *Bestandsaufnahme* (Taking stock).[19] In this collection writers, academics and journalists addressed themselves to a variety of familiar topics, including the consequences of the war and the role of religion in society. The volume does not reflect a single viewpoint, but rather draws attention to the variety of concerns prevalent in the Adenauer era. There are doubts, for instance, about the inequalities produced by the 'economic miracle' and the rigidity of Adenauer's foreign policy. All in all, the book again shows the growing feeling of the 1960s that the Federal Republic was being overtaken by events, was in need of 'modernisation' if it was to face up to the problems of the future.[20] This modernisation, it was felt, was hindered by the large numbers of taboos, ranging from the pure doctrine of the market economy to anti-communism. At the end of his essay 'Vorurteile und Tabus' (Prejudices and taboos), Paul Schallück lists a number of these taboos. He suggests that the use of the word 'so-called' or of inverted commas in connection with the name German Democratic Republic shows that the other German state is a taboo, whilst the slogan 'no experiments' renders all discussion of the internal order of the Federal Republic taboo. Erich Kuby speaks nevertheless of a feeling that one epoch is ending and another one beginning. This feeling may have encouraged the desire to take stock, to look back before moving to a new stage of development. In any case, it was helped by the coincidences of the calendar: 1962 was fifteen years after the banning of *Der Ruf* and the foundation of the Gruppe 47. This fact no doubt encouraged the publication of a collection of articles from the magazine and an *Almanach der Gruppe 47*.[21] Hans Werner Richter was connected with both publications. He contributed an introductory essay to the collection from *Der Ruf*, which stressed its continuing relevance:

> We forget so quickly, and in forgetting we do not feel that we are still living with the same problems without ever dealing with them, let alone solving them. On reading the *Ruf* this becomes frighteningly clear. Then as now we spoke of the Third World War. Then as now we live in fear.[22]

Similarly, in his introduction to the *Almanach*, which itself is essentially a collection of literary texts, Richter spoke of the close connections between the Gruppe 47 and *Der Ruf*. It is true to say that the concerns of Richter's generation in the post-war years, the German question and the need for a different kind of social order, remained on the agenda for the next generation of writers.

A year later, a number of writers and intellectuals addressed themselves to the question explicitly formulated in the title of the collection *Was ist heute links?* (What does left-wing mean today?). Despite the implications of the title, the volume is not ideological in nature but rather another example of writers reflecting their own attitudes and activities within the political life of the Federal Republic. In his introduction, Horst Krüger says that social criticism requires 'a marked individuality, an ability to think in opposition to the tide of the time'.[23] Similarly, the sociologist Ralf

Dahrendorf states: 'Intellectuals are as it were the permanent
critical distrust in society — or they ought to be so in order to fulfil
their task at the head of the "Left".'[24] This was more or less the
position of intellectuals in the first years of the Federal Republic.
Krüger though is quick to dismiss the term 'homelessness', which
he associates with passivity and contrasts with the spirit of analysis
and criticism. This once more reflects the desire for greater involvement prevalent in the 1960s.

Involvement was again the order of the day during the Federal
election campaign of 1965. Another volume of essays with contributions from writers expressing their support for the Social Democrat cause appeared. This time the editor was Hans Werner Richter,
Walser having become disillusioned with the rightward drift of the
SPD. Although the title *Plädoyer für eine neue Regierung oder
Keine Alternative* (Plea for a new government or no alternative)
recalls its predecessor, the general impression of the book is that a
conscious effort is being made to move away from a lukewarm
endorsement of the SPD towards a much more positive stance. The
first section comprises a series of portraits of leading Social
Democrat politicians, reflecting a new emphasis on personalities.
Besides coming close in a number of cases to the election material
that might be expected from professional 'image builders', this part
of the book reflects an even more non-ideological stance, apart
from a general espousal of change and 'progress', than was already
general at this time. In his introduction Richter sums up this
conception of politics:

> But who will or can go into an election today with ideas which, as
> a result of rapid changes, are already obsolete tomorrow and
> who can tie himself to such ideas whilst aiming at policies for
> tomorrow? . . . Thus an alternative through a change in person-
> nel becomes more and more important. By electing new people, I
> am *ipso facto* choosing new initiatives.[25]

Other contributions not specifically about individual politicians
reflect this outlook. In his model of a possible politician, Jürgen
Becker approves of a non-party type characterised by cool pragmatism. Peter Härtling in his portrait of the critical intellectuals of
the Federal Republic sees the use of such labels as 'conservative' or
'socialist' as increasingly irrelevant, preferring to see intellectuals'
criticisms in terms of a generation conflict, in which the young

generation is united in its rejection of past taboos. He adds, with reference to these younger people: 'When Kennedy became president, they saw it as a confirmation of themselves.'[26] Such a statement now appears particularly ironic in the light of the criticisms of the USA that were to come to the fore in the late 1960s. However one reacts to the concentration on personalities in *Plädoyer für eine neue Regierung*, it must be pointed out that one at least is largely negative. That is the portrait by Rudolf Augstein, the editor of *Der Spiegel*, of Herbert Wehner. Wehner is the SPD politician usually associated with the change in the nature of the party encapsulated by the two words 'Godesberg Programme'. Augstein portrays him as an unprincipled tactician willing to pay almost any price to bring his party into government, reflecting a standpoint one might well associate with idealistic intellectuals.

After its series of portraits, Richter's collection has a section providing a view from abroad given by German writers living in various countries. The substance of Reinhard Lettau's argument, significantly entitled in English 'It's time for a Change', is that the SPD enjoys greater confidence than the CDU government in the USA; Erich Fried provides a similar message from Great Britain, even using as evidence an English acquaintance, who in his own country supports the Conservative Party. That such reports from abroad are included and were no doubt considered helpful to the Social Democrat cause is a reflection of West German political culture, in which respect for opinion held abroad plays a significant role. Thus, when neo-Nazism appeared to be gaining ground in the late 1960s with the electoral successes of the National Democratic Party, the argument that was constantly advanced was that this party had to be resisted because of the bad image it gave the Federal Republic abroad. One might have thought that the party's policies offered sufficient grounds for opposition. In contrast to the reports from the Western partners of the Federal Republic, the other two contributions from outside are less sympathetic to the SPD. Robert Havemann, the East German Marxist dissident, reflects on the division of Germany in a way that Richter in his introduction says may well harm the SPD. Peter Weiss from Sweden, whose play *Marat Sade* had first been performed in 1964, makes a more general criticism of the affluent society of the Federal Republic, adding that the general atmosphere of the country has always made it impossible for him to return to the land he left in face of Nazi persecution. His attitude to the Social Democrats, too, can hardly be classed as positive: 'I can hardly differentiate their arguments from the arguments of the conservatives.'[27]

The third and final section of *Plädoyer für eine neue Regierung* is a more varied selection of essays, many of which are very much in keeping with both the concerns of the time and possibly the concerns of intellectuals in general. Hans Schwab-Felisch criticises the cultural policy of the government abroad, which is seen as too restrictive. In the period which was marked by increasing concern that West Germany, because of its outdated educational structures, was facing an 'educational catastrophe', Klaus Wagenbach demands expansion and reform, whilst the scientist Robert Jungk stresses in general terms the need to confront the problems of the future. These contributions underline the general message of the book, the need for a new broom in the shape of the Social Democrats to sweep Germany out of its inertia towards the challenges of the future. The general tone is therefore not surprisingly more bland than that of its predecessor in 1961. Whether, because of this, it contributed more positively to the progress made by the Social Democrats — still, however, not enough for the party to be able to form the government — must remain in the nature of things a matter for speculation.

The above comments do not mean that controversy was entirely foresaken for positive election propaganda. Two articles in *Plädoyer für eine neue Regierung* do deserve specific mention for their radical stance. Ulrich Sonnemann takes the German judicial tradition severely to task in his long essay 'Vom Preis des Unrechts und der Rentabilität des Rechts' (The price of injustice and the value of justice). He concentrates particularly on the role of the judiciary in the Third Reich, pointing out that no judge had ever been convicted for his activities at that time because of the prevailing positivistic view that they were simply administering the law. He finds it particularly ironic that the Federal Republic honours the memory of those who conspired against Nazism in the July 1944 plot, whilst retaining the services of their judicial persecutors. What is more, Sonnemann connects this judicial tradition with the wider, much more dangerous German custom of excessive respect towards authority: towards what he calls 'the nimbus of institutions'.[28] Rather than relying on external authority, citizens should seek 'the restoration of political, human spontaneity'.[29] On a less speculative level, Rolf Hochhuth uses his portrait of the trade union leader Otto Brenner to attack the unequal distribution of wealth in the Federal Republic. This essay entitled 'Klassenkampf' (Class struggle) provoked the most notorious of all Christian Democrat expressions of anger towards critical writers when Ludwig Erhard described its author as a 'pincher'. The title itself was a provocation in view of Erhard's own description of the Federal Republic as a *formierte Gesellschaft* (ordered society). This term was meant to imply that the country had developed a harmonious social structure where class antagonisms had been overcome.

Looked at more closely, Hochhuth's article, despite its title, is far from being a plea for Marxist revolution. What he asks for is a broader distribution of wealth throughout the population. He sees this as the most effective bulwark against communism as more people would have much more to lose. The present tendency towards concentration, on the other hand, would render a takeover by the state a much more feasible proposition. Coupled with this economic argument, Hochhuth's essay reveals the moral concern that underlies all his writing. As an example of this, the following statement could hardly be more direct and forceful:

> This state pays war criminals and judicial murderers, who punished the concealment of a Jewish child threatened with the gas chamber with the guillotine, 1400 marks per month, even more. Eight or nine times as much as the parents or widowed mother of two sons killed in the war.[30]

Even where on other occasions his political arguments and claims appear eccentric, it is impossible to deny Hochhuth's moral courage.

Writers' involvement in the Federal election of 1965 was not restricted to the publication of a single book. As will be seen later, Günter Grass involved himself with the actual campaign, whilst in West Berlin a number of mainly young writers established a Wahlkontor deutscher Schriftsteller (Election office of German writers) to help the SPD. The main aims of this office were to coin slogans and to write or improve the speeches of party politicians. The writer and publisher Klaus Wagenbach was nominally in charge, and other writers involved, who incidentally were paid for their efforts, included Nicolas Born, Günter Herburger and Peter Schneider. One person associated with the group, Gudrun Ensslin, was to achieve notoriety later as a terrorist. Her disillusionment with the SPD, like that of many others associated with the Wahl-kontor, set in when the party entered into the Grand Coalition with the CDU in 1966; on that occasion, the writers joined together in a telegram of protest to their erstwhile patron.

The Federal election of 1965 was the last major occasion where it is possible to speak of a general political consensus among leftist writers and intellectuals. This consensus with its anti-fascist base had developed over the years of the existence of the Federal Republic from a simple rejection of the 'CDU-state' into some degree of support, however grudging, for the Social Democrats. Even in 1965 cracks were beginning to appear. After his efforts in 1961 Martin Walser, as already mentioned, was no longer willing to support the SPD despite the personal efforts of Brandt himself to make him change his mind. Other writers, equally disillusioned with developments in the SPD, advocated voting for the Deutsche Friedens-Union (German peace union). This group, which never achieved anything near the 5 per cent of the vote required for a party to gain seats in parliament, was the only left-wing alternative to the SPD at the time after the traditional communist party (KPD) had been banned in the mid-1950s at the height of Adenauer's anti-communist crusade. A declaration for the DFU, whose signatories included the novelist Christian Geissler, objected to nuclear weapons and the prospect of emergency legislation, a question that was to come to a head in the late 1960s.[31] On both issues, the atti-tude of the SPD was deemed unsatisfactory. If these doubts about the Social Democrats were peripheral in 1965, two years later things were very different. By then and certainly by the next election in 1969, it was more or less possible to discern two sets of writers, those who still stuck by the SPD and those who in some cases went beyond scepticism towards a particular party to something close to a rejection of the whole political system of the Federal Republic. Chapter 4 will deal with the second group, whose ideas became close to those of the burgeoning student movement; the remainder of this chapter, after reference to the events that caused or under-lined the growing divisions among writers, will concentrate on those who still supported the SPD.

It was not long after the defeat of that party in the 1965 election that Günter Grass rounded on those authors whose support for the SPD he deemed inadequate. In his speech 'Über das Selbstver-ständliche' (On the self-evident), delivered in Darmstadt on 9 October 1965 on the occasion of his gaining the Georg Büchner

Prize, he demanded of certain fellow-writers why they had not followed his example and taken part in the recent election campaign.[32] He mentioned Heinrich Böll and Alfred Andersch by name whilst the speech also contained implicit references to Enzensberger. If this showed that the cracks were deepening, a year later the formation of the Grand Coalition destroyed any remaining consensus.

Adenauer's successor, Ludwig Erhard, despite his reputation as the 'father of the economic miracle' and his electoral success in 1965, never cut or was never allowed by his predecessor to cut an impressive figure as Federal Chancellor. The, by subsequent standards, minor economic crisis of 1966 was enough to bring about the collapse of his coalition with the liberal Free Democrats. This provided the chance for the Social Democrats to enter into government, albeit as the junior partner of the CDU. The Grand Coalition was born. What, though, were writers to make of the party they had supported embracing the despised Christian Democrats and, what is more, accepting as the new chancellor a former National Socialist, Kurt Georg Kiesinger? Had they not always objected to the re-emergence of such people in the Federal Republic? Given that jubilation was out of the question, a stark choice presented itself to many writers, either gritting their teeth or breaking with the SPD. A page in the 2 December 1966 edition of the weekly *Die Zeit* encapsulated the choice. In an open letter to Willy Brandt, Grass begs his mentor not to enter into the coalition 'diese miese Ehe' (this wretched marriage) but refuses to break with the party. Next to this, the younger F. C. Delius, who had been active in the Wahlkontor in 1965, declares his dismay at the step taken by the SPD in a bitter poem which announces the end of his support for the party. The first line could not be more explicit: 'Brandt: es ist aus. Wir machen nicht mehr mit.' (Brandt, we are through. We'll go along no more.)

The following year saw another event that reflected the growing divisions among writers, the *de facto* end of the Gruppe 47. Ostensibly, all that happened was that Hans Werner Richter who, given the lack of structure within the group, had sole responsibility for convening subsequent gatherings ceased to do so. Speculation about why this occurred has shrouded this development to the point that it almost seems to belong to the world of myth, but it must be concluded that political differences played a major part. In 1966 the group had met at Princeton University with financial aid

from the Ford Foundation, where it had inevitably the appearance
of being the representative body of German literature rather than a
loosely organised collection of critically minded individuals. As the
fame of many of its authors had spread, meetings had in any case,
regardless of location, tended to develop into a kind of literary
jamboree or market with much media attention. In a polemical
attack in the periodical *Konkret*, the Austrian writer Robert
Neumann claimed that the group was a kind of literary mafia, a
charge that had previously been made by rightist authors like
Krämer-Badoni.[33] His second stricture was that it had now met
amid a blaze of publicity in the country whose Vietnam policies it
had criticised in a resolution a year ealier.

In 1967 the meeting at the Pulvermühle in the idyllic Franconian
Switzerland attracted the attention of student demonstrators. Not
only did they scornfully apostrophise the writers as *Dichter* (poets)
with the implication that they were other-worldly and lacking in
social and political concern; they also broke into the meeting itself.
At the most basic level, those present were torn between calling the
police or entering into discussions with the students. There were
also disputes surrounding a resolution against the Springer Press,
which was printing increasingly vitriolic attacks on the student
movement and any other leftist groups it saw as endangering
society. Even if Martin Walser found the meeting more interesting
because of the varying wings within the group that were emerging,
it appears with hindsight that the once largely homogeneous body
could not cope with the variety of political views emerging in the
turbulent years following the formation of the Grand Coalition.
The physical presence of the students had acted as a catalyst
bringing to light another manifestation of the growing differences
of opinion among previously much more united writers. It is also
worth pointing out that the end of the Gruppe 47 coincided with a
caesura in the development of West German literature. The writers
who had come to the fore in the 1960s, Grass, Walser, Enzensberger
and Uwe Johnson for example, had generally been more directly
concerned with social and political questions than had their predecessors, but nevertheless still shared the same 'oppositional'
stance. In the course of the decade, however, their works and those
of other writers became increasingly beset with doubts about the
writing process itself. In Walser's *Das Einhorn* (The Unicorn) of
1966, for instance, the egregious Anselm Kristlein, advertising
executive turned author, finds it impossible to recount and recall

his love for a young Dutch girl with the novelist's traditional narrative techniques. Similarly, Johnson's title *Das Dritte Buch über Achim* (The third Book about Achim) refers to a work that it proves impossible to write. The direction some writers began to take in the late 1960s will be dealt with in Chapter 4; suffice it to say here that the political crisis brought on primarily by the Grand Coalition and the students was compounded by an aesthetic crisis among many writers.

When the next Federal election came round in 1969, the Social Democrats clearly enjoyed less support from writers and intellectuals than four years previously. Those who still supported the party, however, were determined to make their efforts count. In 1968 the writer and journalist Klaus Harpprecht, who subsequently wrote a biography of Willy Brandt, studied the techniques used in the American presidential election. Out of this visit and from previous experiences in Germany, particularly those of Günter Grass, was born the Sozialdemokratische Wählerinitiative (The Social Democratic voters action group), which has remained a feature of West German political life, especially at election times, until the present. The aim of this organisation, which began to take shape in the months prior to the 1969 election, was to provide a framework for citizens who were not necessarily party members, to express their support for the SPD. The political scientist Professor Kurt Sontheimer, who along with Grass was a founder member, told the Social Democrat party conference in 1969 that the Wählerinitiative favoured the active involvement of the voter in elections which could not just be left to professional politicians. The aim was a dialogue between voters and party members; at the same time rational arguments in favour of the SPD were to be put forward with the intention especially of attracting those social groups traditionally inimical to the SPD to vote for the party.

The Social Democratic Party itself was faced with the problem of how to react to this support from outsiders. Herbert Wehner, never a favourite politician among intellectuals, wrote in a letter to Brandt in 1968 after a meeting with Grass that he was sceptical about the Wählerinitiative and that it should be kept under close party scrutiny. The mutual suspicions between the new body and Helmut Schmidt can be seen in a letter from Grass to Brandt from the summer of 1969 asking him to lead the party with a firmer hand and not to allow Schmidt, presumably suspected of wanting a continuation of the Grand Coalition, too much latitude. Nevertheless, the party leadership, one assumes under the influence of Brandt, accepted the help from outside and provided financial support.

In the election campaign the voters action group set itself a number of tasks. On the one hand, it sought to encourage the formation of groups at local level. This process could perhaps be aided by a visit from one of the celebrities, particularly Grass. It also tried to recruit the famous to the SPD cause, not always successfully, as in the cases of the Frankfurt zoologist Grzimek and the national football manager Sepp Herberger. On 22 January 1969 the Cologne newspaper *Kölner Stadtanzeiger* pointed out that many writers were unwilling to support the SPD any more, including Weiss, Walser, Wagenbach, Böll and Richter, although the last two did modify their stance by election day. Nevertheless, the party did attract the support of many other intellectuals with academics like Sontheimer and the historian Golo Mann possibly more predominant than literary writers. Alongside Grass, the most distinguished of these were the novelists Siegfried Lenz and Peter Härtling and the Swabian regional writer Thaddäus Troll.

Rather than producing a book, the Wählerinitiative chose smaller-scale publications, of which the most important was the glossy magazine *Dafür* (In favour), which appeared twice. The title coined by Grass was reminiscent of that of his play *Davor* (Before) which at the time had just been produced. On its front cover the magazine also sported the symbol of Wählerinitiative devised by Grass in his other profession as an artist, a cock crowing the quasi-phonetic version of the initials SPD 'Es-Pe-De'. The layout was intended to be appealing and modern with the text reinforced with numerous photographs. Even so, the first edition contains an article by Richter in which he endorses the SPD with the time-honoured reluctance. He says that two years earlier he would not have voted for the party because of the Grand Coalition, but concludes that now there is no practical alternative, as small groups, however sympathetic, can never gain sufficient support. Nevertheless, he shows scant enthusiasm for the party: 'I find it difficult. I had and have a lot to criticise.'[34] Unlike previous publications, this tone is generally rare. The aim of *Dafür*, especially the second edition, was according to Grass to appeal to the voter directly. To this end, this second edition was grouped around a series of areas, including transport, education and justice, where the SPD promised major improvements. The most notable coup was an article by Heinrich Böll 'Offener Brief an eine deutsche

Katholikin' (Open letter to a German Catholic lady). Although Böll's article does not contain any exhortation to vote for the Social Democrats — 1972 was the first occasion on which he committed himself — its publication in this context must have added the prestige of his name to the SPD cause.

Although it is impossible in the nature of things to quantify the success of the Wählerinitiative, either through its publications or the speeches of its prominent members, it may well have helped to secure an election result that made a change of government possible. The Social Democrats with the help of the liberal Free Democrats now had a majority, albeit small, and Willy Brandt was duly elected Federal Chancellor. There followed a honeymoon period between writers and politicians — or rather those Social Democrats who approved of intellectuals' involvement in politics. Here was a government that promised both internal reforms — the modernisation of society so long sought — and a new policy of reconciliation towards Germany's former enemies in the East, the *Ostpolitik*. This, too, meant a break with the sterile anti-communism of the past, so despised by many intellectuals. As Chancellor, Brandt appeared to be all that had been hoped for. He soon showed a very different attitude to that of his predecessors. At a writers' conference held in Stuttgart in early 1970, he not only appeared in person but sought to foster a new spirit of co-operation between writers and politicians. He even went so far as to make a personal appeal: 'As a politician, I do not hesitate to ask you the writers for help, so that reason is not again defeated by ignorance.'[35] The implication of this was flattering: namely that writers enjoyed considerable influence in society. Brandt confirmed this by asking them to support his policies, in particular the Ostpolitik. Writers' endorsement of this policy of reconciliation and the new esteem they enjoyed were evident when Grass and Siegfried Lenz, both former inhabitants of Germany's lost eastern territories, accompanied Brandt to Warsaw in 1970 when he signed the treaty that among other things accepted the post-war frontiers of Poland. During this visit Brandt underlined his moral stature by kneeling at the Warsaw Ghetto Memorial, an act of atonement long hoped for by many writers and only possible for a politician with Brandt's impeccable past.

In view of these developments, it is not surprising that writers rallied to Brandt when, faced with the erosion of his parliamentary majority, he had to submit to new elections in 1972. This election

campaign was a high point in the evolution of the Sozialdemokratische Wählerinitiative. There was a great rallying to the SPD,
in particular to save the Ostpolitik, which would have been threatened by a CDU victory. With its new supporters like Böll, the SPD
achieved a remarkable electoral triumph, overtaking the Christian
Democrats for the first and only time in the popular vote. The election was also a personal triumph for Willy Brandt, as it had
developed into something of a plebiscite on his chancellorship. The
Wählerinitiative too had reason to be pleased with the results of its
efforts to secure the continuation of the SPD/FDP coalition.

It is appropriate at this point to assess the role of the Sozialdemokratische Wählerinitiative as a forum for intellectuals to express
their political preferences. In historical terms, it can be clearly seen
as the culmination of writers' attempts to make their commitment
effective in a way that the 'homeless' stance of the 1950s had not
been. In itself, it is something of a hybrid. On the one hand, it seeks
to proceed on the basis of informed argument yet, at the same time,
it is tied to a particular party which may not always act rationally.
It is also true that it attempts to preserve a degree of independence,
but it is helped financially by the party. The most telling criticism
of the whole concept came in an article in the political newspaper
Das Parlament shortly after the 1972 election. The authors Heidrun
Abromeit and Klaus Burkhardt see a danger of voters' action
groups — the other parties too sought to make use of the device in
1972 — being solely an additional source of party propaganda and
hence just another way of manipulating the electorate, particularly
by exploiting the aura surrounding the famous. They also criticise
the general level of argument that does little to make the citizen
more politically aware.[36] If the voters' groups of the other parties
are left aside — it is, however, worthy of note that the Free Democrats have over the years enjoyed the support of Hochhuth and
other well-known writers, including the novelist Walter Kempowski
— these criticisms have some substance in the case of the Sozialdemokratische Wählerinitiative, even if it has never paid its supporters, as some other parties apparently have. A letter from
Brandt's office, for instance, dated 1 September 1972 suggests that
the Wählerinitiative adopts the slogan 'Wähler für Willy Brandt'
(voters for Willy Brandt), something that was taken up and can
hardly be called sophisticated political argument. Nevertheless,
some of the campaigns launched by the Wählerinitiative in 1972,
regardless of their intellectual level, do seem to have been more

effective than the official ones of the party itself. Rather than
seeking to ingratiate itself with the Catholic hierarchy, which was
traditionally hostile to the SPD, it attempted to appeal directly to
Catholic voters through the activities of the affiliated Bensberger
Kreis (Bensberg circle), a group of prominent Catholic SPD supporters, including Walter Dirks of the *Frankfurter Hefte*. When the
election came, the party did make gains among the Catholic
population. That the Sozialdemokratische Wählerinitiative has
generally maintained considerable independence from the party
machine can be seen from expressions of hostility from party politicians who have seen it as a tail wagging the dog. This hostility was
evident in 1972 when Helmut Schmidt, accompanied by the then
Economics Minister Karl Schiller, walked out during an address to
the party by Grass.

What, then, is one to conclude about the activities of the Sozialdemokratische Wählerinitiative? Its longevity speaks for the
validity of the concept. So does the general respect as a force to be
reckoned with which it achieved by 1972, after many had been dismissive in 1969. At the same time, even if it is accepted that it
openly discloses a preference for a specific party and therefore does
not claim to be objective, it cannot be said that it has always contributed to the level of political debate with its glossy brochures and
the like. Ultimately, though, success is a criterion that cannot be
overlooked entirely, and the Wählerinitiative has at least played a
part in successful campaigns. Unless it is held that any intervention
on such a base level of political activity as elections is inappropriate
for intellectuals and that material success is intellectual failure, its
activities can be regarded as acceptable within a democratic society.

The year 1972 can be seen as representing the pinnacle for those
writers who had supported the SPD. They could look back on a
decade or so of activity now having been crowned with success.
Without being immodest, they could claim that their demands for
change and modernisation had contributed to a new mood in the
population. It was now voting for reforms rather than 'no experiments'. That these feelings among writers did not last much longer
cannot just be put down to a natural cycle of events. Something else
occurred in early 1972 that was to cloud the relationships between
writers and politicians for the remainder of the decade, namely the
circular endorsed by the Brandt government in which those responsible for personnel were reminded that public servants should be
loyal to the constitution. The interpretation of this circular, which

came to be known as the *Radikalenerlass* (Radicals decree) led, in
the wake of the student movement, to the exclusion of people
deemed to be extremists from such positions as those of teacher,
and made the term *Berufsverbot* (exclusion from a profession) a
rare German linguistic export. This phenomenon was one factor in
a decisive change of mood in the remainder of the decade following
the 1972 election.

Notes

1. Richter, *Briefe an einen jungen Sozialisten*, p. 124.
2. M. Beheim-Schwarzbach, 'Lieber Freund' in W. Weyrauch (ed.), *Ich lebe in der Bundesrepublik. Fünfzehn Deutsche über Deutschland* (List, München, 1961), p. 98.
3. W. Koeppen, 'Wahn' in ibid., p. 35.
4. G. Hartlaub, 'Die stehengebliebene Stadt' in ibid., p. 40.
5. P. Schallück, 'Zwölf Fragen' in ibid., p. 107.
6. W. Weyrauch, 'Bemerkungen des Herausgebers' in ibid., p. 7.
7. Koeppen in ibid., p. 36.
8. J. Gaitanides, 'Von der Ohnmacht unserer Literatur' in ibid., p. 22.
9. M. Walser, 'Skizze zu einem Vorwurf' in ibid., p. 114.
10. See note 4, Chapter 2.
11. P. Rühmkorf, 'Passionseinheit' in M. Walser (ed.), *Die Alternative oder Brauchen wir eine neue Regierung?* (Rowohlt, Reinbek bei Hamburg, 1961), p. 45.
12. H. von Cramer, 'Es ist so spät wie es schon einmal war' in ibid., p. 92.
13. H. M. Enzensberger, 'Ich wünsche nicht gefährlich zu leben' in ibid., p. 66.
14. H. W. Richter, 'Von links in die Mitte' in ibid., p. 123.
15. F. Schonauer, 'Das schmutzige Nest' in ibid., p. 74.
16. M. Walser, 'Das Fremdwort der Saison' in ibid., p. 126.
17. von Cramer in ibid., p. 87.
18. G. Szczesny, 'Humanistische Union' in ibid., p. 38.
19. See note 2, Chapter 2.
20. It is worth remembering that a similar feeling was abroad in Britain at this time with Mr Harold Wilson endorsing the technological revolution.
21. See note 7, Chapter 2.
22. H. W. Richter, 'Beim Wiedersehen des "Ruf"' in Schwab-Felisch, *Der Ruf*, p. 8f.
23. H. Krüger, 'Das Thema wird gestellt' in H. Krüger (ed.), *Was ist heute links?* (List, München, 1963), p. 27.
24. R. Dahrendorf, 'Links in der Bundesrepublik' in ibid., p. 42.
25. H. W. Richter, 'Die Alternative im Wechsel der Personen' in H. W. Richter (ed.), *Plädoyer für eine neue Regierung oder Keine Alternative* (Rowohlt, Reinbek bei Hamburg, 1965), p. 10.
26. P. Härtling, 'Eine natürliche Opposition' in ibid., p. 181.
27. P. Weiss, 'Unter dem Hirseberg' in ibid., p. 148.
28. U. Sonnemann, 'Vom Preis des Unrechts und der Rentabilität des Rechts' in ibid., p. 166.
29. Ibid., p. 168.
30. R. Hochhuth, 'Klassenkampf' in ibid., p. 83.
31. 'Zur Bundestagswahl 1965' in *Vaterland, Muttersprache*, p. 229.

32. This speech provides the title of the first published collection of Grass's political writing (see bibliography).

33. See Arnold, *Die Gruppe 47*, pp. 237–42.

34. See *Dafür*, no. 1 (1969), 56.

35. W. Brandt, 'Braucht die Politik den Schriftsteller' in D. Lattmann (ed.), *Einigkeit der Einzelgänger* (Kindler, München, 1971), p. 18.

36. H. Abromeit, K. Burkhardt, 'Die Wählerinitiativen im Wahlkampf 1972', Supplement to *Das Parlament*, 15 Sept. 73.

4 TO YOUR MARX, GET SET, GO — WRITERS AND STUDENTS

As was pointed out in Chapter 3, it became finally impossible in the era of the Grand Coalition to speak of a consensus among critical writers and intellectuals. It is now time to look at those writers who took up positions generally to the left of the Social Democrats and whose concerns were similar to those of the student movement, which achieved its peak in 1967 and 1968. The existence of the student movement in itself changed the position of established writers and intellectuals; they were no longer the only radical grouping with a critical attitude towards society. Instead, they had to share the stage with the much more actionistic students. At the same time, there were many shared interests and attitudes. The term *Ausserparlamentarische Opposition* (Extra-parliamentary ooposition) referred to the loose alliance of students and those intellectuals who asserted the right of protest at a time when they felt parliament to be emasculated through the existence of the Grand Coalition.

That there should be such upheavals at the universities in the late 1960s and that, in addition, there should be a reawakening of interest in political ideologies, especially Marxism, seems particularly remarkable in the light of the attitudes that persisted in the early years of the decade. In the volume *Bestandsaufnahme*, the universities were seen as another area of national life that required modernisation after post-war neglect. There had been hopes for a radical change in the system of higher education immediately after the war, but the traditional pattern marked by absolute professorial power soon reasserted itself. Thus, in *Bestandsaufnahme*, the writer on cultural affairs in *Die Zeit*, Rudolf Walter Leonhardt, asserted 'that the German universities have fulfilled nothing of what we had promised ourselves immediately after the war'.[1] Yet he simultaneously held out hopes for reform by expressing the possibility: 'perhaps a renewal of Germany starting from the universities is still before us'.[2] Nevertheless, it is unlikely that the Marxist visions of a new society as propounded by the students at the end of the decade were the kind of renewal Leonhardt either expected or wanted. How strong the anti-ideological tradition of the post-war years still remained in the early 1960s can be seen from the volume *Was ist heute links?* In his introduction Horst Krüger rejects Marxism as a suitable base for criticism of society. He sees no change from the position at the end of the war, of which he writes:

> It was known from the common defensive struggle against National Socialism that the basic theory of Marxism, that all historical processes can be explained solely economically from the relationships of ownership, was no longer acceptable.[3]

Where elsewhere in the volume there is reference to political thought, as in the contribution by Klaus Wagenbach, there is more positive reference to Richard Crossman's 1952 Fabian essays than to Marxism. Despite all this and the negative example for most of East Germany, it should be remembered that the Frankfurt School had kept a form of Marxism alive, and that it was perhaps inevitable that the neglect of ideology would be reversed at some stage.

There remains the need to explain the student movement itself. Besides the causes within the universities themselves — in addition to the hierarchical structures, there was serious overcrowding — the major influences were the Grand Coalition and the Vietnam War, both developments that were open to Marxist interpretation. With Vietnam, it may again be necessary to speak of a process of reaction against earlier attitudes. After the Second World War the United States had been generally seen as the guarantor of freedom and prosperity; now it appeared to be a pitiless aggressor. Writers and students came to share a common concern about Vietnam, which extended beyond the young writers closest to the students themselves. To coincide with an international conference on that subject organised by students in West Berlin in February 1968, a resolution describing Vietnam as the 'Spain of our generation' and calling for the right of self-determination was signed by a large number of writers including Nicolas Born, Enzensberger, Peter Weiss, Martin Walser and the generally less political Wolfgang Hildesheimer, the exponent of 'absurd' theatre. Among non-German signatories were Kenneth Tynan and Raymond Williams.[4] A name that is missing is Günter Grass, an ideological opponent of the students, although he did sign the earlier Vietnam resolution of 1965 instigated by the Gruppe 47. This first resolution had helped to bring the question of Vietnam to a wider public and to stimulate student protest.

There was generally little difference of opinion among intellectuals about the morality of the Vietnam War. Much more controversy was aroused by the question of how writers might effectively protest on this and similar issues. In an article that appeared in 1965 entitled 'Europäische Peripherie' (European periphery), Enzensberger had spoken of the real divide in world politics being between north and south, rich and poor, a bold proposition in divided Germany.[5] The controversy that followed this article involved both Weiss and Walser. In a reply that appeared the following year, Weiss took exception to what he saw as Enzensberger's non-committal approach, and expressed his solidarity with all opponents of capitalism. He sees the divide in the world much more in traditional East-West terms, rejecting any idea that the Soviet Union is part of a rich world indifferent to the struggles of the oppressed. His article concludes with a rhetorical question:

> Are we capable of giving up our doubts and our caution and endangering ourselves by clearly stating: we are solid with the oppressed and we shall seek as authors with all the means at our disposal to support them in their struggle, which is also ours?[6]

Enzensberger's reply to this was that it was impossible to talk of authors endangering themselves: whatever they do, 'there is still always something left to drink in the refrigerator'.[7] He advises people like Weiss to go to Vietnam or Peru and fight a revolutionary war if they want to experience a real struggle. His conclusion is particularly scathing:

> I can do without left-wing Moral Rearmament. I am not an idealist. I prefer arguments to confessions of faith. I prefer doubts to convictions. Revolutionary waffle is anathema to me. I do not need one-dimensional world-views. In cases of doubt, reality decides.[8]

It must be concluded that Enzensberger's precise verbal blows give him much the better of the argument. Nevertheless, Martin Walser sought to balance the account in his essay: 'Praktiker, Weltfremde und Vietnam' (Realists, the unwordly and Vietnam), which concentrates much more exclusively on protests against the Vietnam War. He points out that Enzensberger has inadvertently come up with a new version of the right-wing cry that protesting intellectuals should go to the East. He also puts down Enzensberger's unwillingness to identity with any group to psychological factors. As for the issue of Vietnam itself, he suggests both a 'practical' and a 'non-practical' approach. He is unwilling to concede that moral protest is entirely worthless: 'It cannot be senseless to call a crime a crime',[9] adding that writers' attempts to inform their fellow-men have not proved worthless in history. On the practical level, he suggests the creation of a Vietnam office to disseminate information and the preparation of a petition urging the Federal Parliament to debate the issue, something that did eventually occur during the Grand Coalition.

The period of student disturbances in the late 1960s produced a number of events and issues that provoked comments from writers. West Berlin was already developing into the centre of the student movement when on 2 June 1967 during a demonstration against the visiting Shah of Iran the student Benno Ohnesorg was shot and killed by a policeman. This provoked an open letter from numerous writers and intellectuals, blaming among others the right-wing Springer Press, which enjoyed a near monopoly in Berlin, because of its strident anti-student tone. In addition, the letter, whose signatories included Günter Grass, Nicolas Born and Peter O. Chotjewitz, demanded the resignation of the chief of police and 'a disciplinary procedure' for the Governing Mayor Albertz and the Senator responsible for the police.[10] In the event, the policeman who killed Ohnesorg was acquitted, something that provoked protest from the Austrian writer Peter Handke, at the time frequently criticised by more radical colleagues for being unpolitical. In more general terms, Christian Geissler demanded radical changes after the shooting: 'This system must be changed. And it will be changed too. For this is our country.'[11] This kind of rhetoric reflects the new aggressive mood created by student protest.

That West Berlin developed into the centre of this protest had to do with a reaction against its previous role as the bulwark against communism, the partial loss of its function as a shop-window of the West following the building of the Wall, and with the more banal fact that its inhabitants were not liable for military service — one good reason why it attracted radicals. There were also the politicised writers who had been active for the SPD in 1965 and were now disillusioned. Two of these, Nicolas Born and F. C. Delius, satirically reversed statements made in Berlin to put the case of the students in verse form, both using the line: 'Wir haben es satt, uns von gewaschenen Schlägern schlagen zu lassen.' (We have had enough of being beaten up by washed thugs.)[12] The removal of the prefix 'un' changes the viewpoint totally. The charged atmosphere in the city at this time led to the remarkable suggestion by the historian Golo Mann that Günter Grass, who identified neither with the students nor the city government, should be made Governing Mayor.

Another incident in West Berlin that provoked a great response was the shooting by a right-wing extremist of the student leader Rudi Dutschke in 1968. Once again the Springer Press was widely held to be responsible. Whereas many students took to the streets to try to prevent distribution of the group's newspapers, writers protested in various ways. A telegram was sent by the chairman of the Berlin Writers' Federation Ingeborg Drewitz, blaming the climate of intolerance in the city, whilst in his ballad 'Drei Kugeln auf Rudi Dutschke' (Three bullets at Rudi Dutschke), the East Berlin singer and poet Wolf Biermann, who was subsequently exiled to the West, somewhat simplified the complex relationship between words and actions by directly identifying the three shots with three bodies or individuals, the Springer Press, the new Berlin Mayor, Klaus Schütz and the former Nazi, Chancellor Kiesinger.[13] He also saw the attack as a continuation of the unsavoury tradition of political murders in Germany, referring no doubt to that of Rosa Luxemburg and subsequent ones committed by the Right during the Weimar Republic.

However sensational these two shootings in West Berlin may have been, there was another longstanding issue that provoked even more concern, namely the question of emergency laws. At its inception the West German State had no power to deal with political emergencies; any crisis of that nature would have had to have been resolved by the Allies. By the early 1960s the CDU especially was clamouring for legislation, as the lack of it was seen as a gap in the sovereignty of the state restored in 1955. At the same time, the prospect of such legislation filled with horror all those who knew that Hitler had achieved absolute political power by using the ermergency powers available under the Weimar constitution. The Grand Coalition made the passing of the required laws more likely, as the two-thirds majority constitutionally required was arithmetically available to the governing parties. In due course the laws which made possible the suspension of democracy were introduced.

The hostile reaction of writers and intellectuals, whose fears had been expressed as early as 1961 in *Die Alternative*, was only to be expected. Along with students, they took part in a massive campaign to prevent the passing of the legislation, including a number of congresses and a march in Bonn. Nearly all leading writers were involved, although Grass was reluctant to go too far in criticising the SPD. As early as 1966, with the Grand Coalition imminent and the question already under discussion, a campaign entitled Notstand der Demokratie (Emergency for Democracy) had been launched with Böll, Enzensberger, Walser and Erich Kästner as members of the organising committee. Their proclamation expressed their major fear: 'The danger threatens that the constitutional and free democratic basic order of our state will be abolished for the second time in this century.'[14]

Böll and Enzensberger were particularly prominent in the subsequent campaign which, however, also included writers less known for their political commitment. The poet Günter Eich, for example, wrote a text 'Episode' which describes an imaginary emergency by using literary techniques reminiscent of Kafka to make its point:

> I wake up and am immediately in an emergency situation. I don't know the exact reasons, but as a precautionary measure I immediately arrest my children. Arrests are necessary. I turn on dance music on the radio and turn the aerial in the direction of Luxembourg. Rattling handcuffs, I patrol throughout the building.[15]

Subsequently the police surround the house, and even the narrator is arrested. The purpose of this satirical text is to point to the danger that goes beyond that of an externally imposed 'emergency' — that such laws encourage at all times a submissive mentality alien to any concept of democracy. Emergency laws might well create the 'emergency citizen' who does the state's dirty work himself. In the end, all the protests were to no avail, and the legislation came into force on 24 June 1968. That it has never been used has been cited as proof that writers' concerns were exaggerated; on the other hand the laws are there. It does not follow that because something has not been employed until now that it never will be.

The passing of the emergency legislation lastingly changed the political stance of one major writer, Rolf Hochhuth. After supporting, as already seen, the SPD in 1965, he now began to look towards the Free Democrats, the only opposition party inside parliament during the Grand Coalition and the only grouping to reject the emergency laws, although individuals in the other parties, including one Christian Democrat, did so. In a speech at the time of the passage of the legislation through parliament, Hochhuth castigated the Social Democrats for preventing even the discussion of FDP amendments. He went on to criticise several individual SPD members, justifying this in terms of his overall view of politics, which, as his plays also show, is based on a belief in the moral responsibility of the individual:

> Many *names* have been mentioned here: it will be objected that the importance of these names bears no relation to the seriousness of the threat to freedom that arouses us. But this objection springs from a modish manner of thought. Students especially are inclined to consider as a waste of time the attention given to individuals in politics because of their office, to dismiss it scornfully as 'personalisation of conflicts'. All these men, they reply, are ultimately 'interchangeable at will'. I should like to answer, only the negative manifestations are interchangeable — how rare the positive ones are can be deduced from the way that there are so few of them to see.[16]

This passage shows how much closer Hochhuth's views are to liberalism than to the ideology of the student movement, even if he did make common cause with the students.

Besides reacting to certain events, the student movement or parts of it engaged, as already mentioned, in political and ideological discussion of a kind that had not generally occurred before and which, because of the attention it attracted, inevitably involved older writers and intellectuals. In general, however, they did not contribute to the ideas being developed by the students, being incapable or unwilling to change their attitudes despite being castigated by Enzensberger for not having developed any coherent political theory for all their 'commitment'. Along with the young Berlin writers like Schneider and Delius, it was Enzensberger who came closest to the ideas of the students. In 1968, for instance, he took part in a discussion with student leaders about future society, although here too, as in the argument with Weiss, he retains a good degreee of realism alongside the vague utopianism of his interlocutors, as in this exchange with Rudi Dutschke:

D: Shorter working-time can lead to the total abolition of shift-work and night-work.

E: That is not possible, because there are service functions which are necessary 24 hours a day.

D: That's true. We need, for example, mass kitchens not characterised by their basicness but which develop highly sophisticated needs.[17]

One major question raised by the students and the APO was whether in the light of the Grand Coalition the political system of the Federal Republic was worthy of support or needed to be totally overthrown in favour of an order based on some aspect of Marxism. The students of the Sozialistischer Deutscher Studentenbund (SDS) (Socialist German student league) favoured the establishment, at least for a time, of a democracy based on councils or soviets, of the type that had existed at the beginnings of the Soviet Union or in the German Revolution of 1918–19. Republican Clubs, modelled on those that had existed in revolutionary France, also sprang up. Again Enzensberger appeared to be of a mind with the students by advocating or at least considering the possibility of revolution in a 1967 essay, whereupon the magazine *Der Spiegel* asked a number of in general established writers for their reactions. The general tone of the replies indicates a lack of belief in the possibility of revolution in Germany. Reinhard Lettau leaves himself open to the charge of arrogance by taking a very low view of his fellow-countrymen:

I think Enzensberger is totally correct but do not think that the Germans of all people would be prepared to fight for a revolution, as they have not even either fought for or deserved the present, in reality only most minimal, civil liberties but, on the contrary, under the leadership of the Brandt-Strauss coalition constantly pervert them in the most cynical manner.[18]

The equation of Brandt and Strauss, previously for many writers opposite poles in terms of sympathy, reveals, moreover, a total disillusion with mainstream politics brought on by the Grand Coalition. More optimistic than Lettau are Erich Fried and Martin Walser. Fried speaks of revolution having already begun in many parts of the world, whilst denying that reform and revolution are mutually exclusive. Walser argues dialectically that evolution is only possible where revolution is pursued. Reformism, on the other hand, produces only an 'appearance of movement', which in turn is a trap for self-congratulating intellectuals: 'With a Herculean gesture we occasionally destroy a taboo that has been presented to us to break.'[19] Of the other respondents, only Günter Grass expresses a firm commitment to parliamentary deomocracy, stressing the need for stamina in all attempts to improve it. Jürgen Becker, on the other hand, sees it much more as the lesser of two evils. His comments, like those of the poet Paul Celan, stress much more the role of the individual — it is only by changing people that political changes are made possible, a viewpoint closer to that of Hochhuth than to the Marxist view of history espoused by many students.

The question of parliamentary democracy became acute again in 1969, with the approach of the Federal election, for those writers associated with the APO. Should this event be ignored as a manifestation of a corrupt political system or should support be leant to the leftist grouping ADF (Aktion Demokratischer Fortschritt) (Action for democratic progress) that was participating in the election? This electoral alliance included the pacifist DFU and the newly re-formed Communist Party DKP (Deutsche Kommunistische Partei). In the new literary and political magazine *Kürbiskern*, whose editorial policy has generally been close to that of the DKP, a controversy began to emerge about whether participation in elections was desirable. Two writers who were members of the editorial board, Christian Geissler and Yaak Karsunke, expressed their rejection of such participation before parting company with the magazine, which duly supported the ADF. This argument must be regarded as a storm in a teacup in as far as there was never any chance of the ADF approaching the 5 per cent of the vote needed for entry into the Federal Parliament. This was notwithstanding the support of Martin Walser, Peter Rühmkorf, the playwright Tankred Dorst and Max von der Grün, the novelist who had initiated a Gruppe 61 as an equivalent to the Gruppe 47 for working-class writers. The hope of a broad leftist alliance was clearly illusory in electoral terms.

The non-doctrinaire element in the student movement in its early days may well have favoured such alliances. It owed much more to Marx and Marcuse than to Lenin, whose centralism was generally abhorrent. This was reflected in the aftermath of the Soviet invasion of Czechoslovakia in 1968, which was criticised by many leftists as well as writers closer to the SPD like Grass and Richter.

Richter had apparently hoped that the Gruppe 47 might meet in Prague, and connected its end with the impossibility of this occurring. As for specific protests, writers as different as Peter Weiss, who saw the events in Prague as detrimental to the global struggle for socialism, and Peter Handke condemned the Soviet actions. Handke ironically entitled his comments 'Monopol-Sozialismus' (monopoly socialism), a variation on the prevalent phrase of the time 'monopoly capitalism'. At the same time, he reaffirmed his commitment to Marxism as a movement and an economic model.[20]

It was the question of how Marxism might be applied in practice that helped to destroy any kind of unity within the student movement. Particularly when it became clear that there was no support for the students' ideas among workers, the broadly based revolt against society disintegrated in the early 1970s into a plethora of ephemeral dogmatic groupings whose initials inevitably began with the letter 'K' for 'kommunistisch'. One grotesque incident that occurred in 1969 shows the increasing strife within the protest movement. Ulrike Meinhof, whose stinging commentaries in the magazine *Konkret* had been very much part of the movement, broke at this time with its proprietor and her former husband Klaus Rainer Röhl. A party of her supporters from Berlin took private revenge on Röhl by breaking into his Hamburg house and destroying many of its contents. The signatures of writers, including Enzensberger, Lettau and Peter Schneider, then appeared on leaflets approving of this action, although they may well not have been authentic. Amid all this chaos, it was not surprisingly the more orthodox DKP that proved permanent, after its foundation in 1968 was made possible by the end of the Cold War. Although this party has never achieved much electoral success above the local level and has hardly deviated from the line of its East German mentor, it has enjoyed varying degrees of sympathy from many writers, including Martin Walser, Günter Herburger and the dramatist Franz Xaver Kroetz, particularly in the 1970s. Kroetz especially saw the party whose member he became as a helpful guide in his attempts to portray the life of the underprivileged in the Federal Republic. Sympathy towards the DKP is also visible in Uwe Timm's novel *Heisser Sommer* (Long hot summer), an account of the student disturbances whose protaganist moves from a diffuse anti-authoritarian stance towards orthodox communism. In the 1980s, however, the literary influence of the DKP has declined, with Kroetz having left the party and others less than happy with its policies towards the arts.

As was mentioned in the previous chapter in connection with the end of the Gruppe 47, the student movement helped to exacerbate the feelings of uncertainty about their role and their work experienced by many writers in the mid-1960s. There followed a debate that can best be summed up under the general heading 'death of literature'. Much of it took place within the pages of the magazine *Kursbuch* (Timetable), which had been founded by Enzensberger in 1965. The initial edition speaks of a literary magazine but also one which includes areas that go beyond the traditional sphere of literature. Nevertheless, in the early numbers contributions by established writers, for example Walser, Jürgen Becker and Samuel Beckett in the first edition, enjoy a leading place. There is also a good deal of poetry at this time. Gradually, though, the magazine began to develop into what some saw as a kind of mouthpiece for the APO, with edition 20 in 1970 being the last for a long time to have a largely literary content. Moreover, after this number, the magazine ceased to be published by the literary Suhrkamp Verlag. Edition 21 illustrates the break; under the general title *Kapitalismus in der Bundesrepublik* (Capitalism in the Federal Republic) it sought to show, partly with the aid of tables and diagrams, that the Federal Republic was indeed enthralled by 'monopoly capitalism', a claim that provoked many angry responses elsewhere. *Kursbuch* has remained an important part of intellectual life in the Federal Republic, concentrating increasingly on essays and reports of a more socio-political than a traditional literary nature, although literary texts and occasionally poetry have been published since the hiatus of 1970. Subjects covered in the ten years following that break include children, women, religious cults and morality.

The debate on the state of literature reached its climax in 1968. The view of the students of the SDS at this time was that art had become a 'commodity', because it was tied to a capitalist 'culture industry'. At the same time they maintained the opinion that it was potentially important in the political struggle. By contrast, three essays in *Kursbuch 15* seemed much less certain about the potential of literature. Yaak Karsunke, speaking particularly of literary criticism, claims that it concentrates on aesthetic questions to the exclusion of the social dimension. In this way it fits into the kind of undemocratic society envisaged by the emergency laws. How far Marxist terminology had now entered literary discussion is visible in the claim: 'German literary criticism diligently increases false consciousness.'[21] He himself pleads for a literature that would be 'functional and related to society'.[22] The second essay by Enzensberger's co-editor Klaus Markus Michel 'Ein Kranz für die Literatur. Fünf Variationen über eine These' (A wreath for literature. Five variations on a thesis) takes contemporary literature to task. Not only does he see it as irrelevant to the political struggle, as shown by the students' scorn of the Gruppe 47, but also he accuses it of diverting attention away from social questions even when it sought to be socially aware and committed:

> it tied and satisfied intellectual interests as if they were directly social and political ones, and in this way distorted the view of the latter, simultaneously restricted the dissatisfaction and unrest which it nutured to a cage, where pseudo-battles were fought and Pyrrhic victories were gained, whilst alongside it, it was business as usual.[23]

These assertions, which are as unprovable as those that claim a direct influence for literature, amount to a denial of any social function for literature.

It was Enzensberger's essay 'Gemeinplätze, die Neueste Literatur betreffend' (Commonplaces on the Newest Literature), whose title recalls Lessing's 'Briefe (Letters) die Neueste Literatur betreffend' of two centuries earlier, that made the 'death of literature' a catchword in intellectual discussion. A careful reading of the text, however, shows that he is not crudely dismissing literature as irrelevant or dead. It is rather a case of having his cake and eating it. He begins by pointing out that to talk of the death of literature is itself to use a literary metaphor that has been current for 150 years. His main point is nevertheless that it cannot be shown that literature can help to achieve major changes in society; at least not at the time he is writing: 'An essential social function for literary works of art cannot be stated in our situation.'[24] Writers can only undertake their work 'without any certainty', that is to say unsure whether they will achieve anything.[25] Despite all this, at the end of the essay Enzensberger does suggest types of writing that could be valuable, giving as examples books giving information on the Third World and Ulrike Meinhof's column. Moreover, he castigates those whose political activism exhausts itself in attacking literature; he adds that such people should turn their attention to those parts of cultural life that, unlike literature, can be seen as positively dangerous, doubtlessly meaning the mass media.

Enzensberger's comments on the potentially most socially useful types of writing coincided with developments that brought what was regarded as 'fact' into the realm of literature. In the theatre 'documentary drama' was at its height in the second half of the 1960s, that is to say the overt use of historical sources and documents as the basis for what occurs on the stage. The term itself is broad, in as far as it is used both of plays that consist almost entirely of extracts from judicial or quasi-judicial proceedings, for example Heinar Kipphardt's *In der Sache J. Robert Oppenheimer* (In the case of J. Robert Oppenheimer), and of plays like Hochhuth's *Der Stellvertreter* (The Representative), which is much closer to traditional historical drama in its investigation of the Catholic Church's attitude to the extermination of the Jews. What is important, regardless of terminology, is the attempt to make drama authentic and therefore relevant to social and political questions. In prose writing too there was a move away from fiction. In 1968 there appeared a volume entitled *Bottroper Protokolle* (Bottrop transcripts) with an introduction by Martin Walser, in which Erika Runge presented residents' views of life in the Ruhr mining town during the recession of 1967. In that it is the people of Bottrop who are speaking, the role of the writer, in this case Runge, is reduced to that of recorder and no doubt editor. It was also in the late 1960s that the investigative writer Günter Wallraff began to present his first-hand reports on what it was like being an ordinary worker in the Federal Republic.[26]

The tendency to regard literature as either dead or having a role only in relation to politics, produced statements by writers that might seem a denial of their profession. As early as 1965 Peter Schneider had said there were conditions in which writers might have to turn away from the aesthetic and write manifestos.[27] Although he was thinking primarily of totalitarian societies, he was expressing a view that became prevalent at the time of the student disturbances. In 1969 the critic and writer Reinhard Baumgart implied a low priority for the aesthetic by making the following unlikely comparison: 'If a slap on the ear from Beate Klarsfeld imparts more information than a volume of poetry by Yaak Karsunke, then a slap on the ear is better politics.'[28] Baumgart is referring to the incident when Frau Klarsfeld, an anti-Nazi campaigner and subsequent ADF candidate slapped Chancellor Kiesinger. In itself this statement is ultimately non-committal, but it does imply the primacy of politics, even if it shows scant political nous in the way it disregards the negative aspects of such gestures, not just in relation to the question of violence, but also to whether public sympathy would be on the side of the person slapped. In general, literature and politics became a popular topic at this time and spawned a number of books. The typical conclusion was the one drawn by Urs Jaeggi in the collection of essays edited by Peter Stein under the title: *Theorie der politischen Dichtung* (Theory of political writing), namely that art cannot have of itself any political influence within existing society: 'A politicisation of art without a politicisation of society is pure self-deception.'[29]

Despite all these statements, literature never came close to death: it is often pointed out that Enzensberger himself continued to write poetry. Nor were its advocates only traditionalist critics like Benno von Wiese and Marcel Reich-Ranicki, who were less than enamoured with the dominant role of politics. Not very long after Enzensberger's essay, younger writers too were beginning to look for ways out of the apparent impasse. An essay that pointed in the direction eventually taken by literature in the 1970s appeared in *Kursbuch 20* in 1970, Hans Christoph Buch's 'Von der möglichen Funktion der Literatur' (On the possible function of literature). He speaks particularly of the place of the subjective in literature, whilst expressing fears that such methods as Runge's transcripts and Wallraff's reports do not give workers a chance to express their own needs. He also takes to task those writers who scorn the value of literature that seeks to induce social change:

> That enlightenment that now appears to surfeited intellectuals only a luxury is for the proletariat as important as daily bread. The intellectuals who like to parade their impotence do not recognise that this impotence is a cliché produced by ruling interests; that capital has an obviously transparent interest in keeping them apart from the working masses because in their hands their ideas could become a material force.[30]

Dieter Wellershoff, too, in his essay 'Fiktion und Praxis' (Fiction and praxis) sees literature as not entirely impotent, although his hopes are less directly political.[31] He regards literature as a challenge to the established world, offering the reader the chance to extend his experience. He also criticises Enzensberger for judging literature in terms of its visible achievement and in this way indulging in a crude cult of success. Wellershoff is close to Adorno's view that the influence of literature is achieved more subtly than by direct political statement.

The dominating role of politics for so many writers in the late 1960s and early 70s did not simply consist in their taking sides on questions of the day. They also looked at themselves, at their own position in society, both in material and sociological terms. That this happened at the time of the student movement seems to be more than a coincidence; it was a time for political stock-taking. One disquieting conclusion reached concerned the status of the author in what came to be called the 'culture industry'. No longer was he the Olympian who from his lofty station bestowed master-pieces on a reverential public, but more probably, it was felt, a poorly recompensed purveyor of texts with a subservient position within a huge and profitable industry. Accordingly, in 1969 Heinrich Böll announced the 'end of modesty' and demanded better material rewards for writers. He also stated that writers needed to be much better organised if they were to have any social or political influence: 'whoever is not present in socio-political terms is also not present in political terms, he remains caught in the undergrowth of the cultural supplements.'[32] Böll's remarks coincided with the foundation of the VS (Verband Deutscher Schrift-steller) (Association of German Writers), the first Federal organisation to seek to promote the interests of writers. Within this body writers have attempted to improve their material and social position.

The first congress in Stuttgart in 1970 reflected a new mood of hope. Not only did Chancellor Brandt make, as previously mentioned, an extremely conciliatory speech, there was also a general feeling of optimism encapsulated in the slogan 'Einigkeit der Einzelgänger' (Unity of the loners). The goal was to rectify a situation in which writers faced the prospect of being reduced to being, as one felicitous phrase put it, 'peripheral workers of the wood processing industry'. The material conditions for writers have remained a concern of the VS, the state of affairs in which, according to Siegfried Lenz at the second congress in 1973, writers can die in poverty whilst their works form part of an industry with a turn-over of billions. In this area some success has been achieved, although in 1980 the first chairman of the VS and subsequent SPD parliamentarian Dieter Lattmann, was still complaining that despite steps taken in parliament social security for writers remained inadequate. The second concern of the VS, connected with the first and also raised by Böll in 1969, has been the position of writers in society, how they might exert more influence or, as Lenz put it in 1973, become insiders, an accepted part of the social order. He claims that in their position as outsiders they have achieved little:

> violence in all its forms continues to exist, we have been able to prevent neither the invention nor the use of the most extreme forms of power, we have not created the desired social justice and not abolished hunger.[33]

These remarks reflect the need experienced by writers in the early 1970s to increase their influence by some better form of organisation, even if one is left wondering how any institution created by writers or anybody else for that matter could achieve such utopian goals.

The desire for better organisation, in that it resulted from a sense of being undervalued in society, coincided with writers coining new expressions to express their status, among them 'Wortproduzent' and 'Literaturproduzent' (word-, literature producer). Such ugly neologisms may not bear much witness to literary skill; what they do show is a feeling of kinship with other workers in the productive process. Hence, it is not surprising that one of the major aims of many writers in the early years of the VS was affiliation to the trade union movement. At the Stuttgart congress a number of famous names, including Böll, Enzensberger, Hochhuth and Walser, saw close relationships with the trade unions as mutually beneficial. The unions could help writers by backing their material demands and by supporting the maintenance of freedom of opinion, whilst writers could put their talents at the disposal of unions. Support of the writing workers in the Werkkreis Literatur der Arbeitswelt (Workshop for Literature of the World of Work) that grew out of the Gruppe 61 was one obvious way some felt they could help. At Stuttgart the writers mentioned expressed their wish to back workers in the following general terms:

> It will depend among other things on the direction taken by writers and the persuasiveness of authors whether we can take a step forward in the struggle against the predominance of mono-poly capitalism and the expansion of imperialism.[34]

Linguistically, this statement too may be considered dubious because of its rigid, propagandistic nature; ideologically it was certainly out of tune with those sections of the trade union movement that favour 'social partnership' with the employers. For Martin Walser the ideal solution would have been the creation of an 'IG Kultur' (Industrial union for the area of culture); in the event, the VS affiliated to the existing printworkers' union, albeit one of the more left-wing unions. Although they were guaranteed freedom to write what they wished as union members, some mainly lesser writers did not feel happy with union membership and left the VS.

That writers should seek to improve their lot materially is understandable; nor can the desire to influence events in society be ruled to be inadmissible. Even if it is accepted that some form of organisation might further the second goal, there remains the problem of how and to what ends any influence gained should be used. Clearly, the Stuttgart statement on co-operation with the unions shows a specific political viewpoint. The same is true of the speech by Günter Wallraff at the third congress in 1974, where he demanded that writers incite their fellow-citizens to opposition against hard-hearted technocrats like Helmut Schmidt.[35] Not surprisingly, this viewpoint did not meet with universal approval, with Grass as an SPD supporter being especially sceptical. In fact, after the early euphoria the history of the VS has been marked increasingly by political differences, which became particularly intense in the early 1980s. The main bone of contention in these recent years has been attitudes towards Eastern Europe, following the renewed contacts between writers from both German states to discuss the question of peace and the declaration by the VS that it was part of the peace movement. This has raised the issue of whether Western writers, whilst taking part in such discussions, should ignore other events in Eastern Europe, most specifically the treatment of writers in Poland under martial law and in East Germany itself. Following the expulsion of Wolf Biermann in 1976, the East German authorities have expelled a number of other critical writers, in some cases, for example Jürgen Fuchs, after a period of detention. It is not surprising that these writers once in the West have been less than thrilled about contacts with their erstwhile colleagues, some of whom have put compromise before courage. Stephan Hermlin, a participant in the peace discussions, has, for instance, spoken cynically of exiles leaving with their 'goods and chattels', hardly a true description of the reality of the situation.[36] In the light of such statements it is not surprising that Jürgen Fuchs is worried about a reluctance among some leftists in the West to criticise even the communist authorities. The two major factions in the VS on these issues have been the exiled East German writers and their allies, most prominently Grass, and a group of writers associated with the chairman of the VS until 1983, the historian Bernt Engelmann, whose views have been close to those of the DKP and *Kürbiskern*. An extreme — and many would say — tasteless expression of the second viewpoint was made at the Mainz congress of the VS in 1983 by Erasmus Schäfer, who at least contemplated a comparison between the ten million supporters of Solidarity and the ten million who voted for the Nazis. The 1984 congress in Saarbrücken found the writers in disarray. A resolution calling for a lifting of the ban on the original Polish Writers Union and attacking campaigns against critical intellectuals in the Eastern Bloc was passed by a single vote. If one adds to this the numerous resignations from the VS over the preceding two years, there is not much left of the unity proclaimed a decade or so earlier.[37] That such hopes were in any case misconceived was maintained by Hans Christoph Buch, a strong supporter of the exiled East German writers, in 1983. He stated that it was an illusion to believe that writers, trade unionists and intellectuals all shared the same interests. Moreover, a term like 'Literaturproduzent' reflected a false idea of the position of writers, who cannot be organised as they work individually, and prosper according to the quality of their work.[38]

The ultimately inevitable dashing of the hopes writers entertained for themselves on the foundation of the VS may seem to epitomise the fate of many aspirations nurtured at the time of the student movement. The manner in which the student movement split into impotent dogmatic sects, with a few individuals turning to terrorism, showed that the hopes for revolutionary change in West Germany were totally ill-founded. In as far as writers associated themselves with these hopes, the conclusion seems inevitable that they, too, entertained ridiculous illusions, whilst the debate on whether literature had any purpose implies a lack of confidence or even a failure in their own profession. It is wise, however, to beware of over-simplification. As the student movement waned in 1971, Horst Krüger was quick to point to positive aspects which were worthy of preservation. In particular, he pointed to the dismantling of taboos, the greater tolerance towards minorities and the expression of utopian ideas. He concludes:

> I walk through the streets: nothing but busy people, in other
> words all is business. I see all the exhausted tired faces of the
> West Germans, somewhat grim . . . Nothing can be expected
> from them . . . And so I sometimes wonder: where will the
> courage to be utopian come from tomorrow? It above all ought
> to remain.[39]

The present 'utopian' ideas of the peace and ecological movements can be regarded as proof that Krüger's hopes have been fulfilled, since they represent a continuity in the kind of political
awareness engendered by the student movement. Equally, writers
should not be seen as traitors to their profession because they
questioned traditional forms of literature in the late 1960s. What
happened in part was that new kinds of writing by new kinds of
writers became acceptable so that there was a change in people's
perception of what constituted literature. Moreover, that there was
a student movement at all may well have had something to do with
writers' efforts in the 1950s and 60s to change the political climate
in the Federal Republic. Finally, it should not be forgotten that
there was an aesthetic dimension to student protest, as the many
'happenings' and the use of such slogans as 'Power to the Imagination' in both France and Germany show. That writers and literature
became so entwined at this time with politics was not just an
aberration, as it seemed to be immediately afterwards when the
misplaced revolutionary euphoria subsided.

Notes

1. R. W. Leonhardt, 'Die deutschen Universitäten' in Richter, *Bestandsauf-nahme*, p. 352.
2. Ibid., p. 359.
3. H. Krüger, 'Das Thema wird gestellt' in Krüger, *Was ist heute links?*, p. 24.
It might be pointed out that Krüger ignores more psychologically based explanations
of fascism produced by such Marxist scholars as Erich Fromm and Wilhelm Reich.
4. 'Erklärung zur Internationalen Vietnamkonferenz Westberlin 17./18. Februar
1968' in *Vaterland, Muttersprache*, pp. 260–1.
5. H. M. Enzensberger, 'Europäische Peripherie', *Kursbuch 2* (1965), 154–73.
6. P. Weiss und H. M. Enzensberger, 'Eine Kontroverse', *Kursbuch 6* (1966),
170.
7. Ibid., 175.
8. Ibid., 176.

9. M. Walser, 'Praktiker, Weltfremde und Vietnam', *Kursbuch 9* (1967), 173.

10. 'Zum Tod des Studenten Benno Ohnesorg' in *Vaterland, Muttersprache*, p. 247.

11. C. Geissler in ibid., p. 248.

12. F. C. Delius, *Kerbholz* (Rowohlt, Reinbek bei Hamburg, 1983), p. 80.

13. W. Biermann, 'Drei Kugeln auf Rudi Dutschke' in *Vaterland, Muttersprache*, p. 265f.

14. Quoted from M. C. Krueger, *Authors and Opposition* (Akademischer Verlag, Hans-Dieter Heinz, Stuttgart, 1982), p. 487.

15. G. Eich, 'Episode' in R. Wildermuth (ed.), *Heute und die 30 Jahre davor* (Ellermann Verlag, München, 3 Auflage, 1979), p. 163.

16. R. Hochhuth, 'Die Sprache der Sozialdemokraten' in *Vaterland, Muttersprache*, p. 268f.

17. R. Dutschke, B. Rabehl, C. Semler, H. M. Enzensberger, 'Ein Gespräch über die Zukunft', *Kursbuch 14* (1968), 172.

18. R. Lettau reprinted in *Vaterland, Muttersprache*, p. 259.

19. M. Walser reprinted in ibid., p. 260.

20. P. Handke, 'Monopol-Sozialismus' in ibid., p. 270f.

21. Y. Karsunke, 'Anachronistische Polemik', *Kursbuch 15* (1968), 167.

22. Ibid., 167.

23. K. M. Michel, 'Ein Kranz für die Literatur', *Kursbuch 15* (1968), p. 178f.

24. H. M. Enzensberger, 'Gemeinplätze, die Neueste Literatur betreffend', *Kursbuch 15* (1968), 195.

25. Ibid., 195.

26. His reports were published in three volumes: between 1966 and 1972 *Industriereportagen, 13 Unerwünschte Reportagen* and *Neue Reportagen*.

27. P. Schneider, 'Politische Dichtung. Ihre Grenzen und Möglichkeiten' in P. Stein (ed.), *Theorie der politischen Dichtung* (Nymphenburger Verlagshandlung, München, 1973), p. 154.

28. R. Baumgart, *Die verdrängte Phantasie* (Luchterhand, Darmstadt und Neuwied, 1973), p. 12.

29. U. Jaeggi, 'Das Dilemma der bürgerlichen und die Schwierigkeiten einer nicht bürgerlichen Literatur' in Stein, *Theorie der politischen Dichtung*, p. 207.

30. H. C. Buch, 'Von der möglichen Funktion der Literatur', *Kursbuch 20* (1970), 50.

31. D. Wellershoff, 'Fiktion und Praxis' in Kuttenkeuler, *Poesie und Politik*, pp. 329–40.

32. H. Böll, *Essayistische Schriften und Reden* (3 vols, Kiepenhauer und Witsch, Köln, 1979), vol. 2, p. 385.

33. S. Lenz, 'Das Dilemma der Aussenseiter' in D. Lattmann (ed.), *Entwicklungsland Kultur* (Kindler, München, 1973), p. 67.

34. See Lattmann, *Einigkeit der Einzelgänger*, p. 82.

35. G. Wallraff, 'Autoren Radikale im öffentlichen Dienst' in H. Bingel (ed.), *Phantasie und Verantwortung* (Fischer, Frankfurt am Main, 1975), pp. 24–38.

36. Quoted in *Die Zeit*, no. 16, 13 Apr. 84.

37. Names include Franz Xaver Kroetz, Gerhard Zwerenz, Uwe Johnson and Rainer Kunze. In 1985 Kunze joined the rival — *nomen est omen* — 'Freier Deutscher Autorenverband' (Free German Authors' Association). More positive for the VS is the plan to create a wider media trade union in December 1985.

38. H. C. Buch, 'Herdentiere oder Einzelgänger. Über die Krise des VS und Möglichkeiten zu ihrer Überwindung', *Vorwärts*, no. 13, 24 Mar. 83.

39. H. Krüger, 'Was bleiben sollte', *Die Zeit*, no. 33, 13 Aug. 71.

5 RETRENCHMENT WARFARE — THE 1970s

By the middle of the 1970s any excitement associated either with the student movement or the SPD electoral victories had more or less disappeared. The former had fallen apart, whilst after the initial successes of the Ostpolitik the new government appeared to lose much of its dynamism. The word that seemed to sum up the new state of affairs in the Federal Republic was *Tendenzwende* a term as equally felicitous as Harold Macmillan's expression 'wind of change' and not dissimilar in what it sought to convey. The change it referred to was one of mood, a growing belief that the hopes for reform and modernisation entertained in the 1960s were illusory and that is was time to call a halt or even revive some of the values of the past. One example: if the Left in the 1960s had propagated 'anti-authoritarian' education, conservatives now seized the initiative with the phrase *Mut zur Erziehung* (the courage to educate), which meant that the young should be brought up to accept certain values.

One effective slogan was naturally insufficient to reverse the direction society had been taking; it was rather a reflection of the tangible reasons for a growing disenchantment with the cult of progress as previously espoused. In addition to such factors as terrorism, events like the oil crisis of 1973 dampened the enthusiasm for change and experiment. Moreover, Brandt's plans for internal reforms began to run into increasing difficulties, not just with the official political opposition but also with his cautious Liberal coalition partner and the Federal Constitutional Court. His government had already run out of steam before the discovery of an East German spy in his immediate entourage led to his resignation.

That this step heralded the end of an era as far as relations between politicians and intellectuals were concerned, was quickly picked up by the *Die Zeit* journalist Dieter E. Zimmer in an article entitled 'Ein Kapitel Geist und Macht' (A chapter of intellect and power). Of the era of Brandt and Heinemann, whose term as Federal President also ended in 1974, he wrote:

Willy Brandt and Gustav Heinemann have done more than any German statesmen before them for a reduction of the enmity between 'intelligentsia' and 'politics' that in this country seemed to be as good as a law of nature.[1]

Brandt's successor Helmut Schmidt was a very different personality, at least in his public *persona*, the private man being anything but a Philistine. He also achieved more in material terms for writers than his predecessor, for example in the field of social security, but such factors as his previous scepticism towards the Sozialdemokratische Wählerinitiative and the comment attributed to him at the time of the formation of his first government that 'he had fired the intellectuals from the cabinet' set the tone for a difficult relationship.

The major difference between Brandt and Schmidt was that Schmidt's conception of his political role lacked the moral dimension many writers had so much approved of in the case of his predecessor. In a discussion with Siegfried Lenz and Günter Grass shortly before the Federal election in 1980 — in itself an interesting phenomenon and a reflection of his willingness to meet with writers, something he also did at the time of the Mogadishu hijack crisis of 1977 — Schmidt made clear that he did not consider it part of his constitutional duty as Federal Chancellor to take on the role of mentor. The statement by Schmidt used as the title to the discussion as printed in *Die Zeit* makes this clear: 'Der Kanzler ist kein Volkserzieher'[2] (The chancellor is not a teacher of the people). Incidentally, Schmidt also faced criticism from the right for not giving the country moral or spiritual leadership. His withering reply on this subject in a parliamentary debate to his eventual CDU successor Helmut Kohl makes clear that his abstinence in this area had to do with historical experience, the knowledge of how such leadership can be misused. His comments show him as a member of what the sociologist Helmut Schelsky called the 'sceptical generation', the burnt children of National Socialism:

> I belong to the generation that had terrible experiences as a result of being emotionally misled, which because of this grievous experience looks upon big words with a deep-seated distrust. It is a generation in which many have drawn the conclusion for themselves that they will renounce utopia in favour of that which can in fact be done today and tomorrow.[3]

For those out of sympathy with this viewpoint, Schmidt was *der*

Macher, literally 'the doer' but given its pejorative sense an English equivalent might possibly be 'Mr Fix-it'. Suffice it to say, a different wind blew down from the heights of power towards writers and intellectuals.

Concurrently with this, they in turn were revising their attitudes, particularly about the primacy of politics. By the mid-1970s the catch-phrase in literary circles was: *Jetzt dichten sie wieder* (Now they're writing poetry again). To those who had disliked the politicisation of literature, it must have seemed that a lost sheep was returning to the fold when in 1976 Erika Runge, the doyenne of documentary literature, announced that she was abandoning that method. A year later Peter Schneider, a writer who, as seen in Chapter 4, had been close to the student movement, spoke in an essay of the need for a correction of the 'political jingoism' that had been prevalent in the previous decade. In this essay 'Über den Unterschied von Literatur und Politik' (On the difference between literature and politics), he goes on to accept that there may well be inevitable conflicts between literature and politics, a view always held by Günter Grass.[4] The kind of literature that did come to the fore in the 1970s was marked, as already noted, by a stress on the personal, so much so that it was widely subsumed under the heading 'Neue Subjektivität' (New Subjectivity). This term embraced feminist writing, love stories and autobiographical works, all of which became prevalent. Despite the clear movement away from the documentary techniques of the 1960s, it would, however, be a ridiculous over-simplification to say that the new writing lacked a social and political dimension. An autobiographical work like Bernward Vesper's *Die Reise* (The trip) recounting his life as the son of the Nazi poet Will Vesper and the lover of Gudrun Ensslin could in no sense be called non-political.

At the same time, there is a change of tone, which is particularly visible in works that look back at the recent political upheavals from a standpoint that can be associated with the new subjectivity. Peter Schneider's story *Lenz*, which appeared as early as 1973, tells of a young Berlin intellectual caught up in the protest movement at a time when the students were seeking increased contact with workers. Although one can assume that the work has a strong autobiographical element, the use of the third-person form and the choice of name for the protagonist are significant. Jakob Michael Reinhold Lenz was an eighteenth-century dramatist who, having failed to establish himself and having fallen foul of Goethe, succumbed to mental illness. His sufferings are the subject of a story by that other tormented genius Georg Büchner, with whose work Schneider's *Lenz* shares several parallel incidents. Appropriately, the new Lenz feels alienated from the world around him, not just the consumer society of West Berlin but equally significantly that of the protesters. He cannot come to terms with the sterile impersonality of their world, in which only politics seems to count:

> It appeared . . . so funny to Lenz that all these comrades with their secret desires, with their difficult and exciting biographies, with their active arses did not want to learn any more of each other than these clean-cut sentences from Mao-Tse-Tung. That cannot really be true, thought Lenz. Didn't they possibly want just to be together, to share their enjoyments and difficulties with one another, simply to stop being alone?[5]

Lenz's own solution follows the time-honoured German pattern of escaping the vicissitudes of life in his own country by going to Italy, where he finds political life imbued with human warmth. When he has to return to Germany it appears that he has learned an invaluable lesson.

Another of the Berlin writers who had been politically active in the 1960s, Nicolas Born, sets his 1976 novel, significantly entitled *Die erdabgewandte Seite der Geschichte* (The dark side of events), at approximately the same time as Schneider. The first-person hero, who again bears at least superficial resemblance to his creator, shares Lenz's unease about participation in political life. The following recollection of a May Day demonstration will serve as an example of this:

> These marches under banners seemed to me like a public display from which we, excused through special circumstances, remained distant. I had no answer to certain questions of history, could now only scorn all answers, the more self-assured and righteous they sounded. Answers were something for young curates and unionised social workers.[6]

The novel concentrates on the private feelings of the hero, his personal relationships; that a contrasting figure, Lasski, who continues to throw himself into political activities, dies, appears significant. The stance of the novel is reflected in the collection of Born's other writings published under the title *Die Welt der Maschine* (The world of the machine) after his early death from cancer in 1979. They show a suspicion towards technological progress that occurs at the expense of human qualities. The cult of individuality, which underlies the rejection of the demand for conformity implicit in such measures as the Radikalᴗnerlass, does at times, however, lead him to idealistic positions reminiscent of Rilke, whose famous line 'Denn Armut ist ein grosser Glanz aus Innen' (For poverty is a warm glow from within) not surprisingly provoked a bitter response in the form of a drawing from the more socially aware Georg Gross. On the same subject of poverty Born writes: 'any sense we can give our lives comes from the experience of need, from a deprivation which mobilises our wishes and longings without which we are worthless, chance and poor creatures.'[7] As for literature, Born rejects any restriction to political themes, saying that the imagination and the irrational offer the real alternatives to the wretchedness of the age.

The case of Born illustrates the change of atmosphere in the Federal Republic that was taking place in the 1970s. Many writers were no longer in the mood to assert aggressively the virtues of modernisation and progress; society, in turn, no longer wished to hear such a message. In fact, writers were generally on the defensive on a variety of issues which they perceived as threats arising from the new spirit of retrenchment. One such threat was the already mentioned Radikalenerlass, which Heinrich Böll described simply as shameful. Shortly after it had emerged in 1972, several writers, including Andersch, Koeppen, Schallück and Uwe Johnson, wrote to the Federal Parliament warning against 'another destruction of an embryonic free democratic basic order in Germany under the pretext of defending it'.[8] They pointed out that the Basic Law did not permit discrimination against citizens on account of their political opinions and that the decree was therefore unconstitutional. It was also claimed that different yardsticks were applied in the case of the Left than those used with right-wing extremists:

> As its practice shows, in the Federal Republic it serves almost exclusively to discriminate against left-wing citizens, whereas old and new Nazis infest the apparatus of state without hindrance. This state of affairs has ominous historical precedents in

Germany. Co-operation between the executive apparatus of the state and extreme right-wing conspirators against our first democracy put Hitler in control of the state.[9]

Defenders of the decree, on the other hand, argued that it was actions, not thoughts, that led people to be disqualified from public service, but with opinions being used to project possible future hostile actions, it is hard to reject the writers' protest as groundless.

Reactions to the campaign against political extremists were not just restricted to letters and statements of dissent. Peter Schneider's next prose work after *Lenz* entitled . . . *schon bist du ein Verfass-ungsfeind* (. . . straight away you're an enemy of the constitution) takes as its subject the case of a teacher Kleff who falls foul of the authorities. The term *Verfassungsfeind* in the title, although itself not found in the Basic Law of the Federal Republic, became the umbrella label for those whose loyalty was questioned. Although the work is fictional, it has both autobiographical elements — Schneider himself faced a long struggle before he was accepted as a prospective teacher — and documentary elements, as when the narrator Kleff refers to real people and situations to point to anomalies in the administration of the Radikalenerlass:

> And have you read that the Federal Constitutional Court judge Willi Geiger who has now been involved in formulating: *The liberal democratic constitutional state can and must not deliver itself into the hands of its destroyers*, much earlier defended a German state against alleged destroyers? In 1941, he wrote on the subject of the Aryan Statute, through which journalists were disqualified from their profession solely because of their descent: *The regulation has removed at a stroke the over-powerful influence of the Jewish race with its harmful and subversive effects on the people and its culture from the field of the press.*[10]

At the end of the book, Kleff, whose personal relationships too have been affected by his conflict with the authorities, remains dismissed, although he has not exhausted all the legal channels of appeal open to him.

Probably the greatest stir in the campaign against political discrimination was created by Alfred Andersch's poem entitled 'Artikel 3 (3)' which takes as its starting point the article in the constitution that guarantees freedom from religious, racial and

political discrimination. The poem speaks of 'torture' being used
against those excluded from public service and concludes:

ein geruch breitet sich aus
der geruch einer maschine
die gas erzeugt

(a smell is spreading / the smell of a machine / that produces gas).[11]
Whereas detractors pointed out that torture in the manner of the
Gestapo did not occur in the Federal Republic, others considered
the poem to be an acceptable literary expression to describe the
reality of the situation. Andersch himself, in reply to his critics,
refused to recognise a distinction between what he saw as mental
torture and the techniques of the Gestapo. Even if this view could
be accepted, it remains open to doubt whether Andersch's
language, however literary the context, could have done more than
entrench opinions that were already held.

The protests against the Radikalenerlass were just one part of a
general campaign in the 1970s against what was perceived as the
threat to democracy and civil liberties. As terrorist violence
escalated, culminating in 1977 with the abduction and murder of
the head of the employers' association Hanns-Martin Schleyer, the
Mogadishu hijack and the prison deaths of three original members
of the Baader-Meinhof group, the Federal Parliament passed a
number of laws aimed at combating terrorism — laws which could
also be interpreted as a threat to individual freedom. At the same
time the police were strengthened, and the president of the Federal
Criminal Investigation Office Horst Herold began to predict a time
when computers would be able to pick out prospective criminals
and thus help eliminate crime. This utopia naturally required the
gathering of mounds of information about the individual citizen.
These developments were sufficient to make many writers fearful
about the future. The events of the year 1977 in particular, gave rise
to the evocative phrase *Der deutsche Herbst* (The German
autumn). This not only referred to what actually occurred following the abduction of Schleyer but also to an ominous climate of
opinion in which intellectuals were held responsible for the rise of
terrorism. Once again the response of writers was varied. In the
field of fiction, Peter O. Chotjewitz's novel fragment of 1978 *Die
Herren des Morgengrauens* (The gentlemen of the dawn) centres
round a lawyer and writer, the professions of Chotjewitz himself,

who falls foul of the police and the law because of his political activities. Whereas with Schneider the name Kleff and the events that befall him are in general terms reminiscent of Kafka, Chotjewitz painstakingly builds his work on the model of *The Trial*, right down to its remaining unfinished. The inference is clear: the treatment of those under suspicion in the Federal Republic can be akin to a totalitarian nightmare. More directly, in view of the worries about democracy, writers organised a congress in Hanover in 1978 under the banner of defending the republic. This rallying cry referred in turn to the first of two volumes of letters by prominent authors and other intellectuals which were another aspect of the reaction to the events of 1977.

The first volume *Briefe zur Verteidigung der Republik* (Letters on the defence of the republic), which appeared in the autumn of 1977 and achieved an edition of 110,000 by the end of the year, consists of approximately 25 letters, some addressed to named individuals, some to institutions and some to a non-identified group or individual, for instance a 'neighbour' or an 'educated liberal'. Among the contributors are writers such as Heinrich Böll, Nicolas Born and Siegfried Lenz, the artist Klaus Staeck and the theologian Dorothee Sölle. In the letters of two older writers, Axel Eggebrecht and Hans Erich Nossack, there is a hint of resignation about their fellow countrymen. Eggebrecht points out that democracy has always been imported into Germany rather than being an achievement of the German people itself, whilst Nossack perceives an abiding petty-bourgeois element in the Germans that rises to the surface at certain times: 'This hibernates . . . in the cellar and gradually creeps up the wall again like dry rot as far as the roof and consumes the ideological super-structure.'[12] If Nossack resorts to a mixture of Marx and literary metaphors to express his pessimism, other correspondents adopt a different and much more incisive stance. The journalist and biographer of the first East German leader Walter Ulbricht, Carola Stern, appeals to educated liberals to overcome their reticence and speak out in favour of democracy. Walter Jens turns the tables on those who want restrictive legislation to combat terrorism by claiming that on the contrary only democratic reforms can create the climate in which nobody will support terrorism out of frustration over society's immobilism.

The second volume, *Briefe zur Verteidigung der bürgerlichen Freiheit* (Letters on the defence of civil liberty), which appeared a year later, is a more structured affair with the letters appearing under five headings. The first deals with the plight of five individuals regarded as victims of the climate of intolerance, whilst the second turns more generally to the defence of liberality in the Federal Republic. Of the remaining three sections, the most substantial centres around the Filbinger affair. Rolf Hochhuth, the writer who discovered the skeletons in the cupboard of the prime minister of the state of Baden-Württemberg, writes a long letter to Helmut Kohl following the latter's declaration of solidarity with his party colleague, whilst the novelist Luise Rinser contributes a 'German Midsummer Night's Dream', in which she imagines — possibly a little sanctimoniously — Filbinger's consternation on Judgement Day when he discovers that God's sympathies lie with his unorthodox opponents.[13]

A writer and intellectual who was particularly prominent in the campaigns to preserve democracy in the 1970s was Walter Jens. Given his experience as novelist, essayist and critic, he was able to combine an extensive knowledge of German history and culture with the linguistic skill appropriate to the holder of the Chair of Rhetoric at the University of Tübingen in order to fight for his beliefs. The volume of speeches he published in 1976 *Republikanische Reden* (Republican speeches) reflects his attitudes most clearly. Starting from the ideals of the Enlightenment and of libertarian socialism, he pleads for a radical democracy which runs counter to the German tradition that imposes conformity and quiescence. In his speech on the Radikalenerlass, 'Wider die Isolation' (Against isolation) for instance, he quotes examples of political persecution at his own institution from the sixteenth century onwards and adds:

> Indeed, that's what I call an inventory! Whether as 'blasphemer', 'democrat', 'Calvinist', 'pacifist' or 'communist'': whoever opposes, whoever thinks differently, whoever, as a member of a minority, stands on the wrong side is expelled, blackballed in society, removed from his office. In the sixteenth century as well as today.[14]

He goes on to point out that similar measures were always used by authoritarian governments in Germany and that, by continuing the tradition, Social Democrats are acting against the 'renowned dead in their own ranks'.[15]

Jens concludes that there is a danger that the social and political achievements associated with the Enlightenment are in danger of being reversed, and that a clear statement of this danger is the first step towards preventing its occurring. A second volume of speeches *Ort der Handlung ist Deutschland* (The action is set in Germany) published in 1981 continues in a similar vein. Particularly interesting is the speech given at the 1979 SPD party conference entitled 'Eine Freie Republik' (A free republic). Here he claims that the struggle for human rights and peace, based on the tradition of the 'other' Germany, gives social democracy: 'that trustworthy humanity and credibility, which Thomas Mann meant when he propounded the thesis that solely "in the form of socialism" not otherwise did democracy today find its real, "its moral existence".'[16] The example of Jens shows that political commitment need not exclude linguistic artistry or erudition: his speeches present a challenge through both form and content to not only his political opponents but also to those whose causes he espouses.

One obvious question that has to be asked in the light of the efforts by Walter Jens and others to protect civil liberties, is whether these were necessary, particularly as at no time did the Federal Republic appear on the verge of lapsing into dictatorship. Despite the preservation of democratic forms, the answer has to be in the affirmative. The desire to combat terrorism did provoke over-reaction on a number of occasions. One piece of legislation that was passed made it an offence to advocate in written texts violence that might endanger the constitutional order of the Federal Republic. The danger that arose from this was that any literary description of violence might be deemed illegal, hence the seizure of the book *Wie alles anfing* (How it all started) by the former terrorist Michael 'Bommi' Baumann, although it partially repudiates the path of violence and advises former fellow-terrorists to throw their guns away. This book was, in fact, confiscated by the police in the autumn of 1975 before the new legislation had gone through parliament. Nevertheless, the action was *de facto* the first time it was invoked, as the introduction to the 1977 edition points out.[17] This was prefaced by the names of so many 'editors' including Delius, Enzensberger and Handke along with various publishing houses, that prosecution of them all would no doubt have kept the courts busy for decades. In the event, the legislation was repealed in 1980, something that again might be regarded as a victory over censorship akin to those gained in the Adenauer era. At the same time, the whole episode suggests that the use of legislation or of administrative measures like the Radikalenerlass was not the appropriate means of fighting terrorism, but more likely, as Böll and others pointed out, to create terrorists by encouraging feelings of alienation and frustration.

Another worrying event that came to light in 1977 was the bugging of the home of the atomic scientist Klaus Traube on the pretext that he had connections with terrorists. In the end this action was admitted to be illegal, and the FDP Minister of the Interior Werner Maihofer forced to resign. The episode showed not only the importance of a free press but also that democratic standards still pertained in the Federal Republic. It is important to point out that most writers for all their concern about the threats to civil liberties recognised this, and did not fall into the trap of exaggeration by making similar claims to those of the terrorists that the Federal Republic was a neo-fascist police state or the like. Nicolas Born's contribution to *Briefe zur Verteidigung der Republik* makes the point forcibly: 'One thing this state is certainly not, a police state, a fascist state.'[18]

Another danger writers were aware of was the accusation that by their criticisms they were undermining the state, a claim frequently made, however wrongly, about left-wing critics of the Weimar Republic like Kurt Tucholsky and the Nobel Prize winner murdered by the Nazis, Carl von Ossietzky. Thus, Bernt Engelmann's statement at the press conference during the meeting of the VS in 1977, besides warning of the danger to liberty, contains the phrase: 'This is our republic, too',[19] whereas in his frustration over undemocratic developments in Weimar, Tucholsky had spoken of that republic not being his. In general, writers' campaigns to preserve democracy in the 1970s combined directness with moderation. One possible exception was the support some lent to the International Russell Tribunal of 1978, a body taking its name from Bertrand Russell, whose international membership set out to examine civil rights in the Federal Republic. This episode alienated a good deal of liberal opinion, including the editor of *Die Zeit*, Marion Gräfin Dönhoff, who among other things disliked the failure to make any comparisons with East Germany, the lack of any legal expertise among the members and the self-satisfaction implied by the tribunal's name.[20]

However laudable in themselves the attempts by writers and others to preserve the democratic substance of the Federal Republic may have been, one point remains. Did they possess the moral stature to take on this task? Their right to do so was most vociferously disputed by those who saw critical writers not as the defenders of democracy but as the intellectual begetters of terrorism, and increasingly, as the number of terrorist attacks grew, as sympathisers with terrorism. The general argument was that by their condemnatory attacks on the Federal Republic, intellectuals had encouraged the growth of violence. Franz Josef Strauss, for instance, claimed that there was a direct line from the New Left of the 1960s to the terrorist violence of the 1970s, although many now seek to forget this:

> Today it is common to act as if in ignorance of the fact that from the morass of the 'New Left' underground of the mid-sixties there leads a line of development to those who today wish to destroy our state by violence, blackmail and murder and abolish its free order.[21]

The right-wing CDU politician Alfred Dregger accused intellectuals in parliament of destroying basic values in their efforts to confront the Nazi past, with the result that, along with the twelve years of Hitler, the other 1,188 years of German history were equally vilified. Unfortunately, the assumption behind this viewpoint, that the greatest part of German history is marked by sweetness and light, is utterly untenable. By contrast to Strauss and Dregger, Walter Jens in his letter in defence of the republic sees no need for intellectuals to take anything back or, as he more elegantly puts it, 'to articulate a contrite *pater peccavi*'.[22] He adds that 'we' were always in favour of tolerance and peaceful methods of persuasion.

Before accepting Jens's claim at face value, it would be necessary to determine who is meant by 'we'. Just as it is ludicrous to claim a direct cause and effect relationship between the written or spoken word and specific actions — no doubt propagandists in totalitarian states would be happy if such a clear link existed — it is impossible to deny that a number of things said or written at the time of the student movement were ill-advised. Particularly controversial was an anti-Vietnam pamphlet produced by the then notorious anarchistic commune Kommune I in 1967. In order to bring home the horrors of the Vietnam War and following an horrendous department store fire in Brussels, it was satirically suggested that burning consumers would evoke the realities of Vietnam. The style chosen was that of advertising and the sensational press, as the title shows:

*Neu! Unkonventionell! Warum brennst Du, Konsument? Neu!
Atemberaubend!* (New! Unconventional! Why are you burning,
consumer? New! Breathtaking!).[23] The pamphlet's authors, Fritz
Teufel and Rainer Langhans, were indicted, but acquitted after
literary experts pointed to the satirical tone and intentions. Nevertheless, it was not long after that Andreas Baader and Gudrun
Ensslin did set fire to a Frankfurt store, albeit at night and without
loss of life. This again is not to claim a direct causal relationship,
but in view of the tragedy in Brussels the pamphlet was tasteless
and, given the charged social atmosphere of the time, somewhat
unwise. One writer was definitely involved in violence; Peter Paul
Zahl shot at a policeman whilst trying to escape arrest in December
1972. Although his guilt was generally accepted, many writers did
feel the sentence of fifteen years, of which ten were served, to be
unduly harsh. Looking back in 1984, Peter Schneider admitted that
he had been attracted to terrorism and went on to add:

> The concept of the urban guerilla and of armed struggle in the
> cities by no means arose in the minds of a few isolated loners.
> From the beginning it was part of the thoughts and feelings of
> the generation of 68 and was discussed with a frankness incon-
> ceivable today at teach-ins, in which thousands took part.[24]

It is one thing to agree that there was a violent element in the
student movement that led in some cases to terrorism and another
to claim that writers had directly created it or, even worse, sympathised with its manifestations. The cry of *Sympathisant* (sympathiser) directed at writers and intellectuals from the right was one of
the most distressing aspects of the 'German autumn' of 1977. The
term itself is imprecise, the charge it implies unprovable; all it could
do was re-create an atmosphere reminiscent of McCarthyism.
Writers who found themselves at the centre of the witch-hunt
included Heinrich Böll and Luise Rinser, the latter having had brief
personal contact with two terrorists before they embarked on their
illegal actions, and who changed almost overnight from being
esteemed as a 'Catholic writer' into an accomplice of terror.
Typical is an anti-terrorist publication produced by the CSU's
political foundation in 1978, which includes a documentation
entitled: 'Das geistige Umfeld des Terrorismus' (The intellectual
environment of terrorism). This contains various quotations from
those held to be guilty of sympathising with terrorism, many of

which, it must be said, do appear stupid or regrettable. At the same time it operates largely with innuendo and insinuation, as in a comment on the 'Peymann affair'. The director of the State Theatre in Stuttgart, Claus Peymann, had put up a notice in the theatre saying that the imprisoned terrorists required dental treatment and asking for contributions, in the atmosphere of the time sufficient to lead to his eventual removal and for the CSU to imply clandestine support for terrorism: 'In this situation of left-wing extremists running amok one must ask what it is meant to signify when the Stuttgart theatre-director Peymann collects for the denture of Gudrun Ensslin.'[25] Maybe she intended to bite future victims to death. The inclusion of Günter Grass, a formidable opponent of violence, also shows how shakily based much of this documentation is.

The attack on alleged sympathisers took off following the murder of the Federal Prosecutor Siegfried Buback in April 1977, particularly after the appearance of an obituary written by a Göttingen student who signed himself Mescalero. Although this obituary was interpreted by many as a renunciation of violence, its author nevertheless spoke of having experienced *klammheimliche Freude* (clandestine joy) on hearing of the murder. This was enough to provoke outrage, which intensified after forty-three academics published the obituary once more and their reactions to it. Matters came to a head following the other acts of terrorism that took place in 1977. The CDU politician Bernhard Vogel, the brother of the SPD's Hans-Jochen, said that talking of the Baader-Meinhof group rather than gang was sufficient to betray sympathy. Not surprisingly, the Springer Press countered the attack on it by Günter Wallraff, who had worked clandestinely for the mass-circulation tabloid *Bild-Zeitung* and whose book on this illuminating experience appeared in 1977 under the title *Der Aufmacher* (The page-one revelation), with the claim that he was a sympathiser.[26] The Higher Education Minister of the State of Lower Saxony, Eduard Pestel, demanded that the academics in the service of his state involved in the publication of the Mescalero article should sign a loyalty declaration rejecting violence and declaring willingness to support the state actively. Given that such a demand, albeit within the framework of a different social order, smacks of the kind of world betrayed in *Darkness at Noon*, it is not surprising that writers were quick to react. Peter Schneider ironically suggested that a mere signature under a document was not sufficient as a proof of loyalty and declared his love for Herr Pestel in person. Peter O. Chotjewitz in his 'Beichte des Staatsbürgers' (Confession of the citizen) satirically uses religious language to profess his loyalty:

> Lord, in the light of Your Truth, I admit that I have sinned in thought, word and deed. I shall love my state and lord above all else but I have loved myself more than You.[27]

It was also possible within the volume containing the responses of Schneider and Chotjewitz to point to historical parallels, for instance, that even the philosopher Kant fell foul of the state because of his unorthodox views.

One is forced to conclude that the debate on the causes of terrorism left much to be desired in the way that it was conducted in terms of black or white, guilt or innocence. Frequently omitted was any reference to the social dimension, to the question of the social atmosphere at the time of the student movement. If it is accepted that violence was in the air, statements by writers and intellectuals should then be viewed against this background and judged by whether they might have encouraged the developing tendency towards violence, given that it is impossible to show that individual statements can create violence or love for that matter out of the blue. One example will suffice. There could in theory be no more provocative statement than that made by Rolf Hochhuth about homelessness, the subject of his play *Die Hebamme* (The midwife): he says it is 'a humiliation for the whole human race that children condemned to grow up in accommodation for the homeless do not murder the local politicians responsible for their plight once they have grown up.'[28] In isolation this amounts to an incitement to violence, which, however, never seems likely to have any consequences because it remains an individual, extremely eccentric viewpoint. On the other hand, in the atmosphere of 1977, the closing lines of Erich Fried's poem on Buback:

> Es wäre besser gewesen
> so ein Mensch hätte nicht gelebt

(It would have been better / had such a man not lived) can be regarded as unwise, even if the poem as a whole rejects terrorism with the penultimate stanza being the same as the last except for the word 'died' instead of 'lived'.[29] At the same time it does not follow that consideration of the social dimensions of terrorism must lead to a condemnation of intellectuals and writers. It took a partial outsider, the Swiss writer Max Frisch, to point out in his speech to the SPD party conference in 1977 that the whole of society might be implicated in terrorism:

> How innocent is our society of the reappearance of terrorism? . . . How innocent are we of the reappearance of terrorism — or guilty, not as sympathisers, which we as radical democrats could never have been, but guilty as 'good citizens' through lack of understanding in our families and institutions towards a whole generation?[30]

It was this kind of point that those who campaigned against sympathisers preferred to ignore and which intellectuals were right to raise. In the light of the exaggerated attacks, Jens's total defence of writers becomes understandable, if not entirely accurate.

In view of so many developments in the 1970s that were viewed with suspicion by writers, it might seem that there would be little to say about their relationship with the governing Social Democrats, except that previous support gave way to opposition. Such an assumption would be wrong; it ignores the point that in the federalist system operating in West Germany, the central government does not hold power exclusively. It is the state governments, many of which in the 1970s were in the hands of the Christian Democrats, that most frequently implement the regulations about who may become a teacher or other kind of public servant. In the case of parliamentary anti-terrorist legislation, it should be remembered that the CDU demanded even tougher measures than those implemented by the government. There were therefore still reasons for writers not to abandon the SPD entirely. Nevertheless, it is true that particularly after the resignation of Brandt, enthusiasm for the SPD was much decreased. The journalist of *Der Spiegel* Hermann Schreiber catches the mood of the 1976 Federal election in an article entitled 'Dabei sein ist out' (Being involved is out).[31] He points to the great reduction in the number of voters' action groups supporting the SPD and to the much lesser commitment of Grass, Lenz and Böll. Two years later the party was concerned enough to ask a number of writers why their support had waned. In reply, Peter Härtling speaks of feelings of anger rather than of resignation,

caused by the way the government restricts itself to reacting prag-
matically to events rather than setting itself clear goals. Luise Rinser
complains of a swing to the right: 'The SPD has developed into a
kind of liberal CDU.'[32] She also has harsh words for Chancellor
Schmidt. By contrast, Hans Werner Richter sees psychological
reasons for the estrangement; it is not normal for writers to identify
with political parties and exceptions will generally be short-lived.
Whatever the reasons, relationships were now definitely cooler.

Only at the end of the decade did things improve, though less
through the efforts of the SPD than through actions by the CDU. In
1979 the CDU and the CSU had enough votes in the Electoral
Assembly to make their candidate Federal President. For this
largely ceremonial office, they chose Karl Carstens, a man whose
Nazi past made him unacceptable to many writers. Günter Grass
countered with the politically unrealistic suggestion that his
colleague Siegfried Lenz should be given the post. The eventual election of Carstens may have been bad enough for many intellectuals,
but something even worse loomed the following year when Franz
Josef Strauss became the opposition's candidate for the post of
chancellor in the Federal election. This not only re-opened old
wounds from the days of the Spiegel Affair — much newer ones
were also still festering. In a 1978 speech Strauss had described
critical writers as *Ratten und Schmeissfliegen* (rats and blowflies).
Specifically, on that occasion, Bernt Engelmann was his target; in
early 1980 the CSU's general secretary Stoiber honoured Jens,
Walser and Ingeborg Drewitz with the same zoological comparison.
In fact, this slander rebounded on its initiators not just because it
could be shown to be identical vocabulary to that used by the Nazis
of their enemies, but also for the same reasons that the Kaiser's
scornful phrase 'contemptible little army' rebounded on him. Grass
used his talents as an artist to draw numerous blowflies and writers
could enjoy being the wounded party. The result was that the Sozialdemokratische Wählerinitiative took on a new lease of life, with
Grass enjoying the support of Jens, Härtling and Lenz, and after a
gap of almost two decades, Walser. It mattered little that Helmut
Schmidt's remark about intellectuals returning to the fold probably
contained an element of gloating. The main priority was the duly
achieved defeat of Strauss — although in reality this was clear from
the outset, as the one intellectual of major standing who supported
him, the formerly liberal but much changed Golo Mann, admitted
before the election.

Despite this victory for the SPD/FDP coalition and its intellectual supporters, it would be wrong to conclude that things had returned to where they were in 1969 or 1972. A major publishing event of 1979 shows this most clearly. One of the leading West German publishing houses, especially for modern literary texts, is the Frankfurt Suhrkamp Verlag, part of whose programme has been the paperback series *Edition Suhrkamp*. At its inception this series concentrated on literary and philosophical writing before, in accordance with the changing mood, turning more towards the social sciences at the time of the student movement. The inexorable approach of its thousandth volume, together with the equally inevitable thirtieth anniversary of the Federal Republic, provided the pretext for the mammoth two-volume project *Stichworte zur 'Geistigen Situation der Zeit'* (Key terms on the 'intellectual situation of the age'). The quotation within the title recalls a similar volume written by the philosopher Karl Jaspers in 1931. The editor of the new venture, the sociologist and philosopher Jürgen Habermas, after the somewhat embarrassed admission that he cannot share publishers' love of round numbers, proceeds in his introduction to state his views on the intellectual climate. First, he sees a major change having taken place in the Federal Republic in the 1970s in that intellectual argument is no longer dominated by the Left, who have been challenged by the protagonists of the *Tendenzwende*. Because of this, it has become a major task to defend democracy against those who seek to restrict it. Secondly, he sees the growth of new social movements, for instance the feminist and ecological movements, challenging the whole system of values that had been prevalent in the 1960s. This is a major theme of the book. The artist and art critic Hans Platschek speaks of a new irrationalism. Karl Heinz Bohrer sees the ideas of the Enlightenment, for example the belief that critical intellectual thought can be productive, being replaced by a new subjectivity as manifest in the literature of the decade. For both the sociologist Urs Jaeggi and for Habermas himself, this need not be a negative development. Habermas speaks of a search for 'new symbiotic forms in everyday life in which the cognitive and instrumental, the moral and practical and the aesthetic and expressive come together.'[33] The nature of this search that has gatherered momentum in the 1980s and changed many intellectual assumptions of earlier decades will be examined next.

Notes

1. D. E. Zimmer, 'Ein Kapitel Geist und Macht', *Die Zeit*, no. 21, 17 May 74.
2. *Die Zeit*, no. 35, 22 Aug. 80.
3. H. Schmidt, 'Vom Staat nicht das geistige Heil erwarten' in R. Leicht (ed.), *Im Lauf des Jahres. Deutsche Texte und Dokumente 1981* (DTV, München, 1982), p. 22.
4. P. Schneider, *Atempause* (Rowohlt, Reinbek bei Hamburg, 1977), pp. 162–74.
5. P. Schneider, *Lenz* (Rotbuch Verlag, Berlin, 1973), p. 28.
6. N. Born, *Die erdabgewandte Seite der Geschichte* (Rowohlt, Reinbek bei Hamburg, 1979), p. 97.
7. N. Born, *Die Welt der Maschine* (Rowohlt, Reinbek bei Hamburg, 1980), p. 199.
8. 'An das Präsidium des Bundestags' in *Vaterland, Muttersprache*, p. 287.
9. Ibid., p. 288.
10. P. Schneider, . . . *schon bist du ein Verfassungsfeind* (Rotbuch Verlag, Berlin, 1975), p. 49f.
11. A. Andersch, 'Artikel 3(3)' in *Vaterland, Muttersprache*, p. 298.
12. H. E. Nossack, 'Unser Feind ist immer das Kleinbürgertum' in F. Duve, H. Böll, K. Staeck (eds), *Briefe zur Verteidigung der Republik* (Rowohlt, Reinbek bei Hamburg, 1977), p. 125.
13. L. Rinser, 'Ein deutscher Sommernachtstraum' in F. Duve, H. Böll, K. Staeck (eds), *Briefe zur Verteidigung der bürgerlichen Freiheit* (Rowohlt, Reinbek bei Hamburg, 1978), pp. 207–12.
14. W. Jens, *Republikanische Reden* (Kindler, München, 1976), p. 141.
15. Ibid., p. 145.
16. W. Jens, *Ort der Handlung ist Deutschland* (Kindler, München, 1981), p. 18.
17. M. Baumann, *Wie alles anfing* (Anabas-Verlag etc., Frankfurt am Main, 1977).
18. N. Born, 'Eines ist dieser Staat sicher nicht: Ein Polizeistaat' in Duve *et al.* (eds), *Briefe zur Verteidigung der Republik*, p. 21.
19. B. Engelmann, 'Noch ist dies auch unsere Republik' in *Vaterland, Muttersprache*, p. 310.
20. M. Dönhoff, 'Den Spielraum der Liberalität ständig maximieren' in Duve *et al.* (eds), *Briefe zur Verteidigung der bürgerlichen Freiheit*, pp. 108–10.
21. F. J. Strauss, 'Die Zeit der Entscheidung ist da' in W. Althammer, *Gegen den Terror* (Verlag Bonn Aktuell, Stuttgart, 1978), p. 23.
22. W. Jens, 'Isoliert die Desperados durch mehr Demokratie' in Duve *et al.* (eds), *Briefe zur Verteidigung der Republik*, p. 86.
23. Printed in *Vaterland, Muttersprache*, p. 253.
24. P. Schneider, 'Plädoyer für einen "Verräter" ', *Der Spiegel*, no. 7, 13 Feb. 84, 66.
For a further view of the relationship between Schneider and Boock see: P. Schneider, P-J. Boock, 'Gespräche eines Schiffbrüchigen mit einem Bewohner des Festlandes', *Die Zeit*, no. 15, 5 Apr. 85.
25. Althammer, *Gegen den Terror*, p. 174.
26. G. Wallraff, *Der Aufmacher* (Kiepenhauer und Witsch, Köln, 1977).
27. P. O. Chotjewitz, 'Beichte des Staatsbürgers' in H. Boehncke, D. Richter (eds), *Nicht heimlich und nicht kühl* (Ästhetik und Kommunikation Verlag, Berlin, 1977), p. 38.
28. R. Hochhuth, *Spitze des Eisbergs. Ein Reader* (Rowohlt, Reinbek bei Hamburg, 1982), p. 200.

29. Quoted in Althammer, *Gegen den Terror*, p. 172.
30. M. Frisch, 'Wie unschuldig sind wir?' in *Vaterland, Muttersprache*, p. 312.
31. H. Schreiber, 'Dabei sein ist out', *Der Spiegel*, no. 37, 6 Sep. 76, 46–52.
32. L. Rinser, in 'Schriftsteller und SPD', *Neue Gesellschaft*, vol. 25, no. 11 (1978), 868.
The other references are taken from the same article.
33. J. Habermas, 'Einleitung' in J. Habermas (ed.), *Stichworte zur 'Geistigen Situation der Zeit'* (Suhrkamp, Frankfurt am Main, 1979), vol. 1, p. 35.

6 HOW GREEN ARE OUR WRITERS? — THE 1980s

If the 1980 Federal election can be seen as the restoration of the alliance forged in the 1960s between large numbers of intellectuals and the Social Democrats, it was nevertheless something of an artificial rebirth due almost entirely to common opposition to Strauss. The co-operation of the 1960s, based on the desire for progress and modernisation, could not be restored, as many writers and intellectuals had turned away from the ideal of a society characterised by scientific and technical rationality. The mood of subjectivism that developed in the 1970s did not end with the decade. Politically, it became associated with alternative visions linked to a variety of social movements, especially the peace and ecology movements. The relationship of writers to these movements will therefore be a more significant factor in this chapter than attitudes to the SPD.

It is possible to illustrate something of the mood of the first half of this decade in general terms by reference to a single literary work, Michael Ende's *Die unendliche Geschichte* (The Neverending Story), which, it is true, first appeared in 1979 but occupied a leading position in the West German list of bestsellers until well into the next decade. Its author, who lives in Italy, became a kind of 'guru' to whom pilgrimages were made, primarily by young supporters of the peace and ecology movements. Ostensibly, *Die unendliche Geschichte* is a children's book which juxtaposes the real world with the imaginary Kingdom of Fantastica, a place that ultimately exists only through human imagination. In the novel it has to be rescued by a boy, Bastian Balthasar Bux, in the real world an unhappy isolated individual, but one who is capable of making the necessary leap of the imagination to rescue the other kingdom. He is in fact transported to Fantastica, where he not only has wonderful adventures but also learns important lessons, in particular the value of love. The novel then is clearly didactic and has political implications as well. In one passage, for instance, the world of Fantastica is contrasted with the real world of lies and power. Before Balthasar rescues it, Fantastica is in danger of being sucked into the void, along with its inhabitants. One of these, Atreju, who subsequently befriends Balthasar, is told by a werewolf:

When your time comes to jump into the Nothing, you too will be a mindless servant of power, with no will of your own . . . Maybe you'll help them persuade people to buy things they don't need, or hate things they know nothing about, or hold beliefs that make them easy to handle, or doubt the truths that might save them.[1]

From this, Atreju is able to draw his own conclusion: 'The more of Fantastica that was destroyed, the more lies flooded the human world'.[2] It is not difficult to see how a book which sets imagination against lies and power, should appeal to a generation seeking personal fulfilment and grown weary of the seemingly unprincipled world of traditional politics.

Even the way it is produced, particularly the German edition, seems to say something about the changed values of the time. The parts set in Fantastica have green print, those set in the real world maroon print. There is a leaf pattern at the top of each page, whilst the opening letter of every chapter — there are twenty-six in all, and the opening letters follow the sequence of the alphabet — enjoys a page to itself and its own pictorial setting. One is far removed from the angry social criticism of the 1950s and 60s. The obvious charge that can be levelled is that of Romantic escapism, in the case of a work of fiction a matter of taste on which it is not proposed to arbitrate here. Nevertheless, most people will enjoy what is a charming series of adventures, however they react to the social and political implications of *Die unendliche Geschichte*.

Its author's precise political views can be gleaned more directly from a volume that appeared in 1982 under the title *Phantasie, Kultur, Politik* (Imagination, culture, politics). It is a record of conversations held at Ende's home between himself, an actress and head of a Stuttgart theatre project, Hanne Tächl, and the Social Democrat Erhard Eppler. Eppler was Minister for Overseas Aid in the Grand Coalition and in the Brandt government, but significantly not in the Schmidt years. His increasing support of alternative, especially ecological, positions gained him a large following among young people, but the result achieved by his party in the state elections in Baden-Württemberg in 1980, when he was its candidate for the office of prime minister, was a disappointment to his followers. The discussions between the three reveal a remarkable degree of unanimity about the need for a new kind of politics with Ende, however, being the most radical in his rejection of present-day technological society. He goes as far as to question the whole tradition of logical, Socratean thought: 'From the atomic bomb at the latest, the question of where the whole scientific enlightenment has taken us has become more and more pressing.'[3] Ende's ideal is that of a new human consciousness that will change political life completely. Imagination, culture and politics should not be separate domains but be integrated to create a new kind of politics. One imaginative idea he puts forward is: 'In certain circumstances it will depend on a theatrical production whether a new law is made or not.'[4] Ende's ideas owe something to Rudolf Steiner's anthroposophy — he says that the ecology movement is partly based on the recognition that plants, too, have their own individual existence — and also reveal some kind of religious inspiration. What is visible in the peace movement, for instance, is 'a kind of prophetic instinct'.[5]

It is not easy to place such views on a traditional left-right political scale. Ende speaks of capitalism as the 'real source of the sickness', but includes the Eastern European states in this condemnation as examples of 'state capitalism'.[6] He is also generally opposed to all forms of state intervention: 'I think it is especially bad that the demand for state action is always heard when something is not working in some area'.[7] In Ende's ideal world the state would be banished from such spheres as higher education, where institutions would have to rely on the drawing power of professors to attract students. In a rare disagreement, Eppler takes up the traditional Social Democratic stance against what appears to be an extreme form of liberalism, saying that it is the state that at present protects the weakest and promotes greater equality. Ende's ideal, however, remains the creation of a new form of democracy based on totally different institutions.

At the risk of appearing unimaginative and traditional, one is forced to conclude that Ende's ideas remain largely unpolitical and impractical. His hopes for a change in consciousness amount to the old cry for a 'new man' — in this case, one whose unselfish behaviour will render the state obsolete. It hardly needs saying that history shows that most 'new men' have more faults than the most troublesome new car. Furthermore, his championing of experience and feeling over intellect and understanding represents a return to a Romantic vision of humanity that is as one-sided as its opposite.

The rejection of reason, especially in the form of scientific rationality, is not restricted to Ende. A new periodical of the 1980s published in Tübingen has as its title *Konkursbuch* — literally 'bankruptcy book' — and just as significantly to underline the contrast with *Kursbuch* as a sub-title 'Zeitschrift für Vernunft-kritik' (Periodical for the critique of reason). An article by Wolfgang Schirmacher from 1984 will provide a taste of the ideas it propounds. He claims, for instance: 'The atomic bomb is not a misuse of modern natural sciences but their legitimate child, born out of the "spirit of vengeance" (Nietzsche).'[8] He goes on to dispute the continuing value of the tradition of rationalist thought: 'Our logic is based on causes, whose sense has long disappeared, and whose system is choking us like a garrotte.'[9] All in all, Schirmacher's tone, as the positive reference to Nietzsche implies, is far removed from the rationalist tradition of the Enlightenment, in which, for instance, Günter Grass sees himself.

Another element in this kind of discussion is a general uncertainty about the whole concept of reason. This is clear in the explanation given by the then literary editor of *Die Zeit*, Fritz J. Raddatz, of why he is a pacifist: 'The denial of "reason"-arguments is not necessarily without reason; there is also a force in the non-reasonable.'[10] Raddatz here rejects the rationality of the defence expert, preferring rather to trust some kind of instinctive feeling. His stance reflects the doubts that have developed in the 1980s because of ecological and military dangers about the values of a society geared to material and technological progress. In some cases doubts about the concept of progress have led to a feeling that nothing is worthwhile any longer, hence the decision by the novelist and playwright Wolfgang Hildesheimer to stop writing. Similarly, Günter Kunert, a writer who moved relatively recently to the Federal Republic from the GDR, has abandoned all Marxist ideas of progress to claim that the world is doomed. In a discussion in 1980 with Wolf Biermann, who has retained his hopes for the future, he speaks of the Enlightenment and the scientific tradition as having brought the world to its present plight.[11]

For those writers and intellectuals who reject such apocalyptic visions but search rather for alternative solutions to society's current problems, a key word is *sanft* (gentle). The third volume in the series of publications that began with the letters in defence of the republic bears the title *Kämpfen für die Sanfte Republik* (Fighting for the gentle republic). It appeared shortly before the 1980 election and to some extent formed part of the general opposition among intellectuals to Strauss, labelling him in one contribution as the non-gentle candidate. Elsewhere, again largely in the form of letters, it looks for new solutions to a variety of social and political problems, including the German Question and defence. The kind of environmental danger the writers are aware of can be seen from Siegfried Lenz's letter 'Das Wasser der Republik' (The water of the republic), which is addressed to a young angler. His concern is with the state of his country's rivers and lakes:

> We have managed to let lakes and rivers die. We have managed so to poison and waste the vital raw material of water, whose supply cannot be increased at will, that already there is the possibility of the exhaustion of sources of fresh water in the not too distant future.[12]

In that he requires greater investment on the part of public authorities and suggests making environmental protection a subject in the school curriculum, Lenz's solution to the problem of water pollution remains very much in a social democratic tradition. This differentiates his contribution from those which, as the editors freely admit, consist largely of dreams and visions and as such reflect the increasing rejection of political pragmatism.

Along with *sanft*, the key word of the 1980s has been one that since the beginnings of psychoanalysis has been well known outside German-speaking countries, namely *Angst*. The debate has centred around the question of whether anxiety is an appropriate response to the present state of the world. In other words, is it a sign of self-pity and self-indulgence or rather a sign of courage in face of a threatening reality, as the title of a collection of pacifistic writings *Mut zur Angst* (The courage of anxiety) implies?[13] On the side of those who reject the cult of anxiety, one of the most trenchant contributions has come from the pen of former chancellor Schmidt, in his new role as co-editor of *Die Zeit*, incidentally the publication in which much of the debate has taken place. His leading article adopts, to say the least, an imperious tone in its title 'Fürchtet Euch nicht' (Fear not). Schmidt goes on to admit to having felt fear himself, but regards it as a purely private emotion which has no place in politics, where its effects are likely to be disastrous:

> In this way anxiety comes to be misunderstood as a virtue, there is misuse of the anxiety of others as an instrument in the political struggle, misunderstanding of idealistic utopias as political tasks

achievable in practical terms. In this way, inadequately experienced people or even dilettantes gain in power.[14]

These views are very much in keeping with Schmidt's political philosophy, as explained in Chapter 5. Nor is it difficult to conclude who is not included in the ranks of inexperienced dilettantes. What is more surprising is the conclusion to the article, namely that the existence of God as the ultimate determining force in history makes anxiety inappropriate. Another to reject anxiety is the sociologist Erwin K. Scheuch, who sees arrogance as its motivating force.[15]

By contrast, in the same copy of *Die Zeit* that contains Scheuch's article, Dieter E. Zimmer speaks of his surprise that so few people show signs of anxiety despite the problems facing the world.[16] The novelist Gerhard Zwerenz has applied this to himself, wondering 'how I can sit so calmly here on my chair'.[17] Reaction to this whole question of anxiety will ultimately depend on individual views of the current political situation, especially on the question of nuclear war. It should, however, be pointed out that most of those writers who speak of their fears are not registering a passive emotion, but regard their feelings as the necessary basis for taking action to improve the present state of affairs.

The major force trying to avert the perceived danger of nuclear war is of course the loose grouping generally referred to as the peace movement. It is not intended here to give a full account of its activities or of the role of writers in it but to refer to a number of significant contributions by them. A specific publication worthy of mention, not least because of its impact, is *Frieden ist möglich* (Peace is possible) by Franz Alt, not a writer as such but rather a television journalist and more surprisingly a Christian Democrat. He bases his arguments on the religious inspiration of the Sermon on the Mount, demanding particularly that political action be based on the principles expounded by Christ. In addition to the obvious question of whether such a viewpoint is naïve in the face of Soviet threats, another possible criticism of Alt's book is that it takes an absolutist stance that condemns other approaches to peace out of hand. If politics is about compromises, then a statement like the following is an unsatisfactory framework for political action: 'The ethics of the Sermon on the Mount is not "on the one hand-on the other hand" but "either-or". The Sermon on the Mount cannot be wished. It can only be done.'[18] Despite the tone of this kind of comment, elsewhere in the book Alt is realistic enough to realise that disarmament will be a slow process. His genuine concern for peace also stands comparison with a typically wild statement by Hochhuth within a plea for a referendum on nuclear weapons about what would happen after a nuclear war: 'If Germans were to survive such a catastrophe, then they will execute Kohl for his agreement given without a referendum to put Pershing only *in our* backyard.'[19]

The most remarkable contribution by writers to the whole debate about peace was the two meetings in Berlin in the early 1980s between authors from both German states. That such gatherings took place at all, albeit within the framework of other discussions between European writers from both East and West, was a major new development. Even if it can be argued that the participation of East German writers with their Western counterparts could not have taken place without official approval and should therefore be regarded as part of the general propaganda exercise of the Warsaw Pact countries against American missiles, such approval does imply the existence of a specific German dimension. Moreover, what was said, not least by some GDR writers, was frequently at odds with propaganda standpoints.

The first largely intra-German discussion took place in East Berlin in December 1981, with no further aim in mind than a general exchange of views. The suggestion by Grass that there should be some final resolution or communiqué was not acceptable to the majority. A variety of topics was raised, including the role of the superpowers, the German dimension and the influence writers might be able to exercise on the course of events. Whereas nobody present was willing to defend the policies of the United States, attitudes to the Soviet Union showed considerable variations. Whereas Grass saw both the superpowers in an equally negative light, many of the East German writers, for example Erik Neutsch and Helmut Baierl, identified themselves totally with the official stance of their government and hence with the Soviet Union. Nevertheless, other GDR writers were willing to be critical, for instance Günter de Bruyn about the attitude to unofficial peace movements: 'If they are forced underground, not only are valuable forces for peace lost but one's own credibility is also undermined.'[20] Such a comment shows that not all the GDR writers were mouthpieces of the party line.

As for the German dimension, this, too, was expressed powerfully by a GDR writer, Jury Brézan: 'by the action of the Germans the world can move towards the way out of the threatening catastrophe. Nobody in the world is under a greater obligation to do this.'[21] The question of the role of writers in the peace movement also gave rise to a number of interesting comments. Günter Herburger stressed the connection between writing and the whole idea of survival: as a writer it was his task to preserve things from destruction and, what is more, books, even if they remain comparatively unknown for a century or more, may survive to re-emerge at some future date. For many writers it was important to stress the difference between their world and that of politicians. On this question, Peter Rühmkorf pointed to the significance of language: 'We who write should take care that we do not fall prey to the bureaucrats who administer war technology with their language but that we answer with our language.'[22] Ingeborg Drewitz makes a similar point but reaches a more concrete conclusion. It is the very weakness of writers as peripheral members of society that gives them the strength as part of the peace movement to find alternatives to the present militarised world.

Notwithstanding the variety of views expressed, the general feeling gained from reading the transcript of this first Berlin meeting is that of a common purpose among the writers from the two German states in the search for peace. This is much less the case with the second meeting that took place in West Berlin in April 1983, when controversy was much more the order of the day. It was pointed out, for instance, that the records of the first debate had never been published for the general public in the GDR. Additionally, there was the question of the harsh treatment meted out by the GDR authorities to the unofficial peace activists in the town of Jena. The major controversy, however, centred around the nature of peace itself. Was peace merely the absence of war, in other words, the situation that had existed in Europe since 1945, or did it imply something more? The first view was taken by the GDR writers largely in sympathy with their government's standpoint, with Hermann Kant, at the time president of the GDR Writers Union, rejecting any equation of the superpowers and laying particular emphasis on the Soviet Union's policy of no first use of nuclear weapons. For these writers, the major priority was the prevention of armed conflict. By contrast, other writers wished to connect the question of peace with human rights, specifically the events in Poland and the whole question of the division of Europe following the agreement at Yalta in 1945. It was a Hungarian guest, Gyorgy Konrad, who first raised the question of Yalta. His point was taken up by Peter Schneider in comments on Poland: 'There was . . . no talk in Yalta of establishing a single-party communist dictatorship in Poland . . . it was stated specifically: free, secret, equal elections between different parties.'[23] Hans-Christoph Buch adopts a similar position on human rights: 'that this problem forms part of peace, otherwise it is senseless to talk about peace.'[24] A contrasting position from the West German side comes from Bernt Engelmann who, whilst acknowledging the right to criticise the *status quo* in Eastern Europe, says that the desire to make the other side change is 'no basis for joint efforts for peace and disarmament'.[25] In the case of diplomats this may well be true, but writers should surely have a different vision from negotiators.

The role and nature of writers did, in fact, play a part in the second set of discussions, with stress again being put on special qualities that might aid the peace process. At the start Peter Härtling claimed that 'a considerable portion of guilelessness is required if an atmosphere of trust between different opinions is to be created'.[26] Another West German writer, Eva Demski, totally rejected traditional pragmatic thinking: 'the decision to be pragmatic is for an author an act of self-mutilation . . . We should be utopian.'[27] In the light of such views, it is not surprising that peace and ecology were frequently seen as parallel concerns as values that reflect an opposition to the existing technocratic world. Whether these new modes of thinking could prevail was, however, another point of controversy. Hans Werner Richter spoke of his growing optimism: 'that . . . a change in consciousness was taking place among people.'[28] On the other hand, Günter Kunert maintained his pessimistic outlook. He sees men as victims of their unchanging nature. Referring to all the people involved in the wars that have taken place in the world since 1945, he says: 'they are still the same Neanderthal men, as we are as well of course, with the only difference that our European experience of war provides a certain albeit dropping threshold of inhibition.'[29] Finally, uncertainties extended to the continuation of the discussions. Grass wanted the next meeting near a Pershing base, which led the critical East German author Stefan Heym to suggest an SS20 launching-pad as another possible venue. In the event, the next mass gathering of writers in the cause of peace did take place in the town of Heilbronn, which is close to an American base, but without the presence of writers from the GDR, something which, given the location, would have been extremely awkward.

To mention the difficulties that surrounded especially the second Berlin discussion — and to this could be added the failure to prevent the stationing of the new generation of missiles — is not to dismiss writers' initiatives for peace out of hand. Their right to express their views cannot be denied, particularly as the ultimate goals, peace and disarmament, are shared by all. What is more, in the Federal Republic they were an integral part of a mass movement that attracted and continues to attract great support.

One reason why there was such controversy at the second Berlin meeting of writers was the shadow cast by a group of former East German writers who had left the GDR in the years following the expulsion of Biermann. Although they themselves were not present, their views were more or less represented in the discussion in the statements of Schneider and Buch. In fact, they had refused to take part in a meeting attended by erstwhile colleagues whom they regarded as little more than the emissaries of a despised regime. They made their position clear in a letter to a Berlin newspaper that appeared under the signatures of the poets Sarah Kirsch and Jürgen Fuchs and the prose writer Hans-Joachim Schädlich. A collection of writings published by Fuchs in 1984 under the title *Einmischung in eigene Angelegenheiten* (Interference in my own affairs) allows further insight into his particular views on the question of peace and other related matters. Fuchs quotes the reasons he and his colleagues advanced for not taking part in the West Berlin gathering, drawing particular attention to the role of the GDR Writers Union, some of whose leading members, as already mentioned, were present:

> Among the weapons used by the state GDR and its Writers Union . . . against individual authors there number, for example, hounding, slander, coercion, blackmail, bans on publication at home and abroad, fines, banning of public and private readings, arbitrary call-up into the reserves, expulsion from the Union.[30]

Whilst one can accept this as true, it needs to be pointed out again that the Berlin meetings did provoke genuine discussion, and that those writers from the GDR who identified most closely with their government by no means found things easy.

More generally, Fuchs is concerned about the way the Left in the Federal Republic, in his view, frequently fails to face up to the realities of what occurs in the countries of Eastern Europe. This, it will be recalled, is the issue that has led to the recent controversies in the VS. Fuchs describes in some detail his experience with leftists on his arrival in the West:

> They were quite thorough and passionate in criticising conditions here and what fascism had done and the crimes committed by military dictatorships, for instance in South America. But what inner reserve towards those who had been hastily stamped with the label 'dissident'.[31]

For Fuchs, peace and human rights are indivisible, as he makes clear in his 1983 letter to the Berlin theologian Helmut Gollwitzer and in his comments on Poland. Nevertheless, he is far from being a supporter of Western governmental policies, as his participation in peace rallies shows. In general, he reveals an overall distrust of politicians which leads him to believe that the only way for ordinary people to improve the world is by refusing to obey or, as he puts it, by saying 'no': 'Everywhere where instructions are given, where "defence studies" form part of the curriculum, where uniforms are distributed and uniform thinking prescribed, we should ask questions and delay or refuse to do what we are told.'[32] This plea stands in direct contrast to the German tradition of sub-servience to authority. It is typical of a collection of writings, whose unorthodox radicalism is both worthwhile and thought-provoking.

If a recent fictional work with a particular relevance to the themes of peace and war had to be singled out, the choice might well also fall on work by a writer from the GDR, in this case Christa Wolf's 1983 novel *Kassandra*. In this book the priestess and daughter of King Priam recalls her opposition to war as she awaits execution in Greece following the fall of Troy. Her main concern is with how war develops and then becomes inevitable. Recalling the period before the commencement of hostilities, she asks:

> Did anybody at all in Troy speak of war? No. He would have been punished. In all innocence and with the clearest possible conscience we prepared the ground for it. The first sign: we let ourselves be guided by the enemy.[33]

The story is not a simple allegory of the present — it would suffer as a work of art if it were so — nor does it confine itself to a single issue. Nevertheless, its suggestive power can be seen in the way it provoked the GDR critic and former editor of that country's leading literary magazine *Sinn und Form*, the late Wilhelm Girnus, to repeat his state's official line on peace in an irritating tone that achieves a combination of smugness and officiousness:

> Bourgeois pacifism, which is admittedly perfectly well-meant — and this is what not asking who-whom amounts to — has never yet achieved peace without an alliance with the revolutionary class power of the workers and peasants and their armed strength.[34]

It is a tribute to the challenge of Christa Wolf's anti-war stance that one can imagine comparable arguments in defence of military might being advanced in many countries of the world, albeit couched in different ideological terms.

The change of values apparent in the 1980s, especially in the new social movements like the ecology movement, make it difficult to assess developments in terms of traditional right-left politics. Indeed, it becomes almost impossible to assess what the terms 'right' and 'left' mean. The sub-title 'Confusing variations of a spectrum' given to an article in *Die Zeit* in 1980 entitled 'Die Linken und die Linke' (The leftists and the Left) seems very appropriate in view of the changes the author, the former student leader Knut Nevermann, perceives: 'Left-wing is today no longer internationalist, but regionalist, no longer collectivist but individualist, no longer oriented to the welfare state but towards mutual welfare.'[35] It is not proposed here to discuss the validity of such changes of definition, only to suggest that such a statement underlines once more the movement away from technological rationality, planning and progress. It is, in fact, possible in the writings of the 1980s to find considerable criticism of the concepts of progress and modernity, as embraced by so many intellectuals in the 1960's. The collection of observations by the playwright Botho Strauss that appeared in 1981 under the title *Paare Passanten* (Couples, passersby) is a withering satire on progressives, although it must be pointed out that these include the supporters of the new intellectual and social fashions, for example the trendy professor 'in his late thirties, a reader of the *Tageszeitung*, whose greatest joy is to speak continuously . . . about car-engines, excellent restaurants and exotic holiday destinations.'[36] Equally, aspects of femininism, another social movement of the last decade, do not escape Strauss's acerbic satire:

> The life of the mother-to-be in the circle of mothers-to-be, all showing solidarity . . . pregnancy meets at Helen's on Tuesdays. Enlightened, pale, just having given up smoking, somewhat greasy hair, jeans and T-shirt and an ethnic woolly on top, still thirsting for more and more enlightenment (it's called simply and all-embracingly 'literature'), wanting most of all permanent discussion to protect themselves from happiness, unhappiness and other things that cannot be understood.[37]

Strauss's championing of the uncertain and the mysterious is reflected in his favourable comparison of Hitchcock's *The Birds* with Brecht's *Mutter Courage*; this twenty years after writers had rushed to Brecht's defence after the CDU politician von Brentano had made an odious comparison between Brecht and Horst Wessel.

If Strauss's satire in *Paare Passanten* can be regarded as being in a tradition of cultural conservatism (at the same time, it should not be forgotten that his plays are not traditional in their form), it is more surprising to find criticism of progressives in the magazine *Freibeuter* begun in 1979 by Klaus Wagenbach, the author and publisher who moved well to the left of the SPD after the formation of the Grand Coalition in 1966. Even more surprisingly, this is combined with a willingness to accept a positive dimension in values generally associated with conservative positions. In 1980 Wagenbach himself attacked the Left for its total opposition to Franz Josef Strauss. Besides repeating the frequent criticisms of the SPD made in the 1970s over the infringement of individual freedom, he also speaks in positive terms of such concepts as initiative, risk and the market. He asks:

> Are we *against* 'risk', *against* innovative stimulation through competition, *against* the joys of the market? Why then do the eyes of friends glow (the same people who here submit to the silent picking up of goods from the plastic containers of supermarkets), when they speak of the charm of southern markets?[38]

That the use of the word market in two rather different senses seems somewhat problematic does not alter the major point that these are different tones from those current in earlier decades.

Three years later in *Freibeuter*, Benedikt M. Mülder too showed some sympathy with CDU positions, this time over social policy, in an article significantly entitled 'Nichts gegen die CDU' (Nothing against the CDU). He indulges in criticism of the SPD, before seeing positive aspects in the approach of the Christian Democrats. He refers specifically to the social policies of the CDU in West Berlin, where that party took over what had previously been a stronghold of the SPD in the early 1980s. What he sees is common ground between the new governing party and the Alternative List, the equivalent of the Greens in West Berlin: 'In praise of simple needs and small groups, in search of a safe resting-place and ties, both compete for the uprooted individual who is forced by indus-trialisation into mobility, flexibility and adaptability.'[39] Müller also points out that alternative groups also make use of the grants made available by the CDU for neighbourhood projects.

In his article Müller is not embracing the CDU but, like Wagenbach, seeing less than total opposition between the new social and political attitudes and the conservative values of the CDU. What he calls for is not outright opposition but a more sophisticated confrontation with CDU positions. What alternatives and conservatives do share is a rejection of bureaucratic solutions of the kind favoured by the SPD in government. To sum up: it is impossible to maintain that intellectual fashion has swung to the right in the way it seems to have done in other European countries; it is rather that the propagation of different values has meant a greater affinity to conservative ideology, if not conservative politi-cal practice, to which many intellectuals, not least those in the peace movement, remain strongly opposed. The ideal encapsulated in the word 'gentle' provides one example of this. Whilst writers and intellectuals demand a gentle republic, the former CDU Minister of Health Geissler speaks of the 'gentle power of the family'. This is not just the same word being used in two different senses; the ideal is largely the same, whereas the methods of achieving it remain different. Erhard Eppler has distinguished between *wertkonservativ* (conservative in values), a positive quality, and *strukturkonservativ* (structural conservative), a term to be applied to his political opponents. The use of the word con-servative at all in a positive sense is an indication of the change in values that has recently taken place.

In view of this shift, in some quarters at least, towards conservative values, it again becomes necessary to ask what stances writers are taking towards the Social Democrats. There has, as might be expected, been further erosion of support since the removal of the threat perceived in the person of Strauss in 1980. There was no great outcry when the party lost office in 1982 and in the 1983 election, only those very committed to the SPD cause rallied to the party, for example Günter Grass and Walter Jens. Schmidt's successor, Hans-Jochen Vogel, in any case lacked the charismatic qualities that might have inspired great support. In a conversation with the present writer early in 1984, Heinke Jaedicke of the Sozialdemokratische Wählerinitiative spoke of the need to rethink positions if the party were to appeal to more than those writers of the post-war generation who had supported it since the 1960s. It was especially necessary to find ways of reaching the younger generation who had been unhappy with the policies pursued in the 1970s. For that reason, the Wählerinitiative intended to concentrate over the next two years less on playing an active part in election campaigns and more on wider philosophical issues.

The official party too has been concerned to rebuild bridges with intellectuals. In 1983 it established a Kulturforum der Sozialdemokratie (Cultural forum of Social Democracy), whose original members included Jürgen Habermas and, if only as a guest, Günter Grass. The aim of the forum is to consider and discuss 'questions of cultural development in the Federal Republic of Germany', bearing in mind the relationships of these developments with the 'ideas of democratic socialism'. At the opening meeting Willy Brandt, still the SPD politician with the greatest prestige among intellectuals, spoke of how the CDU had paved the way for its return to power by the propagation of such terms as *Tendenzwende*. The aim of the forum was to suggest different values in order to regain the intellectual initiative. The initial public meeting on civil disobedience that took place in Bonn in September 1983 and at which both Habermas and Böll spoke does not, however, appear to have been a total success, if one looks at the press reports. One major unresolved problem was how the individual can determine when the moment for disobedience has come. Even the report in *Die Zeit* is highly sceptical about the idea of rapprochement between intellectuals and the SPD: 'That the SPD is seeking tentatively to make alliances with intellectuals and artists is new. It can, however, only do so because it is free of that which caused it to suffer for a long time: power.'[40] The truth or otherwise of this statement will only be proved if and when the SPD returns to government. In the meantime it can be pointed out that on a number of issues, such as peace and ecology, the party has moved closer to the positions of many intellectuals. Moreover, the years 1969 to 1972 do suggest that harmonious relations between intellectuals and political parties need not be restricted to the times when a particular party is free of the responsibility of office.

The one political group that one might expect to enjoy a high level of support among intellectuals is the Greens, in that they are the political embodiment of many of their concerns, especially atomic weapons, atomic power and environmental pollution.[41] Accordingly, it is not surprising that this new party has enjoyed a large degree of sympathy, although among writers Heinrich Böll was the only big name to campaign actively for them in the 1983 election. Nevertheless, the party did put Luise Rinser forward as its arithmetically doomed candidate for Federal President in 1984. Some writers, however, remain sceptical, as can be seen in an interesting essay by Peter Schneider that appeared in 1983 with the title 'Keine Lust aufs grüne Paradies' (No desire for the green paradise). The word paradise is especially significant. Schneider accuses elements within the Greens and the peace movement of having an unrealistic vision of a harmonious world from which all conflict can be eradicated. Because of this, they come to regard all that is evil as extraneous to the true nature of man, something which makes them more akin to a revivalist movement than a political grouping. Hence, they come to make absolute demands that are ultimately unpolitical: 'The necessarily experimental character of the political project is replaced by a self-opinionated, basically totalitarian pose.'[42] Whether the word totalitarian is fair, is open to debate. What does seem true is the general point that there is much that is unpolitical in the peace movement at least. A *Kürbiskern* report on a demonstration that took place in 1983 at what was then the projected Pershing base at Neu-Ulm is in many ways typical. Jürgen-Peter Stössel reflects on the human chain that was formed between the base and the city of Stuttgart and connects it with Marx and Engels — something not surprising in itself given the connection between *Kürbiskern* and the DKP. What is remarkable is the stress on emotions and feelings:

When I was part of this chain, . . . when I felt the warmth of the people, . . . when I passed on the warmth to the people to whom I gave my right hand; and when my arm grew and through the pressure of so many hands grew strong so that it reached to Stuttgart without any difficulty — then I could hear Karl and Friedrich who were getting an overview from a helicopter calling out of the sunny autumn sky: 'Carry on. Into the factories. Then you'll manage it.[43]

One fears on reading this that, rather than the helicopter blades, it will be Karl and Friedrich who will be gyrating — in their graves because their names are being invoked when realistic political analysis is being superseded by emotional phantasies.

In conclusion, the question of how one should react to the new postures being adopted by writers and intellectuals in the 1980s — specifically to the new values they have propagated and to their rejection of the traditional kind of commitment that expressed itself principally in support for the SPD — must be faced. On these issues they have been strongly criticised by the political scientist and co-founder of the Sozialdemokratische Wählerinitiative Professor Kurt Sontheimer. He sees the indifference to the change of government as a withdrawal from politics. The excessive zeal of the late 1960s and early 70s has given way to a non-political indifference.[44] What this view ignores are the political issues that have led to writers' rejection of the SPD. On the general question of the change of values, it depends on how one answers the question posed in the title of Sontheimer's 1983 book *Zeitenwende?* (A new era?).[45] Whereas Sontheimer rejects the need for a new kind of politics despite the threats to the environment and to peace, others see the present dangers as resulting from the failure of traditional politics. What is incontrovertible is that trees and lakes are dying in the Federal Republic and that nuclear arms are being amassed. Even if some of the ideas put forward in the 1980s have been unrealistic and open to criticism, the need to respond to a worrying situation cannot be denied.

Notes

1. M. Ende, *The Neverending Story* (Penguin, Harmondsworth, 1984), p. 127.
2. Ibid., p. 127.
3. E. Eppler, M. Ende, H. Tächl, *Phantasie, Kultur, Politik* (Thienemanns Verlag, Stuttgart, 1982), p. 33.

4. Ibid., p. 52.

5. Ibid., p. 72.

6. Ibid., p. 53.

7. Ibid., p. 45.

8. W. Schirmacher, 'Post-Moderne — ein Einspruch', *Konkursbuch 11* (1984), 10.

9. Ibid., 12f.

10. F. J. Raddatz, 'Warum ich Pazifist bin', *Die Zeit*, no. 42, 9 Oct. 81.

11. 'Wenn ich so dächte wie Kunert, möchte ich lieber tot sein. Ein Zeit-Gespräch zwischen Wolf Biermann, Günter Kunert und Fritz J. Raddatz', *Die Zeit*, no. 47, 14 Nov. 80.

12. S. Lenz, 'Das Wasser der Republik' in F. Duve, H. Böll, K. Staeck (eds), *Kämpfen für die Sanfte Republik* (Rowohlt, Reinbek bei Hamburg, 1980), p. 89f.

13. I. Krüger (ed.), *Mut zur Angst* (Luchterhand, Darmstadt und Neuwied, 1982).

14. H. Schmidt, 'Fürchtet Euch nicht', *Die Zeit*, no. 52, 23 Dec. 83.

15. E. K. Scheuch, 'Die Arroganz der Ängstlichkeit', *Die Zeit*, no. 47, 13 Nov. 81.

16. D. E. Zimmer, 'Deine Angst und meine Angst', *Die Zeit*, no. 47, 13 Nov. 81.

17. G. Zwerenz, 'Deutschland, automatisiertes Schlachtfeld', *die Tageszeitung*, 22 Apr. 83.

18. F. Alt, *Frieden ist möglich* (Piper, München, Zürich, 1983), p. 28.

19. R. Hochhuth, 'Kohls Armageddon oder Sedanlächeln und Seife' in H. Albertz (ed.), *Warum ich Pazifist wurde* (Kindler, München, 1983), p. 39.

20. *Berliner Begegnung zur Friedensförderung* (Luchterhand, Darmstadt und Neuwied, 1982), p. 82.

21. Ibid., p. 43.

22. Ibid., p. 92.

23. *Zweite Berliner Begegnung, Den Frieden erklären* (Luchterhand, Darmstadt und Neuwied, 1983), p. 113.

24. Ibid., p. 95.

25. Ibid., p. 134.

26. Ibid., p. 35.

27. Ibid., p. 75.

28. Ibid., p. 128.

29. Ibid., p. 73.

30. J. Fuchs, *Einmischung in eigene Angelegenheiten* (Rowohlt, Reinbek bei Hamburg, 1984), p. 157.

31. Ibid., p. 162.

32. Ibid., p. 153.

33. C. Wolf, *Kassandra* (Luchterhand, Darmstadt und Neuwied, 1983), p. 74.

34. W. Girnus, 'Wer baute das siebentorige Theben', *Linkskurve*, no. 1/1984, 23.

35. K. Nevermann, 'Die Linken und die Linke', *Die Zeit*, no. 41, 3 Oct. 80.

36. B. Strauss, *Paare Passanten* (Carl Hanser Verlag, München, Wien, 1981), p. 68. (*die Tageszeitung* is a new, independent newspaper which runs on alternative principles.)

37. Ibid., p. 25.

38. K. Wagenbach, 'Über das geistige Befinden der Republikaner angesichts eines Landesfürsten', *Freibeuter 3* (1980), 23.

39. B. M. Mülder, 'Nichts gegen die CDU', *Freibeuter 18* (1983), 83.

40. U. Greiner, 'Mut ohne Macht', *Die Zeit*, no. 39, 23. Sep. 83.

41. The campaign against the construction of a storage and re-processing plant for nuclear waste at Gorleben, close to the GDR frontier, has been a major concern

of writers. Several, including Peter Schneider and Günter Grass, signed a manifesto in 1977 demanding re-forestation rather than the atomic project. A book about the experience of protest is H. C. Buch, *Gorlebener Tagebuch* (Verlag 2001, Frankfurt am Main, 1983).

42. P. Schneider, 'Keine Lust aufs grüne Paradies', *Kursbuch 74* (1983), 187.

43. J. P. Stössel, in *Kürbiskern*, no. 1/1984, 13.

44. K. Sontheimer, 'Brauchen wir eine Vision der Zukunft', *Neue Rundschau*, vol. 95, nos. 1/2 (1984), 155–62.

45. K. Sontheimer, *Zeitenwende?* (Hoffmann und Campe Verlag, Hamburg, 1983).

PART TWO:
CASE STUDIES

GÜNTER GRASS — THE CAMPAIGNER

When Günter Grass's first novel *Die Blechtrommel* (The Tin Drum) was published in 1959, it appeared to many, and still does today, that a new era in post-war German literature had begun. The generation whose youth had been betrayed by National Socialism had found its voice. Using Grass's home town of Danzig as its setting, the novel showed for the first time the ugly banality of Nazism, whilst reflecting on the political immaturity that made it possible. In its form it represented an imaginative parody of the German tradition of the *Bildungsroman* (novel of education), whilst also drawing on the model of the picaresque novel. What is more, the sexual descriptions broke one of the major taboos of the Adenauer era with Grass seen in some quarters as a pornographer and blasphemer. The sense of scandal and outrage engendered by the novel was furthered by the impression conveyed by Grass as a person. With his distinguishing moustache, he seemed to embody to the public at large the quintessential Bohemian living at the periphery of bourgeois society. If one adds to this the publication of two more controversial works in the meantime, the novella *Katz und Maus* (Cat and Mouse) and the novel *Hundejahre* (Dog Years), now frequently grouped together with *Die Blechtrommel* as the *Danzig Trilogy*, it is easy to see why Grass's full-blooded entry into the political arena in 1965 as an independent speaker supporting the SPD in the Federal elections should cause a considerable stir and attract widespread media attention. The title of the first novel itself provided journalists (and continues to do so) with such irresistible headlines as 'Grass drums for the SPD' or 'Tin-drummer Grass speaks'. It is the aim of this chapter to show what use Grass has made of the political opportunities given, if the hackneyed metaphor may be continued, by the drum of his literary fame.

Grass's first entry into specifically political writing is his contribution to *Die Alternative* in 1961, although it should not be forgotten that his previous fictional work, that is to say *Die Blechtrommel*, has an important political dimension. In the case of his contribution to Walser's volume, however, entitled 'Wer wird dieses Bändchen kaufen?' (Who will buy this slim volume?), whatever the intention, the political dimension is of very modest proportions. After he has wondered whether certain people he meets in everyday life will vote SPD, the essay becomes increasingly fanciful, with Grass telling former fellow-citizens of Danzig that on a visit to his former home he heard the sea and the pigeons advocating a vote for the Social Democrats. What is more, the gap between the real world of politics and that of literary fiction completely disappears when Grass turns to the voting habits of the characters of *Die Blechtrommel*. The overall impression is of a literary writer indulging himself from a supposedly political starting point. Practically the only really political point of interest is that Grass shares the scepticism towards the SPD of many of his fellow contributors, characterising the party as the 'lukewarm, goodygoody, musty SPD'.[1] This contrasts with his subsequent wholehearted support.

Four years later Grass made two contributions to Richter's *Plädoyer für eine neue Regierung*, with the literary element again very much to the fore. One is a poem on the German Question, whilst the other takes the form of a one-act play set during a flight with Willy Brandt from Berlin to Stuttgart. This play *POUM oder die Vergangenheit fliegt mit* (POUM or the past is a fellow passenger) — the initials are those of a small Spanish anarchist party at the time of the Civil War — has a lot in common with the kind of theatre written by Grass at the beginning of the decade, which is usually classified as 'absurd'. These contributions pale into insignificance, however, beside Grass's personal intervention in the election campaign. Independently, as the extremely cautious hierarchy of the SPD was at pains to point out, though not without contact with party politicians, he travelled the country seeking support for the party, choosing towns and areas where the Social Democrats were weak. Expenses were defrayed by an admission charge, and surpluses were to be used to provide libraries for the Federal army and for a competition for a more appropriate school reader for the subject of German.

The texts of the four standard speeches delivered by Grass during his two tours — he spoke in all on fifty-two occasions — are contained in the first collected volume of his political works *Über das Selbstverständliche* (Speak Out!). They were 'Es steht zur Wahl' (The Issue), which seeks to follow the example of Walt Whitman in praising democracy; 'Loblied auf Willy' (Song in praise of Willy) whose title is self-explanatory; 'Was ist des Deutschen Vaterland' (What is the German's Fatherland), where the title refers back to a

poem written by Ernst Moritz Arndt in the first half of the nineteenth century in a period of national ferment and which asks the
German people to accept the loss of those territories in the east
including his own home, the former Free City of Danzig, whose
German inhabitants were expelled after the war; and finally, 'Des
Kaisers neue Klieder' (The emperor's new clothes), a fierce attack
on Ludwig Erhard and his government. As the last three titles have
literary nuances and the first speech is based on the model of
Whitman, it is plain that Grass the writer of literature is still very
much present in his political commitment. Indeed, in 'Es steht zur
Wahl', he characterises himself as a story-teller and admits by
implication in a series of rhetorical questions that he is not the
typical political expert: 'Who is speaking? A story-teller. A man
who is always saying: Once upon a time. Ought he to raise or lower
his voice? . . . Oughtn't he to have columns of figures in front of
him? Aren't statistics sacred nowadays?'[2] This speech is marked by
frequent anecdotal references to types of voters, whilst throughout
all the four there are endless stylistic flourishes, as in the following
comment on the electoral promises of political parties:

> For in a forest of equally uninspired election posters we are
> wandering like Hansel and Gretel without path or guide. Every-
> where gingerbread houses are promised us. In the tones of a
> Children's Hour storyteller we are promised satisfaction and
> security.[3]

Here the literary rhetoric is amusing and appropriate; doubts arise,
however, when he himself lapses albeit ironically into the tone of
the professional advertiser by concluding his eulogy of Brandt with
the slogan 'Put a Willy in your tank'.[4]

Although following his scepticism of 1961 Grass continued to
speak in 1965 of elections not being clear-cut issues offering a
choice between black and white, a considerable portion of his four
campaign speeches is devoted to blistering attacks on the Christian
Democrats. These reach their climax in 'Des Kaisers neue Kleider',
in which the political bankruptcy of the Erhard government is illustrated by reference to Andersen's fairy-tale. Of the government's
performance Grass says:

> No planning, no rationality, there is nothing except Ludwig
> Erhard's fear of losing the office of Federal Chancellor. The

usual cigar smoke, his vacuous language and cheap self-praise
can no longer clothe him.

The Emperor is naked. Everybody knows it, everybody has
nightmares about it; and already the children are beginning to
point with their childish fingers: 'He has nothing on!'[5]

Whatever their validity, these comments again reflect Grass's
literary talents. Elsewhere, he is simply vitriolic, as when he castigates the then Minister of Health Frau Schwarzkopf, who is
generally accused of neglecting the nation's health and specifically
condemned over the Erhard government's outright rejection of
abortion and the consequent death of numerous women each year.
Schwarzkopf is accused of having failed 'in a murderous manner'.[6]
In as far as Grass is speaking of a minor, in the meantime largely
forgotten minister, his tone appears exaggerated and misplaced,
reflecting a tendency to dwell too exclusively on personalities. In
fact, one impression of the four election speeches of 1965 is that
they are often stronger on polemics and rhetoric than on argument
and policy.

Nevertheless, it would be wrong to dismiss Grass's intervention
in the 1965 election outright. As the above quotations show, his
contribution was anything but boring. Nor was he entirely a dilet-
tante on policy matters. His frankness on the question of the
former German areas in the east, something the SPD prévaricated
on in 1965, was to be vindicated when, as part of Brandt's
Ostpolitik, the Federal Republic accepted Poland's post-war frontiers. The willingness to appear in areas where the Social Democrats
were weak brought their cause notice in places where without the
personality of Grass it might have been ignored. Moreover, the
reactions of the CDU and its supporters in such strongholds
revealed something about that party. In Cloppenburg, a town in
Lower Saxony where the Christian Democrats habitually gain more
than 60 per cent of the vote, the party issued a statement following
the visit of Grass in 1965 which seems to imply that the good people
there had withstood an alien invasion: 'Günter Grass spoke on
Tuesday evening in Cloppenburg. We thank the population of
South Oldenburg that it did not let itself be provoked.'[7] Most
important of all was that Grass had actually participated in the
election and added a new dimension to the political commitment of
West German writers. However sceptical critics or some fellow
writers might have been or might have become over Grass's public

appearances over the past twenty years, this first entry into the
political arena should in the context of its time be seen as a bold
experiment. Finally, the four speeches do show in embryo the ideas
that Grass was to formulate in the following years, and which will
be discussed in the next part of this chapter.

Following his involvement in the 1965 election, Grass turned his
attention almost exclusively to political questions. This is reflected
not least in his literary writing, which begins to concentrate on
current political issues. The novel *Örtlich Betäubt* (Local Anaesthe-
tic) and the play *Davor* (Before) of 1969 have linked subject matter
related to the student movement, whilst the volume of poetry
Ausgefragt (Interrogated) of 1967 contains several political poems.
If the play *Die Plebejer proben den Aufstand* (The Plebeans
Rehearse the Uprising) of 1966 is not strictly contemporary in that
it is set at the time of the 1953 conflicts in East Berlin, it nevertheless takes as its subject the political role of the artist, a major
concern of Grass in the 1960s. Finally, *Aus dem Tagebuch einer
Schnecke* (From the Diary of a Snail) of 1972, a work not easily
classified in terms of literary genre, encapsulates much of Grass's
political thinking in the late 1960s and early 70s.

The first aspect of Grass's commitment that requires explanation
is the basis on which he justifies it. A key word here that is
repeatedly used by Grass is *Bürger* (citizen). For him, the writer and
intellectual are not the inhabitants of either an ivory tower or
Mount Parnassus but first and foremost citizens of their country.
Thus, he is quick to criticise those colleagues who stand aloof from
political life. The speech given in 1965 'Über das Selbstverständliche' — already referred to as a manifestation of growing tensions
among writers — contains many examples of such criticism. In the
rhetorical style of his election speeches of the same year, he asks:
'What disaster must descend on this country before a scholar will
look up from his papers for a few hours and take a position here,
now and today?'[8] In the same vein, the idea of the writer as the
'conscience of the nation' is dismissed in a scathing reference to
'the platitude spewing conscience of a non-existent nation'.[9] The
traditional German dichotomy between *Geist* and *Macht* is also
rejected by Grass. The election speech 'Des Kaisers neue Kleider'
makes this clear:

There is no cause to reconstruct the antiquated opposition
between intellect and power. For we do not pay our taxes and

vote on some Parnassus among muses and incense, and not in
sensitively created republics of scholars but here in the Federal
Republic we have to pay and open our mouths.[10]

A speech made in Princeton in April 1966 significantly entitled
'Vom mangelnden Selbstvertrauen der schreibenden Hofnarren
unter Berücksichtigung nicht vorhandener Höfe' (On Writers as
Court Jesters and on non-existent Courts) goes further into this
question with Grass saying that writers cannot expect to influence
political events unless they are prepared to compromise. They must
abandon the criteria they apply in their literary work: 'a poem
knows no compromises, but men live by compromise'.[11] In short,
the writer should take on a different *persona*, that of the citizen,
when he involves himself in politics. And politics for Grass means
the workaday world of political life.

It is this view of the writer's role within politics that led to Grass
involving himself in the election of 1965 and before the following
election to be a founder member of the Sozialdemokratische
Wählerinitiative. Grass's explanation of this body made in an
election speech in 1969 encapsulates the nature of his political commitment: 'We favour the active involvement of the voter in
elections so that this most important democratic event is not solely
left to the parties.'[12] Significant here is the stress on the phenomenon of elections along with the belief in the primacy of the
citizen in the role of voter. Just as he himself is motivated as a
citizen to involve himself in politics, Grass desires that other
citizens take a similar interest. It is also worth noting that Grass's
election speeches in 1969, under the auspices of the Wählerinitiative, lack the flamboyance of those of 1965, in this way underlining
the new sense of responsibility for the democratic process. Ringing
denunciations of his political opponents have largely given way to a
concern for the minutiae of policies pursued by the Social Democratic members of the originally despised Grand Coalition. The
claim made in connection with the policy for the coal industry of
the then SPD Economics Minister Karl Schiller: 'The coal revival
law protects the coal industry from a new crisis',[13] whatever its
merits as a statement of political fact, is hardly sparkling prose, nor
is it meant to be. It reflects rather Grass's view of the writer in
politics as a knowledgeable and responsible citizen.

The form of Grass's political commitment implies much of its
substance. Involvement in elections presupposes a belief in Western

parliamentary democracy. Even if it appears somewhat self-impor-
tant, a statement of this belief made in 1968 could hardly have been
expressed more clearly:

> For my part I shall continue to defend this first promising
> attempt to establish democracy in Germany. And whoever . . .
> lessens the in any case weak and always endangered basis for
> democratisation in the Federal Republic, whoever . . . thinks he
> must destroy parliamentary democracy . . . he has in me a politi-
> cal opponent with a fair degree of stamina.[14]

These words aimed at the revolutionary students also suggests an
acceptance of the Federal Republic as a state and a commitment to
it.

Grass's commitment to the parliamentary democracy of the
Federal Republic leads in turn to the rejection of those forces perceived as a danger to it. In the late 1960s he was an implacable
opponent of the National Democratic Party, whose electoral successes at the state level seemed to herald a revival of neo-Nazism.
On the occasion of the state election in Bavaria in 1966 he
addressed a speech 'to a young citizen who feels tempted to vote for
the NPD'.[15] One of his major objections to the Grand Coalition
and particularly the choice of a former member of the Nazi Party
as Federal Chancellor was that such a choice made the Nazi past
appear more respectable and thus helped the NPD. On the Right
too he showed strong opposition to the Springer Press, which in
1967 he accused of using fascist methods in a report on the East
German writer Arnold Zweig.[16]

Although such a statement inevitably provoked controversy, it
was Grass's opposition to what he perceived as the extremist Left
and his unabashed equation of both Right and Left under the label
of undemocratic extremism that created the greatest stir among
intellectuals. His opposition to the political tendencies within the
student movement led Rudi Dutschke to declare that combating
Grass was the main political priority. There are many instances of
Grass equating both political extremes, which typically he sees as
united in their opposition to the SPD: 'Because right and left-wing
extremists see in this party the main guarantor of parliamentary
democracy, they wish to weaken it and finally destroy it.'[17] Specifically, he fears a repeat of what happened at the end of the Weimar
Republic, whose downfall was caused in his view not solely by the

extreme Right but also contributed to by the extreme Left. On many occasions he pulls no punches when comparing both political extremes. After some leftists in his opinion had not shown enough interest in the fate of Czechoslovakia, he accused them, following the Soviet intervention, of a general intolerance reminiscent of Goebbels.[18]

This strong opposition to the Left is based on his dismissal of any idea of revolution or violence. He never believed that there was any possibility of revolution at the time of the student disturbances, nor did he consider one desirable. In his view, the dialectic of revolution leads inevitably to dictatorship and oppression.

> I am an opponent of revolution. I fear sacrifices, which invariably have to be made in its name. I fear its suprahuman goals, its absolute demands, its inhuman intolerance. I fear the mechanism of revolution. . . Revolutions have substituted dependence with dependence, replaced compulsion by compulsion.[19]

The title of the speech made at a writers' conference in Belgrade in 1969, from which this quotation is taken, could hardly be more explicit: 'Literatur und Revolution oder des Idyllikers schnaubendes Steckenpferd' (Literature and revolution or the idyll writer's snorting hobby-horse). In contrast with those of a revolutionary temperament, Grass is proud to describe himself as a revisionist, a term of abuse among his opponents.

If this general rejection of revolution were not enough for Grass's student adversaries, he was also unwilling to concede that the German students were in any sense true revolutionaries. Although he is willing to concede that Marxism is a scientific doctrine, he is dismissive of those students who claimed to act in its name. First, he maintains that the motives for their actions were largely sociological. It is a case of a privileged middle-class group indulging in a phase of pseudo-revolutionary activity before settling down in a conventional manner: 'It cannot come as any surprise if the sons from all too good a family use their time at university to let off a bit of left-wing radical steam.'[20] Grass's second objection to the students' revolutionary ideology is that it is less Marxism than a new version of German Idealism, that is to say a philosophy that is abstract and non-political in its absolute demands. He speaks of the protesters owing more to Fichte than to

Marx and asks: 'Where do these all or nothing demands come from, if they have not always been a youthful strong-man act arising from the well-fertilised cottage garden earth of German Idealism . . . ?'[21] In other words, the student movement is another episode within the German anti-democratic tradition.

Grass generally regarded the students' predilection for distant political systems and admiration for distant revolutionaries as another manifestation of this German Idealism. He showed nothing but scorn for the adulation directed at such figures as Ho-Tchi-Minh and Che Guevara. Although there is no evidence to suggest that he supported American actions in Vietnam, he did not make this favourite cause of the time his major concern. Nor was he a vociferous opponent of the 1968 emergency laws, despite his reservations about them. His view was that the students and others should direct their efforts primarily at supporting the progressive policies advocated by the SPD ministers within the Grand Coalition. Thus, he welcomed the declaration of support given by Social Democratic students to Willy Brandt's foreign policy and called on all students to change the emphasis of their political activities:

> I should like to ask the students in the spirit of this declaration and according to their opportunities to give student protest a direction which is first and foremost oriented towards political reality and the Federal Republic and the existence of two German states.[22]

Similarly, he asks the students to support the policies of the SPD justice minister and subsequent president Gustav Heinemann. These requests also show that Grass's condemnation of student political activity was not total; he differentiated between those who wanted, as he did, educational reform and what he perceived as a revolutionary minority.

As already seen, an essential component of Grass's commitment to parliamentary democracy and his rejection of political extremism has been from the outset his support for the SPD. This expressed itself in the 1960s and 70s not in the form of party membership but through a body like the Sozialdemokratische Wählerinitiative, the embodiment of his conception of the role of the citizen in a democracy. A prime reason for his continuing support of the party lies in the way he identifies it with democracy. This identification has first a historical basis. He speaks glowingly of the way the SPD in the late nineteenth century changed from being a revolutionary party to an evolutionary, parliamentary one, of how it established democracy in Germany at the end of the Great War, and how it was the only party to vote against Hitler's Enabling Act in 1933 that destroyed the democracy of the Weimar Republic. As for the Weimar Republic itself, he claims in a 1965 election speech that it was rescued by the Social Democrats 'on several occasions'.[23] By contrast, he sees the Christian Democrats as a product of an authoritarian German tradition and not wedded to democratic principles.[24] Secondly, in the context of the Federal Republic, Grass equates the SPD with his own values, namely the rejection of absolute goals in favour of continuous democratic reforms. 'Not ideological demands but achievements based on reason show the worth of political action'[25] is a statement of this view taken from a 1969 election speech significantly entitled 'Rede von den begrenzten Möglichkeiten' (Speech on limited opportunities).

Grass's support for the Social Democrats is not restricted to the approval of its democratic credentials. As a 'democratic socialist' he regards their general policies too with favour. What Grass means by socialism is less to do with the ownership of the means of production than with a system of moral values coupled with, in economic terms, an extension of co-determination and democratic control. In his 'Sieben Thesen zum Demokratischen Sozialismus' (Seven theses on democratic socialism) he is unwilling to lay down any hard-and-fast rules about how socialism is to be achieved, saying as well that there is as yet no clear definition of the concept.[26] Such a viewpoint clearly fits in with the reformist approach of the SPD's Godesberg Programme.

Despite Grass being highly sceptical about the theoretical approach of his political opponents, especially the students, he nevertheless seeks to justify his own support for the SPD in terms of political ideology. In particular, he regards the party as the child of the European Enlightenment. He associates it directly with the Enlightenment values of reason and tolerance: 'The SPD with its reformist tradition is based on reason and enlightenment.'[27] The other Enlightenment virtue manifested by the SPD on which Grass sets great store is tolerance. He gives his 1974 speech on tolerance a significant place in his second collection of political writing *Der Bürger und seine Stimme* (The citizen and his voice) by making it the final contribution or 'epilogue'. The charge of intolerance is one that Grass makes frequently against the Left, whereas he is keen to stress his own tolerance by speaking not of political enemies but of opponents in the democratic process. It is not just dogmatic Marxists that he picks out as opponents of the Enlightenment values. Among philosophers he criticises Hegel, whose dialectical system is seen as the fatal inspiration for subsequent theorising that puts abstract systems before all else.

Alongside these questions of theory and probably of much greater significance as the starting point for Grass's political thinking, is the role he attaches to personalities in politics. After the Second World War Grass was impressed by the Social Democrat leader Kurt Schumacher, but of much more significance subsequently has been the figure of Willy Brandt. It was admiration for Brandt, whose performance as Governing Mayor of West Berlin and whose unblemished past he found so exemplary, that led Grass to take an interest in politics and to lend his support to the Social Democrats. In particular, he was appalled at the way Brandt was vilified by his opponents because he had emigrated to escape from National Socialism. Much of this sympathy for Brandt is encapsulated in the 1965 election speech 'Loblied für Willy'. Of Brandt's policies, it is the Ostpolitik that Grass with his special feeling towards Poland approved of most strongly, whilst he has also praised Brandt's personal qualities. In his arguments with students, Grass frequently sought to portray Brandt as a model of tolerance, citing his acceptance of the left-wing views of his son Peter. Equally, Grass has generally approved of Brandt's tolerant style of leadership, although there were occasions, particularly just before Brandt's resignation as Chancellor, when he demanded a more forthright approach.

Besides the generally complimentary references to Brandt, to read Grass's political speeches and other writings is to find oneself confronted with a series of names of politicians, some hardly remembered, whatever their previous prominence, whose performance at the time is either praised or denigrated. This reflects a belief in the importance of the individual and specifically a belief in individual moral responsibility, which cannot be explained away by reference to the climate of the age or other extraneous factors. Thus, Brandt is a person who was equal to the test presented by National Socialism and consequently enjoys moral authority, whereas Kiesinger remains discredited because as a responsible adult he acted 'contrary to all Christian morality'.[28] How far Grass goes in accordance with this attitude can be seen from a speech made in Israel in 1967, when he spoke of two of the Auschwitz guards Kaduk and Boger, who were brought to trial in 1965, as necessary members of any list of people in history who have committed horrific crimes.[29] He rejected the view that they were 'little men' — anonymous sadists in the service of a political ideology.

If most of the above suggests that Grass has been a more or less uncritical supporter of the Social Democrats, such an impression would be misleading. In accordance with the importance he attaches to personalities, he has criticised SPD politicians, for instance at the beginning of the Grand Coalition Herbert Wehner, whom he saw as the architect of that undesirable alliance.[30] In 1965 he described the party as a mixture of strengths and weaknesses, noting its inability to project itself and its 'petty fear of its own proletarian background'.[31] After two election successes, he was afraid in the 1970s that the party might begin to regard the state as its property, as the CDU had before it. Nevertheless, it is the continuing support of the Social Democrats that is the hallmark of Grass's commitment and the factor that differentiates him from so many of his colleagues and from predecessors in the Weimar Republic, like Tucholsky and Ossietzky, who turned away from the party with — in Grass's view — disastrous consequences for that democracy.

As already stated, *Aus dem Tagebuch einer Schnecke* presents within a single unified work many of the political ideas and opinions expressed by Grass up to the beginning of.the 1970s. With its mixture of fact and fiction it is a difficult work to sum up. The diary element, although the term diary is not entirely appropriate — jottings might be more accurate — consists of an account of Grass's pre-election speaking tours for the SPD in 1969. The chief fictional element is the story of how an anti-Nazi Danzig teacher Hermann Ott manages to avoid persecution by hiding in the cellar of a bicycle repairer. At the same time this fictional account, which itself is partly based on the true experiences of the literary critic Marcel Reich-Ranicki, provides a framework to recount the fate of the Jewish community of Danzig. The third major element in the book concerns a speech Grass was asked to give in Nuremberg in 1971 to commemorate the 500th anniversary of the birth of the artist Dürer. The preparation of this speech forms a motif throughout the book, whilst its text provides an appendix to the main narrative.

All these various elements of the *Tagebuch* make it a complex work, particularly as Grass constantly shifts, sometimes confusingly, from one element to another and from one time-level to another. These various time-levels, necessitated by the telling of the story of Ott, underline, however, how much Grass's political commitment arises out of the past, specifically the unhappy recent history of Germany. His view is simply that the past must in no way be forgotten but rather its lessons must be learned. Grass describes the writer as 'someone who writes against the passage of time.'[32] In other words, he prevents the past falling into oblivion, for example the past of individuals like Kiesinger, who can only benefit from the natural tendency of the majority to forget. In the general political context Grass seeks through his knowledge of the past to influence the present and the immediate future. The nexus between past, present and future is made clear by him in an interview when, after having repeated his description of the writer, he adds: 'Politics for me as a writer is the attempt to anticipate the time that will shortly pass, to make use of it or stamp it, before it has passed.'[33] The problem that arises from this standpoint is whether all the parallels Grass seeks to draw between past and present can be accepted, for instance his comparison in *Aus dem Tagebuch einer Schnecke* between the student SDS and the SS, both seen as idealistic conspiracies based on a false sense of community. Given the anti-authoritarian element in the student movement, this particular comparison does not hold water.

The narrative situation of the *Tagebuch* consists of Grass giving the account of his election tours and telling the story of Ott for his four children, whose often impatient reactions are included in the text. His intention is that they should learn the appropriate political lessons. This context, besides providing some of the book's lighter moments through the descriptions of family life, underlines the pedagogic quality in Grass's political writing. His fictional writing abounds with pedagogues, and here too there is the fictional character of Ott, who is a far more positive figure than his predecessors. Much of the *Tagebuch* is Grass as teacher repeating at times in a patronising tone many of his political ideas to the address of his children, as in the following passage:

It may be, Franz and Raoul, that when you're in search of something later on, Communism will give you hope . . .
Some day, because in Germany theory is put before practice, you may try to find a solution in that totalitarian system, which

claims to reconcile the contradictions and promises painless
transitions (A pacified existence.) . . .
I say: you may . . .
I say: over my dead body.[34]

Although it does not affect the substance of the ideas, this personal
element is a difference between the *Tagebuch* and the speeches. It
allows him to react more directly to his opponents, both in his comments about the students who disrupt his speeches and about the
CDU leader of the time Barzel, his adversary in a television debate,
whom he bitterly combines with the *bête noire* Strauss into a single
name 'Strauzel'.

Another major difference from the political speeches is the way
Grass seeks to put his political ideas into a wider conceptual framework. The major concepts he invokes are utopia, progress, doubt,
melancholy and resignation. The snail of the title is a literary metaphor for progress, which in a democracy can and should come only
at a very slow pace. In keeping with his metaphor, Grass describes
revolutionaries particularly as those who want snails to be able to
jump — a utopian demand. Melancholy is an important motif in
the book in that it is the drawing *Melancholia I*, around which
Grass centres his Dürer lecture. Melancholy is also associated with
the schoolteacher Ott, who not only collects snails, but is also preparing an academic treatise entitled 'On the snail as a mediator
between melancholy and utopia'. Equally importantly, Ott's nick-
name is *Zweifel* (Doubt), a word he uses frequently in keeping with
his generally sceptical outlook on life. In the contemporary setting,
it is Brandt who is seen as the sceptic: 'A man of the tribe of
Doubt.'[35] The — for the optimistic revolutionary — negative concepts of doubt, resignation and melancholy are vindicated in terms
of Grass's political philosophy in the Dürer lecture, which concludes: 'Only those who know and respect stasis in progress, who
have once and more than once given up, who have sat on an empty
snail shell and experienced the dark side of utopia, can evaluate
progress.'[36] These are the qualities and feelings of the person of
experience, the experience Grass believes young bourgeois revolutionaries lack.

Within this short account it is impossible to do justice to *Aus
dem Tagebuch einer Schnecke* with all its diffuse themes and
settings. Grass reveals a great sureness of touch in combining and
contrasting, creating connections and parallels. Characters

especially are balanced and contrasted, for instance the sceptic Ott with the partly fictional, partly factual Augst, who commits suicide during the Synod of the Lutheran Church at Stuttgart in 1969. His life is presented as a search for absolutes, hence his involvement at various times of his life with such apparently different bodies as the SS and the anti-nuclear groups of the 1950s. For Grass, these both represent the idealist as opposed to the pragmatic principle. The task of holding all the various elements together falls to the metaphor of the snail, as the narrative follows the principle which Grass enunciates at the outset and which clearly applies to politics as well: 'Hardly anything, believe me, is more depressing than going straight to the goal.'[37] At times, however, it must be admitted that the burden put upon the snail metaphor is too great, as when one specimen even becomes the force through which the daughter of Ott's landlord, Lisbeth Stomma, is freed from her grief and frigidity to become Ott's sexual partner rather than a service provided by her father. Nevertheless, as a whole, the book represents a remarkable literary experiment at the boundary of fact and fiction.

Following the 1972 election triumph of the SPD, Grass came to share the mood of many other intellectuals: frustration at the lack of direction of the Brandt government, followed by unhappiness at Brandt's replacement by Schmidt. He found it hard to come to terms with Brandt's resignation since he did not believe that there were adequate grounds for such a drastic step. As for Schmidt, it has already been seen that the relationship between him and Grass was never easy, although it cannot be overlooked that both ultimately shared the same anti-ideological, pragmatic approach to politics. Grass's change of mood following the advent of Schmidt is reflected in the, by his standards, peripheral involvement in the 1976 election and his comments after the SPD's less than convincing performance. He speaks of the party having lost its way by not providing any leadership and setting any goals that could inspire people to active support. He goes on to demand 'that the SPD, in accordance with its tradition thinks, plans and prepares further ahead than is possible for politicians restricted by demands of the day and the force of circumstances'.[38] He himself sought to aid the process by becoming involved in a new periodical *L76*, at the end of the decade *L80*, whose overall concern was questions relating to democratic socialism. In addition to these political reasons for Grass's partial withdrawal from the arena of daily politics, there were equally important professional ones, in other words the desire to devote more time to literature. Thus, there appeared in 1977 the novel *Der Butt* (The Flounder), which marks a return to the epic style of the early works.

His subsequent full-blooded return to the political battleground, as was the case with many other writers, was the result of concern about the possibility of Strauss as Federal Chancellor and about environmental and nuclear issues. Another work, similar to *Aus dem Tagebuch einer Schnecke* in that it mixes factual and fictional elements, appeared in the election year of 1980: *Kopfgeburten oder Die Deutschen sterben aus* (Headbirths or the Germans are Dying Out). The book is partly the description of a visit to China by Grass and partly the outline of a planned film about a young couple, both teachers, agonising about whether to have children and also undertaking a visit to the Third World. Both major elements provide a framework for speculation about themes connected with Germany, not least, as the second part of the title implies, the possibility much discussed in recent years that the number of Germans will decline considerably in the next century if the present birth-rate continues. Equally, the approaching election and the contemporary political scene in the Federal Republic play an important part in the work. In addition to Strauss, the political opponent Grass now perceives is the Greens, who have taken over the role of the students in *Aus dem Tagebuch einer Schnecke* as the grouping bringing an undesirable Messianic element into politics. Although Grass shares their concern about the environment, he rejects the tendency to 'drop out' and sink into despair, especially when at the same time they seek the privileges of the public servant enjoying security of tenure: 'Our Mama's darlings want to get out as soon as the travel expenses of their peregrinations are guaranteed. Plaintively (and under protest) yesterday's revolutionaries escape into the civil service. And everyone claims to be afraid.'[39] However vital its themes, *Kopfgeburten* is something of a disappointment in that it lacks the sparkle of much of Grass's earlier writing including the *Tagebuch*. The fictional characters, particularly the couple Harm and Dörte Peters, appear very contrived.

Since 1980 a new metaphor has partly replaced the snail in Grass's political writing. He has increasingly described political activity as being akin to the ordeal imposed on Sisyphos by the gods. There is continuity from the snail metaphor in as far as both ideas refer to an unending task without the prospect of an ultimate goal being achieved. The major difference lies in the change of attitude towards the concept of progress. Whereas *Aus dem Tagebuch einer Schnecke* espouses a general idea of slow progress, Grass has recently been at pains to stress the negative aspects, especially in ecological terms, of technological progress. In his speech in Rome in 1982 on the occasion of his being awarded the literary Antonio Feltrinelli Prize, he used the opportunity to point to the environmental dangers facing man, referring appropriately enough to the forecasts of the Club of Rome in the previous decade. He also takes his leave from the snail metaphor in its original sense:

> After all the experiences with time and its contrarotating course, I chose a slow animal for my literary coat of arms and said: Progress is a snail. At that time many wished — and I, too, wished — that there might be jumping snails. Today I know . . . the snail is too quick for us. It has already overtaken us. Yet we, fallen from Nature, we, the enemies of Nature, still feel to be in advance of the snail.[40]

Even if, in an interview with *Der Spiegel* later in the same year, Grass spoke somewhat confusingly this time of the snail being too slow, the point remained the same, namely that the post-Enlightenment tradition of equating reason with technical progress and doing all that is technically possible is no longer desirable. The prhase he uses here is: 'We must learn to do without.'[41] What separates this from the pessimism he strongly rejects in *Kopfgeburten* is explicable in terms of the Sisyphos metaphor. Grass has frequently stated that Sisyphos must now be regarded as a happy man in his task. In other words, political activity is still to be regarded as worthwhile. The Sisyphos metaphor takes on both a practical and philosophical aspect at one point in *Kopfgeburten*. Fighting for the same values of peace, freedom or justice is a Sisyphos-like task but, at the same time, the pushing of the stone gives his human existence meaning: 'It doesn't want to be freed from me nor I from it. It is human, in my measure. It is also my God, who without me does not exist.'[42] The use of the Sisyphos metaphor, taken as it is from Camus, adds a new dimension to Grass's political commitment, gives it a greater personal, subjective element than the previous more abstract doctrine of progress. Thus, in a television interview in 1984, Grass accepted that there were reasons for throwing in the towel, as his colleague Wolfgang Hildesheimer had done by announcing his intention of stopping writing, but confirmed his own intention of pressing on by saying: 'I am of the house of Sisyphos.' The personal element, always significant in Grass's political writing, has now taken on a new, almost metaphysical dimension.

Alongside ecology it is the nuclear issue that has led Grass to continue his political struggle in recent years. In 1980, along with Peter Schneider and two writers who had recently left East Berlin, Thomas Brasch and Sarah Kirsch, he addressed an open letter to the Federal Government, warning about the danger to peace and specifically criticising the United States, whose Vietnam policy — something Grass did not condemn as vociferously as others at the time — was said to have destroyed its moral standing.[43] This letter came at the beginning of the controversy about the stationing of the new generation of American missiles in the Federal Republic, a plan opposed by Grass from the outset. His concern about peace has become so paramount that he has been a leading participant in the discussions on the subject with East German writers, despite his consistent opposition to communism, visible in his championing of Solidarity in Poland. The climax to these efforts was an open letter to the deputies in the Federal Parliament shortly before the debate in which it was being asked to sanction the deployment. He appealed to the parliamentarians to follow their consciences and reject the missiles, comparing an eventual vote in their favour with Hitler's Enabling Act of 1933.[44] Whatever the general merit of Grass's case, the way in which it was expressed did little to advance it. As Professor Hans-Adolf Jacobsen, the chairman of an institute for peace and conflict research in Bonn, was able to point out, the comparison with 1933 is totally invalid, as this time there is no party to the debate who favours war; the argument is about the best way to preserve peace.[45] Jacobsen also castigated Grass for his overall tone, specifically the use of the word 'infantile' of those in favour of deploying the missiles, whilst complaining at the same time about those who describe the Soviet Union as 'the enemy'.

Not surprisingly, given the state of the parties in parliament, Grass's pleas fell on deaf ears. Undaunted, his next step, along with other writers including Peter Härtling, Hans Christoph Buch and Luise Rinser, was the Heilbronn Appeal of December 1983. This resulted from the meeting of writers in the town of Heilbronn, referred to in Chapter 6. The appeal calls on those concerned to refuse military service in the West German army, as the new missiles — seen by the writers as offensive weapons — give the army as part of NATO an unconstitutional role, as the Basic Law speaks of a purely defensive role for the armed services. This appeal created considerable controversy, particularly because in his speech at Heilbronn he had used the word *Wehrkraftzersetzung* (subversion of military strength) to describe his future tactics towards the military.[46] Afterwards he was to say that the term was meant ironically. Be that as it may, one must again question the effects of Grass's tactics. A volume of replies by a group of officers published later in the same year showed that Grass and his colleagues had alienated moderate military opinion. Wolf Graf von Baudissin, a former high-ranking officer who at one time was associated with the Sozialdemokratische Wählerinitiative, criticised Grass's mode of argument because it rejects the possibility of different opinions being sincerely held and claims 'to have a monopoly of morality and conscience'.[47] He makes the further point that nobody voted for the missiles to abolish democracy, the issue of 1933. The wise decision by the legal authorities not to prosecute Grass for the comments — as some on the Right demanded — only underlines Baudissin's point.

If Grass's arguments on the nuclear question and the tone in which they are expressed seem out of keeping with the anti-extremist stance he took up in the 1960s, it needs to be stressed that he himself is at pains to reconcile them with the democratic order of the Federal Republic. It has already been pointed out that he regards the opponents of Pershing missiles as the true supporters of the constitution, a claim repeated in an interview with *Die Zeit* in February 1984.[48] As for the legality of his own campaign against the missiles, he has based it on the constitutional right of resistance. An addition to the Basic Law incorporated as a safeguard at the time of the 1968 emergency laws, gives all Germans the right to resist anyone attempting to overthrow the democratic constitution 'if no other means are available'. Grass claimed this right for those opposing nuclear weapons at an SPD meeting in January 1983 to mark the fiftieth anniversary of Hitler's coming to power. Whilst accepting that violence is out of place and that no spectacular event similar to those of 1933 is imminent, he nevertheless expresses his belief that the time to resist has come, in the light of both the nuclear threat and a perceived erosion of civil liberties. He also makes a prophecy about the significance of the year 1983:

In this year . . . it will be proven whether the Federal Republic of Germany in contrast to the Weimar Republic can count on enough democrats. On critical democrats, who are not to be appeased, on non-violent yet militant democrats, who if necessary are ready to resist.[49]

Now that some missiles have been deployed, one must conclude that Grass will have been disappointed. In fact, with hindsight, it seems that he greatly exaggerated the significance of a single year, possibly moved to such hyperbole by the anniversary of Hitler's accession. Dubious comparisons with 1933 are what make the whole idea of resistance problematical. It is an exaggeration to claim that the democracy of the Federal Republic has degenerated so much that individual or collective extra-parliamentary resistance is the only way to preserve liberty or prevent war. That Grass in his January 1983 speech prefaces his belief that the time to resist has come with the words 'I think' also suggests how subjective the whole idea is. In terms of Grass's own political development, it nevertheless represents a major change. How great this change has been since 1980 can be seen in the 1984 television interview already referred to. Whereas he had once criticised the young for their cult of fear, he now talks of his own justifiable *Angst*.

These changes in Grass's political attitudes raise the question of his relationship to the SPD, the major governing party until 1982 and thereafter the chief opposition grouping. Despite everything, his support for the party has never wavered; indeed, immediately on hearing of the fall of the Schmidt government in 1982, he changed his previous stance and finally joined the party, in his own words 'as a sign of solidarity'.[50] To some extent this seems to have been an emotional gesture, although it should not necessarily be condemned for that. In the 1983 election he again supported the party actively, re-writing his 1980 speech 'Orwells Jahrzehnt' (Orwell's decade). Its title reflects the restrained mood adopted in *Kopfgeburten*, the 1980s being seen as the decade when both peace and freedom are threatened. The 1983 version, however, is most remarkable for its vitriolic attack on the new Chancellor Kohl:

Without any ideas of his own and untroubled by expert knowledge, this man takes pleasure in the dignified verbosity of the toastmaster. This is not the way a chancellor speaks and acts; at most it is the way a chancellery clerk speaks and acts.[51]

One is strongly reminded of the 1965 election speeches, the time when Grass was not a universally welcome supporter of the SPD. This, though, has not generally been the case recently, even if all the party's right wing is not delighted by his membership and he himself has shown himself aware of possible conflicts with the SPD. Nevertheless, it should be pointed out that his recent forceful views, at least on nuclear weapons, have not estranged him from the party. By rejecting the deployment of American missiles in the autumn of 1983 it has moved to a position much closer to that of Grass than of former Chancellor Schmidt.

When seeking finally to assess the political role of Günter Grass over the past twenty years or so, it is impossible to ignore the extremes of opinion that have been held about him. The critic and publisher Heinz Ludwig Arnold accorded him something of a representative pedagogic role in 1969 by stating: 'Grass, one can say, has become, either by accident or design, a kind of *Praeceptor democratiae germaniae*.'[52] This title is to award him a status akin to Thomas Mann. On the other hand, for the cultural critic of *Der Spiegel* Hellmuth Karasek in 1984, Grass was little more than a tiresome busybody who cannot restrain from expressing a view on every possible subject.[53] Karasek's comments reflect an impatience with the form Grass's commitment takes, his concern with apparently trivial issues, his involvement with politics at a basic or 'grass-roots' level. That he is attracted to elections and generally to the daily stuff of politics is conceded by Grass in *Aus dem Tagebuch einer Schnecke* with the frequent references to *Mief* (fug). He uses the word to connect his self-understanding as a writer with his political activities:

> In case you didn't know, children, a writer these days is just a fug measurer. What they call stable smell. Back from Verden, Cloppenburg, Osnabrück, Lünen. Fug-filled bell jars ring in the evening. Last stop the Scholl High School. For my table: Catholic fug.[54]

The author of *Die Blechtrommel* describes the 'fuggy' world of the petty-bourgeoisie; Grass the politician seeks out the 'fuggy' provinces of the Federal Republic for the scene of his political commitment. It might seem from this that Grass's political activity is some kind of self-indulgence, based largely on his own temperament and the interest he has in the seedy, finally compounded with a desire to shock or create attention in keeping with his image as a writer. It would, however, be grossly unfair to see Grass's political involvement in such crude psychological terms. It surely cannot be held against him that his political commitment takes on the form most suited to his nature and that he might even enjoy what he does. Its durability also suggests that it is more than some form of self-gratification. Where Grass is on weaker ground is when he seems to claim that the form his commitment takes is the only legitimate one. In an interview with Heinz Ludwig Arnold, for instance, he said: 'Perhaps some writers have not yet realised that political involvement is something other than flying intellectual kites on late-night radio programmes.'[55] This ignores the possibility that some writers with legitimate political concerns might not be capable of facing hostile election crowds in rural Bavaria.

When it comes to political issues, it is probably impossible to make hard-and-fast judgements on Grass, unless a particular ideological standpoint is adopted. With hindsight it appears that he was right to warn against the danger of violence arising out of the student movement, but that on the other hand his worries over the Grand Coalition were exaggerated. Rather than draw up some kind of list of issues past and present and subject Grass to some kind of marking scheme — no points for being wrong in prophesying a crisis-free future for the coal industry, for instance — it is more sensible to examine the basis of his ideas, the conceptions upon which he builds his political commitment. In this the intention is again not to judge, for example, Grass's views on parliamentary democracy or on the role of the individual in history from a particular ideological standpoint, but to look more at questions of internal consistency. One is immediately faced with a paradox here, namely that Grass strictures the Left for its theoretical predilections, whilst at the same time attempting to build a theoretical basis for his own non-ideological approach.

It is this body of theory that has attracted possibly most criticism from Grass's many detractors, especially those with an academic background. Peter Rühmkorf is particularly scathing, though not necessarily objective, in his view of the theoretical basis of Grass's political activity: 'In keeping with his petty-bourgeois grocer's way of thinking, post-Godesberg social democratship was the most he was willing to subject himself to in terms of basic political research.'[56] Whatever motives one attributes to such criticism, it is nevertheless true that particularly the claims made by Grass about his political commitment reflecting the values of Reason and the Enlightenment are dubiously founded, often amounting only to unproven assertions. In his introduction to the second edition of *Über das Selbstverständliche*, he expresses somewhat immodestly the hope that his book will contribute 'to achieving a broader basis for Reason in the sense of the European Enlightenment'.[57] The impression given is that the views Grass advocates are reasonable and that those he dislikes are unenlightened. This is particularly visible in the speech 'Des Kaisers neue Kleider', where the two terms are simply incorporated into rhetorical questions: 'When finally will in our country as well the age of enlightenment begin? When will ignorance finally vacate the ministerial chair and make way for Reason?'[58] Similarly, referring to his 1969 election tours in *Aus dem Tagebuch einer Schnecke*, he speaks of being 'in the service of enlightenment'.[59]

Equally questionable is Grass's interpretation of the history of the SPD. By merely referring to positive parts of that history, he ignores such questions as whether its caution in 1919 destroyed the chance of creating an effective democratic basis for the Weimar Republic, and whether in 1933 it contributed to its own downfall. As for this downfall, Grass is right to refer to the SPD's courage in voting against Hitler's Enabling Act, but forgets that in the same year the party appeared to accept much of Nazi foreign policy. Although he associates the party with his preferred doctrine of revisionism, he neglects to mention that two of his revisionist models, Rosa Luxemburg and even Eduard Bernstein, generally regarded as the father of revisionism, left the SPD, albeit temporarily in the second case. That he classes Luxemburg at all as a revisionist is somewhat eccentric, as she always remained a revolutionary for all her criticisms of the Bolsheviks. Such factors make it impossible to dispute that there is at times a lack of intellectual coherence in Grass's political thinking.

A possibly more important question is whether Grass abides in practice with the principles he expounds, particularly those of moderation and tolerance. Michael Hollington describes him in inverted commas as a 'fanatical moderate, who, in proselyting for tolerance, often reveals himself as surprisingly intolerant'.[60] One incident that cost him a lot of sympathy with fellow writers will serve as an example. In 1971 Heinar Kipphardt planned a production in Munich of a play by Wolf Biermann, at that time still in East Germany, entitled *Der Dra-Dra*, 'Dra' being the first syllable of the word *Drachen* (dragon). The dragon of the title that needed to be slain was, roughly speaking, the 'political enemy'. In connection with the performance, a programme — not itself the work of Kipphardt — was considered that would contain the names of twenty-four West German 'dragons', mainly industrialists and politicians, but including the then mayor of Munich and subsequent SPD minister Hans-Jochen Vogel, who at that time was in conflict with the party's left wing. In the event, the planned programme was rejected after Kipphardt referred it to his superior, and the eventual programme contained two blank pages. When Grass heard of the original project he launched into a bitter attack on Kipphardt, accusing him of inciting violence and murder in the tradition of the political murders of the Weimar Republic. Subsequently, he went on to talk of left-wing fools whom he equated with the extreme Right. The outcome was that the already controversial Kipphardt was dismissed from his post. Even if the portrait project was stupid, it was not logical that in his attack on what he perceived as dangerous extremism, Grass should use terminology like 'lynch justice' and 'witch hunters', particularly as it was directed at someone who had been instrumental in stopping the 'extreme' material reaching the public.[61] As for more recent issues, many would not call the recent statements on the need to practise resistance 'moderate'. Lack of moderation is a criticism that can also be applied to much of Grass's rhetoric long after the rumbustious election speeches of 1965. To compare his left-wing opponents with Goebbels, Stalin and even Freisler, the notorious judge at the infamous Nazi People's Court, appears especially dubious if it is recalled that Grass's political adversary Franz Josef Strauss, too, has described those demonstrating against him as 'pupils of Goebbels'.

Another criticism of Grass's rhetoric must be that at times it seems an end in itself. One example of this is in an article on Nicaragua following a visit there, in which, incidentally, he appears to go back on his previous doctrine about the negative mechanism of revolution. As part of the article he makes an appeal to the Pope to support the Nicaraguan people:

> O much-travelled, Polish Pope, who visibly suffers on account of this world and its injustices, Wojtyla! May one be familiar with you? Can it still be hoped that, as you have shown in Poland, the poor, the suffering, the persecuted are close to you.[62]

The sentiments may be laudable but, given that the Pope was unlikely to read the article, the technique seems inappropriate. In the light of such prose it is not surprising that Grass has devoted a lot of attention to how the SPD presents its policies. A frequently made criticism is that the party does not know how to project itself, not necessarily a question an intellectual should address himself to.

It might seem that all these points which could be added to — whether it is justifiable for him to label his political opponents as typical German idealists, for instance — render Grass's political commitment invalid. Despite the numerous problems, it would be wrong to dismiss it for at least two major reasons. First, through his unstinting concern with everyday issues and his courage, Grass has gained for the political writer a new status in the Federal Republic. His activities and those of other writers have to be taken seriously and can no longer be regarded as 'drum beating' or publicity-seeking. The Sozialdemokratische Wählerinitiative, for instance, has proved to be a lasting phenomenon largely through his efforts which has helped to create a situation where all political parties have had to accept a widening of the political debate to include more than just professional politicians. In the light of the German tradition, this is an achievement for which Grass must take a lot of credit. As the critic Hanspeter Brode puts it: 'Grass . . . has helped to mould the political consciousness of the German public.'[63] Secondly, the content of Grass's political remarks has to be taken seriously. If it is remembered that a major starting point of his political thinking is a belief in the moral responsibility of the individual, then his comments can be accepted as stemming from his conscience, whatever simplifications and inconsistencies they may contain. His political commitment has, in fact, through its tenacity an almost Faustian quality. Without being patronising or assuming divine qualities, one can say, as with Goethe's Faust, that his constant strivings deserve, if not redemption in this secular age, at least respect and recognition.[64]

Notes

1. G. Grass, 'Wer wird dieses Bändchen kaufen' in Walser, *Die Alternative*, p. 76.

2. G. Grass, *Speak Out!* (Secker & Warburg, London, 1969), p. 15.

3. G. Grass, *Über das Selbstverständliche* (DTV, München, 1969), p. 47. The English version is not a complete translation of the German original — hence

the necessity to refer to the German text.
   4. Ibid., p. 31.
   5. Ibid., p. 51.
   6. Ibid., p. 55.
   7. H. L. Arnold (ed.), *Günter Grass — Dokumente zur politischen Wirkung*
(Richard Boorberg Verlag, München, 1971), p. 51.
   8. Grass, *Speak Out!*, p. 35.
   9. Ibid., p. 28.
   10. Grass, *Selbstverständliche*, p. 45.
   11. Grass, *Speak Out!*, p. 53.
   12. G. Grass, *Der Bürger und seine Stimme* (Luchterhand, Darmstadt und
Neuwied, 1974), p. 57.
   13. G. Grass, 'Die runde Zahl zwanzig' in Arnold, *Politische Wirkung*, p. 175.
   14. G. Grass, 'Die angelesene Revolution' in ibid., p. 129.
   15. Grass, *Speak Out!*, pp. 54–60.
   16. Grass, *Selbstverständliche*, pp. 163–6.
   17. Ibid., p. 188.
   18. Grass, *Speak Out!*, p. 140.
   19. Grass, *Der Bürger*, p. 67.
   20. Grass, 'Die angelesene Revolution' in Arnold, *Politische Wirkung*, p. 132.
   21. Ibid., p. 131.
   22. Ibid., p. 135.
   23. Grass, *Selbstverständliche*, p. 47.
   24. G. Grass, *From the Diary of a Snail* (Secker & Warburg, London, 1974),
p. 102.
   25. Grass, *Der Bürger*, p. 64.
   26. Ibid., pp. 178–81.
   27. Grass, *Selbstverständliche*, p. 47.
   28. Grass, *Speak Out!*, p. 70.
   29. Grass, *Selbstverständliche*, p. 132.
   30. Grass, *Speak Out!*, p. 69.
   31. Grass, *Selbstverständliche*, p. 56.
   32. Grass, *Diary*, p. 141.
   33. G. Cepl-Kaufmann, *Günter Grass* (Scriptor Verlag, Kronberg/Ts, 1975),
p. 305.
   34. Grass, *Diary*, p. 143f.
   35. Ibid., p. 254.
   36. Ibid., p. 310.
   37. Ibid., p. 9.
   38. G. Grass, *Denkzettel* (Luchterhand, Darmstadt und Neuwied, 1978), p. 231.
   39. G. Grass, *Headbirths or the Germans are Dying Out* (Secker & Warburg,
London, 1982), p. 68.
   40. G. Grass, *Widerstand lernen* (Luchterhand, Darmstadt und Neuwied, 1984),
p. 56.
   41. G. Grass, 'Wir müssen lernen zu verzichten' in *Der Spiegel*, no. 41, 11 Oct.
82, 252–63.
   42. Grass, *Headbirths*, p. 81.
   43. Grass, *Widerstand*, pp. 13–14.
   44. Ibid., pp. 84–90.
   45. H-A. Jacobsen, 'Vom Vergleich des Unvergleichbaren', *Die Zeit*, no. 50,
9 Dec. 83.
   46. Grass, *Widerstand*, p. 95.
   47. W. Graf von Baudissin, 'Eine Neuauflage der Reichswehr sollten wir uns
ersparen' in F. H. U. Bortkenhagen (ed.), *Wehrkraftzersetzung* (Rowohlt, Reinbek

bei Hamburg, 1984), p. 17.

48. Grass, 'Wir sind die Verfassungsschützer', *Die Zeit*, no. 9, 24 Feb. 84.

49. Grass, *Widerstand*, p. 64.

50. Grass, 'Wir müssen lernen zu verzichten', 252.

51. G. Grass, 'Orwells Jahrzehnt' (quoted from typed copy in possession of author).

52. H. L. Arnold, 'Grosses Ja und kleines Nein' in Arnold, *Politische Wirkung*, p. 148.

53. H. Karasek, 'Der unermüdliche Querkopf, e.V.', *Der Spiegel*, no. 20, 14 May 84, 215.

54. Grass, *Diary*, p. 222f.

55. Quoted from H. Brode, *Günter Grass* (Verlag C. H. Beck, München, 1979), p. 122.

56. Rühmkorf, *Die Jahre*, p. 134.

57. Grass, *Selbstverständliche*, p. 8.

58. Ibid., p. 55.

59. Grass, *Diary*, p. 304.

60. M. Hollington, *Günter Grass* (Marion Boyars, London, 1980), p. 131.

61. This controversy can be followed in Arnold, *Politische Wirkung*, pp. 355–405.

62. Grass, *Widerstand*, p. 46.

63. Brode, *Grass*, p. 133.

64. An entirely positive view of Grass as a political writer is taken by the Literary Editor of the *Guardian*, W. L. Webb, reviewing a new English collection of Grass's political writings, which should prove useful to non-speakers of German: G. Grass, *On Writing and Politics* (Secker, London, 1985). He wishes for an English Grass but asks 'Who would that be. . .?' (*Guardian*, 27 Sep. 85).

8 HEINRICH BÖLL — THE GOOD CATHOLIC

The award of the Nobel Prize for Literature to the late Heinrich Böll in 1972, the first time that a writer from Germany had been honoured outright in this way since the war (if one excepts the 1946 award to Hermann Hesse, who by then was both a resident and a citizen of Switzerland), was widely interpreted as not just a reward for individual merit, but also as a sign that there was no longer any stigma attached to German culture or anything else German for that matter. Incidentally, the same year saw the award of the Nobel Peace Prize to Willy Brandt for his Ostpolitik. One might have thought that Böll's prize at least would have been greeted joyfully in the Federal Republic and that the contribution of literature to the prestige of the still new state that had been formed in such unpropitious circumstances would have been universally recognised. No such thing occurred. The early part of 1972 had seen Böll the target of vicious attacks because of the stance that he had taken up over the terrorism of the Baader-Meinhof group, a state of affairs that never fully abated and which reached another peak following the sad events of 1977.

In 1972 Böll found himself described as a drawing-room anarchist and as more dangerous than the Baader-Meinhof terrorists themselves. In 1977 it was suggested by the CDU politician Mayer-Vorfelder, at the time of writing — sad to relate — the Minister of Education in the State of Baden-Württemberg, that Böll should emigrate if he was unhappy with the state of affairs in the Federal Republic, whilst at the Federal level, the Bavarian politician Friedrich Zimmermann, Minister of the Interior in the post-1982 Kohl government, attacked him in a parliamentary debate on terrorism. He spoke disparagingly of the Nobel Prize holder, and suggested that he had reacted in a lachrymose way to the searching of his son's house during the hunt for terrorists. Zimmermann pointed out that thousands had had to put up with such searches, implying no doubt that how an individual reacted revealed his general strength and virility.

What lay behind all these polemics? The first cause was an article by Böll published in early 1972 in *Der Spiegel* about the Baader-Meinhof group, on whose basis he was accused of being on the side of terrorism. Shortly before Christmas 1971 Springer's *Bild-Zeitung* had published a front-page report on a bank robbery in the town of Kaiserslautern, part of whose headline was the claim 'Baader-Meinhof gang continues murdering'. Böll's contentious reply appeared in *Der Spiegel* under the title 'Will Ulrike Gnade oder freies Geleit?' (Does Ulrike want mercy or safe conduct?). Böll objected to the way *Bild* had prejudged the case at a time when the police had no clear evidence of who was responsible for the robbery and the murder that occurred during its course. Böll's other major concern in the article was that in the climate of hysteria created by Springer, members of the Baader-Meinhof group might well not receive a fair trial. He combined the two issues in one sentence that refers specifically to Ulrike Meinhof: 'Nevertheless she should be offered safe conduct, a public trial, and, at the same time, Herr Springer should be publicly tried for incitement.'[1]

In as far as it appeared to equate Meinhof and Springer, such a statement was bound to create controversy. What is more, even some of those who agreed with Böll on his two major points referred to above were unhappy that he did not seem to be taking the phenomenon of terrorism seriously enough. In the article he admits that the terrorists have declared war on society, but regards it as an unequal struggle of six against sixty million, continuing: 'It is a declaration of war by desperate theorists, by people now persecuted and denounced, who have put themselves in a corner, have been driven into a corner and whose theories sound far more violent than their praxis.'[2] What is interesting in such a comment, apart from the problematical assessment of terrorism, is the way Böll is prepared to see the terrorists partially as victims. He went even further in this direction when he turned to the questions of the possible arrest and trial of the terrorists. He seeks to remind his readers, particularly any who were once persecuted by the Nazis, of what it is like to be an outcast: 'Were they, those formerly persecuted, not once declared opponents of a system, and have they not forgotten what lay concealed behind the charming expression "shot while trying to escape"?'[3] Compassion for those he sees as victims is also a marked feature of Böll's novels, as is anger against the powerful. This is visible in this article in his description of the journalism practised by *Bild* as 'naked fascism, lies, filth'.[4]

According to Böll, his aim in writing 'Will Ulrike Gnade oder freies Geleit?' was to defuse a highly charged situation. That he did not achieve his aim can be seen from the reactions to the article, which were so numerous and violent that they were collected and published in book form. Thus, they remain an invaluable document on the relationship between writers and politics in Germany. It is hardly surprising that the Springer Press reacted vehemently to the attacks on it. Besides its own journalists, it was able to field the rightist duo Krämer-Badoni and Hans Habe, the latter a best-selling novelist, who had been an émigré and had returned to Germany with the American army. Krämer-Badoni's first shots were fired the day after the appearance of Böll's article. It took the form of frequent rhetorical questions which aimed at calling into question Böll's logic, along with scathing references to Böll's position at that time as President of the International PEN club. Hence, taking into account the role of this club in the struggle to preserve authors' rights, he coins such an unlikely compound as *Meinungsfreiheitspräsident* (freedom-of-opinion-president), which to say the least smacks of demagogy.[5] In his comments Habe combines Böll's apparently lenient attitude towards Baader-Meinhof with another controversy of the day, the imprisonment of the Soviet writer Bukovsky, who had been sentenced to two years imprisonment, five years forced labour and five years internal exile. In a television interview Böll had said that he was not permitted by the statutes of the PEN club to protest in his role as president and that, before making private protests, he would have to consider whether these would do more harm than good. Such an eminently sensible tactic, which was in no sense a condonement of Soviet actions, did not meet with Habe's understanding. His polemics reach their heights or rather depths when he insinuates that a person like Böll would not have stood up to the Nazis:

It had become urgent, Böll said in London, for PEN to take up a position on environmental pollution. *But Moscow's western darling, who presents himself, as the Americans would say, as a 'goodie-goodie', as a Lord Bountiful, does not want to know about Soviet intellectual pollution. He, the president, has no arrogant concepts of freedom. He would presumably, if he had been PEN-President at the time of Ossietzky, have respected the Hitlerian concepts of freedom.*[6]

Even allowing for Habe's emigration, it is somewhat surprising to see him use as a model the case of a left-wing victim of Nazism such as Ossietzky.

Behind such attacks were first the innuendo that Böll, as a popular writer in the Soviet Union, did not wish to jeopardise this state of affairs, and secondly a desire to harm the SPD's Ostpolitik, which had reached a critical stage in 1972. In fact, Böll was a consistent critic of the Soviet Union's policies towards dissidents, being reported, for instance, in February 1984 as wanting a harder line to be adopted towards cultural functionaries from the Eastern Bloc.[7] It also seems unlikely that Solzhenitsyn would have stayed with Böll immediately following his exile if he had perceived him to be a friend of Soviet officialdom. As for the Ostpolitik, Habe's own attitude is revealing. In an article written in February 1972 he criticised government policy in the following terms: 'This government has opened the door, through which the East creeps into the West.'[8] Habe is entitled to his rigid anti-communism, but in reality the reverse has happened much more, as not least the events in Poland over recent years have shown, with the process of détente awakening a desire for greater democracy among the citizens of Eastern Europe.

It was not just the Springer Press that attacked Böll. Large sections of the regional press, which has such a significant role in a country without a truly national press, were critical, including the paper from Böll's home town of Cologne, the *Kölnische Rundschau*, which saw Böll's 'understanding words' for terrorism as part of an intellectual climate breeding violence.[9] What is more, harsh criticism emanated from the Federal Republic's public service braodcasting system despite the legal requirement for 'balance'. On 24 January 1972 a television commentary by Ulrich Frank-Planitz spoke of drawing-room anarchists in general and of Böll specifically as the 'advocate of anarchist gangsters'.[10] In response, Böll described Planitz's commentary as denunciatory and fascist, and declared his unwillingness to work in future for the station responsible for the broadcast. Böll was then accused of being unwilling to accept freedom of expression for others, an accusation to which he gave the tongue-in-cheek reply that he had only limited his own freedom of expression by rejecting this particular avenue of communication with the public. By contrast, he had to deny a report that he had broken with the Second Channel of West German television (ZDF) after he had been denounced as a sympathiser with left-wing fascism on that station's political programme *ZDF-Magazin* by its presenter Gerhard Löwenthal, a controversial political journalist not renowned for even-handedness.

Not everybody lined up against Böll, which at least showed a degree of pluralism in the media. He was defended in the liberal weeklies *Die Zeit* and *Der Spiegel*, and in sections of the daily press. One influential newspaper generally seen as conservative, the *Frankfurter Allgemeine Zeitung*, presented different viewpoints within one edition, that of 2 February 1972. Dolf Sternberger accused Böll of feigning impotence whilst using his undoubted influence irresponsibly. He also attacked him for comparing Baader-Meinhof with the opponents of Nazism, pointing out the differences between the Third Reich and a democracy.[11] By contrast, Karl Heinz Bohrer, one of the paper's writers on literary matters, shows considerable sympathy for the writer who involves himself in politics. In a thoughtful article he sees the moral attitude of the writer as bound to create conflict with the state. The only alternatives are to ban poets in the way advocated by Plato or to accept this state of affairs. As for Böll himself, he 'should bear the contrast to his critics, who view from a different angle'.[12] In the event, Böll was unable to comply with this demand, which given the vitriolic nature of the criticism, must be viewed as rather idealistic. By June 1972 he was speaking of being at the end of his tether as a result of the attacks on him and the general climate being engendered in the Federal Republic.

It cannot be disputed that much that was said about Böll at this time was disgraceful in both tone and content, with the charge that he was a sympathiser with terrorism totally contemptible. This is not to say that the original article in *Der Spiegel* is without flaws, although it was correct on the two major points it sought to make. The German Press Council censured *Bild* for its reporting of the Kaiserslautern incident, whilst the danger of individual terrorists becoming so isolated and condemned that their future re-integration into society would be impossible, however penitent they might be, was a problem that came to be recognised later in the decade. Even where Böll may seem extreme, for instance when he talks of people being shot in the back, it can be pointed out that there were occasions when the police appeared to use firearms somewhat injudiciously during the hunt for terrorists, for instance when they shot the Scot Iain Macleod, who was suspected of being involved with Baader-Meinhof, in Stuttgart in 1972. Nevertheless, it must still be asked whether Böll should have reacted to the provocation from *Bild* so emotionally and used such terms as 'fascism' so freely. That the political content of the article is by no means beyond criticism was shown by one response from a practising politician.

Diether Posser, at the time the SPD Minister of Justice in the State of North Rhine Westphalia, published his comments in *Der Spiegel* two weeks after the appearance of 'Will Ulrike Gnade oder freies Geleit?'. After condemning the *Bild* report, which aroused Böll's wrath, he goes on to criticise Böll on four counts. First, whilst accepting that Böll does not sympathise with terrorism, he points out that the terrorists' own claim quoted by Böll that they do not shoot first, is not borne out by the facts. Examples are given. His second point is that Böll, by stating that the terrorists were more violent in theory than in practice, is playing down the offences committed by them which in fact range from murder to arson and armed robbery. Hence, it is totally inappropriate to compare them in any way to the victims of National Socialism. Posser's third point concerns the prosecution of captured terrorists. Quoting examples of terrorist trials, he claims that they are conducted in an appropriate manner and that acquittals are not unknown. Fourthly, he takes exception to the terminology used by Böll, particularly the two terms used in the article's title 'mercy' and 'safe conduct'. He points to a disparity between their usage by Böll and the requirements of statute. In conclusion, Posser says:

> Böll has raised his voice on an important subject. But anger emotionalised his criticism and rendered it unobjective. His polemics not only exaggerated — they were harmful. He wanted to call for reflection and wrote himself without reflecting.[13]

Replying to Posser, Böll showed some acceptance of the criticisms made: 'In general terms, in some details, too, I must concede that Dr Posser is right.'[14] Nevertheless, he goes on to justify himself in terms of his role as a writer, a point that will be returned to later. As for the original article on Baader-Meinhof one must conclude, however much one may admire his sense of compassion, that Böll's erroneous political assessment of terrorism and the state of democracy in the Federal Republic harms its overall impact.

The literary aftermath of this particular feud between Böll and the Springer Press is well known. In 1974 he published the story *Die verlorene Ehre der Katharina Blum* (The Lost Honour of Katharina Blum) about a young woman who becomes the victim of a press campaign because of her association with an alleged terrorist. The outcome is that she shoots the journalist who has destroyed her existence, a reporter on a tabloid newspaper very reminiscent of *Bild*. The choice of a literary form was not enough to save Böll from similar criticisms to those made at the time of the article in *Der Spiegel*. The CDU politician and subsequent Federal President Karl Carstens said in a speech in the Ruhr city of Duisburg in December 1974:

> I call upon the whole population to disassociate itself from terrorist activities, especially too the poet Heinrich Böll, who just a few months ago wrote a book under the pseudonym Katharina Blum, which presents a justification of violence.

The question that immediately arises, once one has got over the demagogic tone and the anachronistic word poet (Dichter) — incidentally also used by Chancellor Kohl in his statement on Böll's death — is whether Carstens had read the book to the extent of noticing that it was not even written in a first-person style. Nevertheless, once such an accusation has been made by a prominent person, it has to be examined. The full title of the story provides in itself an indication that Carstens was misguided. It is *Die verlorene Ehre der Katharina Blum oder: Wie Gewalt entstehen und wohin sie führen kann* (The Lost Honour of Katharina Blum or: How Violence Develops and Where it Can Lead). The second part of the title implies a kind of case study, and it is the objective tone appropriate to such a study that Böll wishes to convey. The fact of the murder is revealed at once, so that the reader does not identify with the heroine's deed to the extent that he or she might be carried away to an emotional reaction by the development of events. The film version by Volker Schlöndorff did not follow the book in this, so that there was a much greater danger that the audience might feel Katharina's action was a justifiable response to unbearable provocation. By contrast, Böll's narrative retains an ironic distance to the events described, which at times in fact appears overdone, as when at the end the descriptions of some of the problems experienced by Katharina's friends are presented in an entirely humorous form. As for the murder itself, it is always made clear that Katharina has committed a crime; that it is described by one character as 'almost logical', is not the same thing as Böll himself saying it is justifiable.[15] The building of the Berlin Wall can be regarded as a logical step from the point of view of the East

German State; this is not to say that it was morally justifiable. Carstens is overlooking the point that an explanation is not a justification.

Böll's book is principally a critique of a certain kind of journalism. He calls the sensational newspaper simply *die ZEITUNG* (The Paper), a cleverly chosen name in that it raises the question of the whole nature of the press, although at the same time it is made clear that there are different kinds of journalism. Whether, as in the initial article in *Der Spiegel*, Böll partly spoils his good case by exaggeration remains, however, a vital question. Is it credible that a cool-headed young woman, which is the way Katharina is presented, would be totally destroyed and driven to violent revenge by a newspaper campaign, however vicious? The answer might seem to be in the negative if the line followed by the present writer is accepted, namely that the origins of violence are extremely obscure and not attributable to any single source. In this case though, it is not a question of somebody being spurred to politically motivated violence by intellectual argument; it is rather a question of direct personal response to an antagonist. The situations are not parallel. Böll is claiming that people may react violently to attacks on their integrity, a much more plausible proposition. Thus, the question of whether the actions of the fictional character Katharina Blum are credible is a matter for the individual reader's aesthetic judgement. Where Böll might be on weaker ground is in the presentation of Götten, the young man with whom Katharina consorts. Whereas *die ZEITUNG* describes him as a dangerous terrorist, it is said at the end of the narrative that he is an army deserter who has stolen arms and money from the military. This can be viewed as playing down terrorism in that the reality of more heinous offences is not referred to. On the other hand, a work of fiction is not an encyclopedia of crime. To sum up: Böll can be absolved of the charge of justifying violence; whether he has written a convincing work of fiction remains, in the nature of things, a question subject to personal interpretation. The sale within just over a year of almost half a million copies of the paperback edition does, however, suggest that Böll dealt with highly relevant social issues.

To understand Böll's political commitment, it is necessary to look in some detail at his conception of the role of the writer. As already mentioned, in his reply to Posser's criticisms he seeks to justify himself in terms of this role. His first demand, one that is consistently repeated, is that all his work is considered before any judgement is made. After conceding Posser's points, he asks: 'Can I not assume with a man of his political responsibility, education and sensitivity that he possibly knows more of my work than this article; that he takes into account the differences of expression as well?'[16] The corollary of this is that he refuses to distinguish between his fictional work and political writings, as he says elsewhere:

> I believe that it cannot be separated at all, that an essay, too, or a pamphlet, a polemic or such which I write is just as — let us say — literary as a novel I write. And the liberty which is given me as a novelist . . . I find it uncanny.[17]

In other words, fictional and non-fictional works should be viewed on the basis of the same criteria, both aesthetic and in terms of content.

Another aspect of Böll's view of his role is the relative freedom he claims for himself as a writer. This too is revealed in his reply to Posser, where he differentiates himself as a writer from members of other professions: 'I am a writer and the words "persecuted", "mercy", "criminality" have a different dimension for me than they of necessity have for a civil servant, lawyer, minister and also for police officers.'[18] He goes on to specify that he uses the word persecuted 'existentially and with a touch of metaphysics'.[19] Another liberty Böll claims for the writer is that to provoke, to test how far it is possible to go. He speaks of 'the natural right of literature to the most extreme criticism',[20] or as he put it more impishly in 1983: 'I am not only disreputable, I am extremely disreputable.'[21] These comments can be seen as the other extreme to the right to be utopian Böll also demands for writers. This right he claims to be socially both necessary and useful. In a 1978 speech he said:

> And if the portion of hope that is within every illusion and also within every utopia and the large portion of hope that is within hope are denounced, a society or youth without hope or full of despair is created.[22]

At the same time, Böll is willing to concede that it is this utopian dimension that leads to conflict between intellectuals and politicians. In an essay about André Sakharov written in 1981, he criticises the narrowness of politicians whilst claiming a different dimension for the statements of intellectuals: 'They do not understand, they do not grasp that behind the apparently fantastic there lies reason, behind the apparently utopian demand precision, which might also be called the aesthetics of authenticity and justice.'[23] The point Böll is making in this essay is that there is a direct connection between the exact sciences and the support for human rights. Finally, it should be remembered that Böll believes that emotional responses like the anger displayed in the article on Baader-Meinhof are perfectly permissible.

At face value these statements would seem to amount to Böll putting himself and his fellow writers on to some kind of pedestal. Nevertheless, he always sought to deny that writers enjoy a special position within society. He frequently stated that he regarded himself as a full citizen of the Federal Republic, even referring to his status as a taxpayer. One occasion when he made his position clear was in 1978 when it came to light that, along with Günter Grass and Siegfried Lenz, he had been approached about whether he would accept an official honour. In the event all three refused, whereupon there were complaints that despite writing about the Federal Republic, they were setting themselves apart from their fellow citizens. Both Böll and Grass justifiably replied that all citizens had a right to choose on this issue, with Böll pointing out that many years previously no less a person than Chancellor Schmidt had refused an honour. He also added that his refusal had nothing to do with a rejection of the Federal Republic. He concluded: 'I shall continue to play my part.'[24] It is in keeping with this attitude that Böll, like many of his colleagues, always scorned the idea that writers enjoyed a special role as 'the conscience of the nation', a cliché he felt to be particularly dangerous:

> The really highly dangerous concept of the 'conscience of the nation' was coined without it being borne in mind that the conscience of a nation is first of all its parliament . . . Then there is public opinion as well, that is to say the newspapers, the various media and within this natural constellation intellectuals do of course play an important and necessary role. To place the role . . . of the 'conscience of the nation' . . . solely on them means in reality putting the public in a state of being without conscience.[25]

What this statement shows is a desire to spread responsibility over the whole of society.

That this is no easy task is admitted by Böll in the same interview where he speaks of writers being forced more or less against their will into the position of outsiders.[26] One reason he advances for this state of affairs is the lack of literary sensitivity amongst politicians, including many Social Democrats. This leads to a lack of communication between writers and politicians. Another relevant factor he perceives results from the nature of German society, where there is a shortage of democratic awareness among the public. What Böll calls the lack of 'a permanently critical public opinion'[27] has of course been a matter of concern for writers since the days of *Der Ruf*.

In conclusion, it is hard to avoid the suspicion that there is a dichotomy in Böll's conception of the role of the writer in politics. It is hard to reconcile what he says about, for example, the relationship of the writer to language with the rejection of any elite status. In itself, the view that the writer is always a writer might be more honest than Grass's belief that his literary work as a writer can be separated from his political activity, when, as he himself concedes, the latter depends on his literary fame to achieve widespread attention. On the other hand, by not making concessions to the world of politics, Böll leaves himself open to the charge of ignorance of political realities. Whereas it is possible to dismiss the epithet 'tin drummer', as applied to Grass's political activity as a superficial journalistic cliché, the equivalent term used of Böll — 'the clown' — which relates to the novel *Ansichten eines Clowns* (The Clown) reflects the vulnerability of his position, although it nevertheless remains a cheap insult.

An example of how Böll's role in society has been criticised can be found in the sociologist Helmut Schelsky's book *Die Arbeit tun die anderen* (The others do the work). As part of his general attack on intellectuals, Schelsky singles out Böll for negative comment, referring to him as 'cardinal and martyr'. He is a cardinal in that he represents the new type of intellectual seeking power in society by preaching a new social gospel of salvation: 'He is concerned with the ownership and the monopoly of the means of production and domination that is "publicity".'[28] According to Schelsky, this was seen at the time of the foundation of the VS, when Böll demanded that writers should exercise more influence. He is a martyr in the way he responds to criticism. Referring to the controversy that followed the Baader-Meinhof article, which he cleverly presents as the outline of a five-act play, Schelsky claims that Böll had as many supporters as detractors but chose to play the role of martyr:

> In those days Böll must have been a masochist in reading newspapers . . . He no longer conveyed arguments, but only a pitiable impression. At this time, too, the words were spoken that this was a country in which it was impossible to live. The martyr of the vicious 'anti-intellectual campaign' directed against him presented himself to the public.[29]

The charge is one of self-pity, something that is often said to be a characteristic of Böll's fictional heroes, for example the clown Hans Schnier.

Although Schelsky's polemic is skilfully presented, it does not hold water in a number of respects. It is for example presumptuous of him to suggest in support of his thesis about the power-seeking nature of intellectuals that in his criticisms of the Soviet Union Böll is only interested in Soviet intellectuals, not the plight of the Soviet people in general, when one remembers that his literary work could almost be summed up as a championing of the weaker members of society. Schelsky regards his view as being further confirmed by Böll's support of communist intellectuals in the Federal Republic who are opposed to the values of the Soviet dissidents. In reality, Böll is surely arguing for freedom of expression in all kinds of society, a perfectly consistent stance. What Schelsky's position reveals is that he is only opposed to those intellectuals who do not share his conservative views. This is shown further in his comments about Böll's claim to be persecuted. Besides claiming that Böll seems to enjoy this state of affairs, something that cannot be proved, he says that it was those intellectuals who opposed the ideas of the student demonstrators who were really persecuted, in many cases along with their families. No doubt harassment did take place and must be viewed as entirely reprehensible. A more logical standpoint, however, would be to attack all persecution rather than draw up a league table of who suffered most.

A study of Böll's political commitment cannot restrict itself to his conception of the role of the writer. It is also necessary to turn to the particular social and political issues that concerned him over his long career. Given the amount he wrote, it will only be possible to deal with these in general terms. If this is borne in mind, it is possible to describe the 1950s as a time when Böll was extensively concerned with religious questions, as his novels of this decade also show. It is not proposed to concentrate here on whether Böll was a Christian or specifically Catholic writer, that is to say whether his writing reveals Christian beliefs, but on his views on the Church, particularly the Catholic Church, as a social institution. Nevertheless, it can be pointed out that he himself was aware of possible conflicts between his religious beliefs and his profession as a writer. In his essay 'Kunst und Religion' (Art and religion), he says it is impossible to define Christian literature, speaking of conflicts between his conscience as a writer and his conscience as a Christian.[30]

Conflict with the Church or its representatives began early in Böll's literary career. One small episode from 1953 illustrates this and also something of the atmosphere of the time. A priest, in this case a Protestant, had complained about the satirical story *Nicht nur zur Weihnachtszeit* (Not just at Christmastide), in which a disturbed middle-class lady insists on the ritual singing of the famous Christmas song 'O Tannenbaum' every day of the year. This was taken by the priest as an attack on German traditions and a slight on those Germans living under communism who needed the comfort of tradition in their unenviable situation. This attack is an archetypal example of the type of thinking prevalent in the 1950s: by criticising the Federal Republic, critical writers were somehow undermining the struggle against communism. Böll's reply came in the form of an open letter. He pointed out that people from the East approved of the freedom they found in the West, but disliked the crass materialism. He considered his story useful 'to give a shock to our restorative West German consciousness'.[31]

Towards the end of the decade Böll published what remains his most substantive criticism in essay form of the Catholic Church in Germany, his 'Brief an einen jungen Katholiken' (Letter to a young Catholic). It is addressed to a new recruit and deals primarily with the Church's attitude to war. Böll draws heavily on his own experiences as a soldier in the Nazi era, when the Church was not generally in conflict with the state and propounded the doctrine of the right of defence. He points out, for instance, that the Vatican was the first state to conclude a treaty with Hitler. Additionally, as in his fictional writing, he speaks of the futility of much of the soldier's everyday life. His major criticism is that, despite the lessons of the past, the Church in no way seems to have reconsidered its attitude to the morality of war. It continues rather to equate morality with sexual morality, being primarily concerned about soldiers' propensity to visit brothels. It is not surprising that Böll is scathing on this point. One basis for all his writing is anger at having had to serve in the army of an odious regime, coupled with the desire to prevent a recurrence of any similar state of affairs.

In the second half of the letter, Böll extends his criticism of the Church to the way it, in the term used by another critic Carl Amery, has capitulated to the CDU.[32] By its subservience to the CDU, Böll claims, the Church is risking the end of theology. It prefers to use its influence in support of the crude political proposition that Adenauer and Strauss should be condoned because they are Catholics. For Böll, this means that the Church is supporting a questionable materialism, something he makes most clear in another essay 'Hast Du was, dann bist Du was' (Money talks). After referring in this essay to the Church's support for CDU policies on wealth creation, he goes on ironically to question the appropriateness of previous doctrines on wealth and poverty:

> The canonisation of the have-not of Assisi was presumably a mistake, like the canonisation of the have-not Johannes Maria Vianney . . . ? Perhaps an attempt should be made to raise them a little socially by smuggling into their estate a savings account previously kept secret or a posthumously discovered share portfolio.[33]

The instance Böll sets against the official Church in his letter to the young recruit and elsewhere is individual conscience. He makes the point that the Christians in Germany who formed part of the resistance to Hitler were following their consciences rather than official teachings. This championing of conscience brought a reply from a prominent Catholic layman Walter Weymann-Weyhe, who said that the Church itself rather than individuals must be the keeper of conscience. Interestingly enough, two decades later he had come round to Böll's view, disappointed by the lack of reform in the Church.[34]

Böll's interest in religious questions did not end with the decade of the 1950s. In fact, his attitudes hardened subsequently as the 1963 novel *Ansichten eines Clowns* shows. This contains particularly scathing attacks on the Catholic Church, especially over questions of sexual morality. Nevertheless, Böll was to claim in the same year: 'my views on organised Catholicism are more bitter, harder than those of any of the characters in my novels.'[35] In 1966 a sequel to the original letter appeared, this time for a non-Catholic and specifically addressed to Günter Wallraff. This 'Brief an einen jungen Nicht-Katholiken' adds a new, more political dimension to the original letter's moral arguments about the Church and the military. Böll claims that the majority of Germans opposed rearmament in the 1950s and that the Catholic Church betrayed this opposition by supporting the new army: 'The Catholics as the one large statistical mass would have had a chance of keeping this people peaceable.'[36] This view is somewhat idealistic. However critical one may wish to be of the Catholic attitude to rearmament, it cannot be overlooked that it was ultimately the division of Europe that made the creation of a West German army inevitable.

To discuss at length Böll's personal religious beliefs would be inappropriate and presumptuous. Nevertheless, it does seem that his growing disillusionment with the Church in society left a mark. In 1966 he spoke of being tired of his role as critic of German Catholicism, what he called fulfilling 'the function of an internal Catholic cheeky monkey'.[37] In the following decade he more or less broke with the Catholic Church following his decision to stop paying Church Tax. Parallel with this estrangement there went a growing uncertainty in his statements of religious belief. In 1957 he was still categorical: 'I believe in Christ and I believe that 800 million Christians on this earth could change the countenance of this earth'.[38] Although he goes on to concede that the history of the Church is full of horrors, he also feels able to cite examples of good. In the letter to the non-Catholic too, alongside the criticism, he still expresses the hope he might die a Catholic, and refers specifically to his willingness to pay Church Tax. By 1973 he is much less categorical: 'Thus I can neither call myself a Christian nor be a follower of Jesus of Nazareth. I can only believe in the presence of Him who became man. No more and no less.'[39]

However Böll's personal religious attitudes may have evolved and however much he may have despaired of German Catholicism, it nevertheless remains the case that he always retained Christian terminology and ideals. The ideal of mercy, raised in connection with Ulrike Meinhof in 1972, was again to the fore twelve years later in a verse reaction to the sentences of life imprisonment passed on the former terrorist Peter-Jürgen Boock, despite his rejection of his former confederates. Böll's poem suggests that the maxim 'justice without mercy is cruel' applies only to those in uniform who murdered people considered to be less than human.[40] In the same year, in an article in *Der Spiegel*, Böll recommended to the new Federal President Richard von Weizsäcker that he should receive members of peripheral social groups in his residence, mentioning foreigners, those seeking political asylum, gipsies and the unemployed. This suggestion, because of its very impracticality in wordly terms, may also be said to be a product of religious inspiration, if the company kept by Christ is borne in mind.[41]

If the 1950s were the decade when Böll devoted much of his attention to religious questions, then the decade following proved to be the time when he became more overtly political. He moved away from a general suspicion of politics towards both a greater interest and to specific political commitment, expressed in support for the Social Democrats, by implication in 1969 and openly in 1972. At the inception of the Federal Republic, Böll had been — if not a CDU supporter — a CDU voter in keeping with his religious and social background. The disillusionment with this party apparent in his letter to the young Catholic seems to have led to a general rejection of politics. The failure of theologians, that is to say their submission to the CDU, may, he says, have rendered politics all-important but, according to Böll, politics is 'dubious fare'.[42] Equally noteworthy in this letter is a rejection of conventional political terminology. In his references to the 20 July plotters against Hitler, Böll describes the terms 'right' and 'left' as insignificant and foolish in comparison with the factor of individual conscience.

The wish for a political force or institution to identify with or simply to respect only begins to manifest itself very slowly in the 1960s. That such a force does not exist at that particular time seems to be the main message of Böll's contribution to the 1963 volume *Was ist heute links?*[43] A similar feeling was apparent in 1965 when he was extremely scathing about intellectuals supporting the SPD. A year later he turned his attention to the state in a speech made in Wuppertal, which contains some of his most controversial remarks: 'There where the state might have been or should be, I only see some festering remnants of power, and these obviously precious rudiments are defended with rat-like fury.'[44] This is not part of a plea for the return of a centralised Prussian-type state. He says that as a writer, he does not need the state, but that others do, another example of a distinction being drawn between writers and the mass of citizens. Such a distinction may be dubious but, not surprisingly, it was the characterisation of the state that provoked a storm. As late as 1974 the right-wing journalist Mathias Walden picked up these comments, or rather misquoted them, in blaming Böll for the outbreak of terrorism. The result was a court case and 40,000 DM damages for Böll. To return to the remarks themselves: despite their harshness, they are not a total rejection of the West German State. It must also be remembered that they were made at a time when the Erhard government was seeking to cling to power despite a general lack of confidence.

Towards the end of the decade Böll's greater desire for commitment comes through not least in his efforts to promote the status of writers through the newly formed VS. During these efforts he made yet another controversial remark: 'We owe this state nothing, it owes us a good deal', referring to the role of literature in restoring the esteem of Germany in the world.[45] Schelsky predictably seizes on this and expresses his own gratitude to the state for allowing him to write and carry on his profession freely. It all depends no doubt on how far one should be grateful to the state for the fundamental right of freedom of expression. Whatever its merits, Böll's claim should be seen in context as part of the expression of a wish to play a greater role in society.

As already indicated, this search for commitment manifested itself in part in increasing support for the SPD. In 1972 Böll expressed his approval of Brandt, typically basing his endorsement on Brandt's being a representative of the ordinary people rather than belonging to the privileged strata of society.[46] He spoke at the SPD party congress in 1972 and to the party's parliamentarians two years later. That he switched his support to the Greens a decade later was not in his view to be interpreted as opposition to the SPD, a position that is tenable in an electoral system based on proportional representation and the necessity of coalitions.

Another indication of Böll's increased commitment was his greater participation in the political events of the moment. This became particularly apparent at the time of the student movement. Böll sympathised with the students, especially the campaign against the Springer Press, which he accused of wishing to seize power in a manner comparable to the Nazis in 1933. He even uses the word *Machtergreifung*, the term frequently employed to describe the Nazi takeover.[47] As a comparison, this is somewhat far-fetched — in some ways it is parallel to Schelsky's exaggerations — since a press group, however influential, cannot wield absolute power. Böll was on firmer ground in his rejection of student violence, what he called 'senseless actions'.[48] During this same period he also took an active part in the campaign against the emergency laws, speaking against them in meetings in Bonn and Frankfurt. He spoke of the passing of such legislation as equally ominous as rearmament. In the 1970s he campaigned against the 'Radikalemerlass', whilst in more recent years he was a keen supporter of the peace movement, speaking for instance at the big demonstration in Bonn in the autumn of 1981 against the stationing of American missiles. If Grass's political commitment was marked more or less from the outset by the adoption of a public role, then it can be said that by comparison Böll over the years gradually developed one, as he devoted an increasing amount of energy to current political questions.

There is one further seminal aspect of Böll's political writing that permeates much of what has already been described and which must now be considered in its own right: namely the view that the Nazi past is of enduring significance for the society of the Federal Republic. On one level, the enormity of what occurred means that it will not be forgotten for a long time if ever, or, as the title of a 1978 book review puts it: 'The area is far from having been cleared of mines.'[49] Böll's stress on the continuing presence of the past, though, is anything but a mechanical statement of fact; his concern is that important lessons should be learned. This involves initially a willingness to remember and to inform the next generation about all the horrors of National Socialism. Conscience cannot be stirred where there is a desire to forget or suppress: 'As the ignorance of the children proves, the conscience of the parents — our conscience — is dead'.[50] Two years after this statement, in a speech made in 1956, Böll explained in more detail what he sees as the consequences of this failure of conscience. This speech 'Wo ist dein Bruder?' (Where is your brother?) was made on the occasion of a Brotherhood Week and, as the title shows, is centred around God's question to Cain. The brothers Böll thinks of are the victims of war, from whose fate few lasting conclusions seem to have been drawn. Most importantly, the values of society have not improved after the catastrophe. He asks poignantly: 'Did our brothers die, were our neighbours murdered and whole peoples, whole generations exterminated so that we should become a society of snobs basking in the certainty that we are all doing well enough or too well?'[51] In keeping with his overall theme, Böll notes the lack of fraternity in society:

> We were ready for a new fraternity after the catastrophe, after the hunger, we had a kind of birthright for this new fraternity, because we were neither collectively innocent nor collectively guilty — but we sold this birthright not for a mess of potage but for a cracker in which there were really fine novelties.[52]

How far Böll considered these novelties to be dross in moral and spiritual terms can be seen from a comment made in 1960 that 'feelings and memories' are not required in the purely materialistic society of the Federal Republic.[53] In other words, little has been learned from the past to improve the moral quality of society.

That there was a fateful continuity between the Third Reich and the Federal Republic remained a constant concern for Böll. On an individual level, this means, as the poem about Boock implies, that it is former Nazis who prosper, and more generally that the strong and unfeeling do well at the expense of the weak. This is expressed symbolically in the novel *Billiard um halb zehn* (Billiards at Half-past Nine), where society is divided into lambs and buffalos. There is no need to spell out on whose side Böll stands.

Böll's reaction to the Nazi past is one reason why he is so frequently described as a moralist, a definition with which it is impossible to disagree. One consequence of his moral stance that is particularly relevant in connection with his political writing is the individual or personal motivation of his commitment. One small incident will underline this point. Böll's reaction when the anti-Nazi campaigner Beate Klarsfeld slapped Chancellor Kiesinger was to send the lady flowers, a gesture that was criticised by Grass. Defending his action, Böll cited various personal reasons for his gesture: the death of his mother in an air-raid and the fate of his generation at the hands of the Nazis. He went on to compare such an action favourably with the futile efforts of writers who are only 'the famous token idiots' of the Federal Republic.[54] Böll endorses spontaneity and directness, the qualities that mark his own writing.

This personal approach is not only open to the criticism that it can lead to misjudgements, as it may well have done with the Klarsfeld incident, but also on academic or intellectual grounds, even from those whose views are similar to his own. The unconventional theologian Dorothee Sölle, for instance, complained that his review of Bernard Vesper's *Die Reise* was too emotional. He replied by describing himself as one of those persons 'whose imagination is described as a "lack of theory", this imagination, which is always playing them tricks, because it deviates from "theories".'[55] This admission separates Böll from an academic writer like Enzensberger; Grass too, for all his non-academic background, entertains academic pretentions. Quite clearly, Böll's political writing does not reveal the approach of the political scientist or theorist, nor does it contain much reference to detailed policies. It would be arrogant to dismiss it as 'unscientific' because of this, especially as he admits that he does not aim at 'scientific infallibility' when he uses a term like fascism.[56] Nevertheless, it would be equally arrogant to be totally uncritical because of the personal approach: that would be to condemn him to the despised role of 'token idiot'. Once Böll's individualism is accepted, it is necessary to treat his comments on their merits. This will inevitably lead to a certain degree of subjectivity on the part of the critic, however fair he or she might try to be. It goes without saying that only a small amount of objectivity will be required to reject the invective of those who labelled him a supporter and comforter of violent political extremists.

Böll's concern with political issues lasted until his untimely death in July 1985. His last major piece of non-fictional political writing appeared in 1984 under the title *Bild Bonn Boenisch*.[57] In this work he analyses the journalism of Peter Boenisch, formerly of *Bild*, who was press spokesman for the Kohl government until his precipitate resignation in 1985 after it came to light that he had been on the payroll of the Daimler-Benz (Mercedes) company. Böll's point is that Boenisch's kind of journalism — he is seen as the person responsible for the *Bild* phenomenon — does not qualify him for his official post. This is coupled with the worry that Boenisch's appointment gives *Bild* a greater presence in Bonn. In the event, Boenisch's departure has made this worry superfluous. It might also be claimed that Böll chose an easy target in Boenisch's columns for *Bild*. Nevertheless, particularly on the occasions where he uses irony rather than resorting to anger, Böll has written a book that is a delight to read, and that is frequently a more effective weapon against the Springer Press than the 1972 polemic in *Der Spiegel*.

Böll's death naturally occasioned a considerable number of obituaries. One that was entirely predictable appeared in the East

German communist organ *Neues Deutschland*.[58] Whilst praising Böll's generally 'progressive' attitudes, it deprecated his criticism of Eastern Europe. Elsewhere there were attempts to encapsulate the essence of his writing in a few words. Wolfram Schütte in the *Frankfurter Rundschau* coined the epithet 'A dissident in his own country',[59] whilst the headline in the *Sunday Times* over the piece by J. P. Stern 'Germany's Conscience' would surely not have met with its subject's approval.[60] Some of the most perceptive comments came, albeit in a somewhat cynical tone, from Hans Magnus Enzensberger in *Der Spiegel*.[61] He speaks of Böll having had the failing of not being able to be indifferent to injustice. Because of this he was exploited by others into taking up every cause. As a result of this burden he is for Enzensberger — not entirely originally — in the title of the medieval German poem 'der arme (poor) Heinrich'. Others might think that this refusal to ignore wrongs was rather a source of great, non-material wealth.

Notes

1. Böll, *Essayistische Schriften und Reden*, vol. 2, p. 548.
2. Ibid., p. 543.
3. Ibid., p. 548.
4. Ibid., p. 545.
5. F. Grützbach (ed.), *Freies Geleit für Ulrike Meinhof: Ein Artikel und seine Folgen* (Kiepenhauer und Witsch, Köln, 1972), p. 36. Since most of this collection consists of brief newspaper extracts, it is not proposed to refer to each text separately.
6. Ibid., p. 56.
7. *Marbacher Zeitung*, 9 Feb. 84.
8. H. Habe, *Leben für den Journalismus* (3 vols., Knaur, München und Zürich, 1976), vol. 3, p. 146.
9. Grützbach, *Freies Geleit*, p. 70.
10. Ibid., p. 85.
11. Ibid., p. 152f.
12. Ibid., p. 156.
13. Ibid., p. 84.
14. Ibid., p. 142.
15. H. Böll, *Die verlorene Ehre der Katharina Blum* (DTV, München, 1976), p. 7.
16. Grützbach, *Freies Geleit*, p. 142.
17. 'Gespräch mit Heinrich Böll' in Eggebrecht, *Die alten Männer*, p. 123.
18. Grützbach, *Freies Geleit*, p. 142.
19. Ibid., p. 142.
20. H. Böll, H. P. Riese, 'Schriftsteller in dieser Republik', *L76*, no. 6 (1977), 20.
21. H. Böll, 'Keine Angst vor Systemveränderern', *die Tageszeitung*, 4 Mar. 83.
22. H. Böll, *Vermintes Gelände* (Kiepenhauer und Witsch, Köln, 1982), p. 49.

23. Ibid., p. 222.
24. *Frankfurter Allgemeine Zeitung*, 30 May 78.
25. Böll/Riese, 'Schriftsteller in dieser Republik', p. 7.
26. Ibid., p. 26.
27. 'Gespräch mit Heinrich Böll' in Eggebrecht, *Die alten Männer*, p. 124.
28. H. Schelsky, *Die Arbeit tun die anderen* (DTV, München, 1977), p. 462.
29. Ibid., p. 480.
30. Böll, *Essayistische Schriften*, vol. 1, pp. 318–22.
31. Ibid., vol. 1, p. 78.
32. Böll wrote an appendix to Amery's book (*Essayistische Schriften*, vol. 1, pp. 540–3).
33. Böll, *Essayistische Schriften*, vol. 1, p. 457.
34. Ibid., vol. 1, pp. 606–11.
35. Ibid., vol. 1, p. 597.
36. Ibid., vol. 2, p. 219.
37. Ibid., vol. 2, p. 249.
38. Quoted in H. Mölling, *Heinrich Böll — eine 'christliche' Position?* (Juris Druck und Verlag, Zürich, 1974), p. 14.
39. Böll, *Essayistische Schriften*, vol. 3, p. 15.
40. H. Böll, 'Für Peter-Jürgen Boock', *Die Zeit*, no. 29, 13 Jul. 84.
41. H. Böll, 'Tausend Asylbewerber im Palais', *Der Spiegel*, no. 21, 2 Jul. 84, 40–1.
42. Böll, *Essayistische Schriften*, vol. 1, p. 276.
43. Ibid., vol. 1, pp. 531–4.
44. Ibid., vol. 2, p. 229.
45. Ibid., vol. 2, p. 385.
46. Ibid., vol. 2, pp. 535–41.
47. Ibid., vol. 2, p. 283.
48. Ibid., vol. 2, p. 357.
49. Böll, *Vermintes Gelände*, pp. 69–83.
50. Böll, *Essayistische Schriften*, vol. 1, p. 134.
51. Ibid., vol. 1, p. 175.
52. Ibid., vol. 1, p. 177.
53. Ibid., vol. 1, p. 372.
54. Ibid., vol. 2, p. 346.
55. Ibid., vol. 3, p. 503.
56. Ibid., vol. 2, p. 568.
57. H. Böll, *Bild Bonn Boenisch* (Lamuv Verlag, Bornheim-Merten, 1984). The posthumous novel *Frauen vor Flusslandschaft* that appeared in 1985 also has a political context in that it is set in the political world of Bonn.
58. H. Haase, 'Eine Moralist und Meister des Wortes', *Neues Deutschland*, 18 Jul. 85.
59. W. Schütte, 'Entfernung von der Truppe', *Frankfurter Rundschau*, 18 Jul. 85.
60. *Sunday Times*, 21 Jul. 85.
61. H. M. Enzensberger, 'Der arme Heinrich', *Der Spiegel*, no. 30, 22 Jul. 85, 137–8.

9　HANS MAGNUS ENZENSBERGER — THE WILL O' THE WISP

On hearing that a chapter on Hans Magnus Enzensberger was to form part of this book, a member of staff at the Marbach Literary Archive in the Federal Republic told the present writer, with a hint of sympathy in his voice, that he had chosen 'a chameleon'. Another comparison that has been made by a fellow writer is with Shakespeare's Ariel.[1]

There is indeed no doubt that Enzensberger is a restless spirit, whose stances appear to shift with bewildering frequency. It is not difficult to find instances of his saying one thing and then more or less its opposite some time later. One small example of this tendency will suffice at this point. In the early 1960s his political writing contained a number of positive references to Scandinavian society. In 1983, however, in the magazine *Stern*, he published an article 'Armes Schweden' (Poor Sweden), which repeats the frequently made criticisms of that country for its excessive social welfare provisions and state interference in the private lives of citizens.[2] If this small example provides in itself a hint of changing political attitudes, then Enzensberger's physical mobility too seems to reflect the same phenomenon. He has spent significant periods of his life in Norway, Berlin, Cuba and Munich, to mention just a few of the places where he has lived. To refer to all these changes is not a device to beg the reader's indulgence because of the difficulty of the task presented by the phenomenon of Enzensberger. The intention is rather to show why this chapter will have a particular structure. The first part will devote itself to the changes of attitude and viewpoint that have generally been perceived, then there will be some discussion of how significant such changes may have been before an attempt is made first to find any consistent elements — Enzensberger himself claims not to have changed over the past two-and-a-half decades or so — and secondly to evaluate his political writing.

Hans Magnus Enzensberger first became widely known with the publication of the volume of poetry *verteidigung der wölfe* (defence of the wolves) in 1957. This collection of poems which contained an unusually large amount of aggressive social comment helped to earn him the reputation of being Germany's own 'angry young man'. The poem that gives the volume its title, for instance, 'The wolves defended against the lambs' is a strong attack on the passivity of ordinary citizens:

> and tell me who sews the ribbons
> all over the general's chest? who
> carves the capon up for the usurer?
> who proudly dangles an iron cross
> over his rumbling navel? . . .[3]

Notwithstanding the social and political themes of these early poems, Enzensberger did not at this time wish to subsume poetry in any way under politics. The essay 'Poesie und Politik' (Poetry and Politics) of 1962 makes this clear. Here he points out that poetry was traditionally written on commission from those in power, but claims that now such a form of writing has become impossible. Referring to the anthem of the GDR written by the poet Johannes R. Becher, who became that country's Minister for Culture, as well as to the proposed anthem for the Federal Republic written by Rudolf Alexander Schröder, he concludes that 'these anthems bear no more relation to poetry than does an advertising slogan for margarine'.[4] Enzensberger does not make any ideological distinction here, preferring simply to stress the primacy and independence of poetry. It is in fact only through its distance from official politics that it can gain a truly political, that is to say essentially subversive dimension:

> Its mere presence is an indictment of government announcements and the scream of propaganda of manifestos and banners. Its critical function is simply that of the child in the fairy tale. No 'political engagement' is necessary to see that the emperor is wearing no clothes. It is enough that a single verse breaks the speechless howl of applause.[5]

The views expressed here are similar to those of Theodor W. Adorno referred to earlier. Committed art is rejected in favour of the opposition seen as inherent in the use of new poetic forms. In addition, Enzensberger's stance reflects the general abhorrence of ideology prevalent among intellectuals in the first fifteen years or so of the Federal Republic's existence.

In addition to the poems, Enzensberger's early reputation as a social critic was established by essays and articles that appeared in such publications as *Konkret*. His contributions to collections of political essays include not only his lukewarm endorsement of the SPD in 1961 but also a letter from Rome — another stopping point on his peregrinations — included in *Ich lebe in der Bundesrepublik* and entitled, angrily enough, 'Schimpfend unter Palmen' (Cursing beneath palms). It consists of a contrast between the joys of life in Italy and the horrors of affluent Germany, for instance the city of Düsseldorf. German coffee houses with their elegant décor and their whipped cream are said to teach 'fear of the eternity of hell'.[6] More seriously, he goes on to criticise the policy of rearmament in the Federal Republic, before totally damning the whole German way of living. Again East and West are equated, this time in an inspired aphorism: 'On the two disputing piles known as Germany there live in part people partially.'[7] The letter ends with Enzensberger proclaiming that he does not live in the Federal Republic, but there is a postscript dated two months after the original letter announcing a return and saying that it is impossible to stay permanently on the outside. The return to the fold coincides with the 'positive' stance of *Die Alternative*, but the contribution to Richter's collection following the building of the Wall speaks of departure again, this time to Norway.

Enzensberger's early prose writing also announces his interest in a field which, regardless of changes in political outlook, has remained a constant concern for him, the mass media. His essays on this subject from 1957 to 1962 were first collected and published under the title *Einzelheiten* (Details) in 1962. Some of the texts originated as radio broadcasts, a sign of Enzensberger's practical experience in the field. The major essay in this volume, the one that gives it its subtitle and has given a new term to discussion on the media is 'Bewusstseins-Industrie' (Consciousness Industry). In it Enzensberger defines the present age as one of mass communication, a state of affairs that cannot be changed and one which is an inevitable consequence of industrialisation. His major concern in this situation is the uses the media can be put to. His conclusions are not entirely pessimistic. Although those in power wish to harness the media to their own ends, this goal can never be fully achieved, as it is inevitable that people's critical faculties will be aroused. Equally paradoxical is the position of intellectuals working within the media. They are dependent as employees, but are needed as the only group with the required creativity. In this way there is the chance to change society which should be used by the intellectual: 'He must try, at any cost, to use it for his own purposes, which are incompatible with the purposes of the mind machine.'[8] As with the poet, subversion is the order of the day.

The remainder of this part of *Einzelheiten* deals with a variety of topics. There are critiques of two publications, the *Frankfurter Allgemeine Zeitung*, whose coverage of news is unfavourably compared with that of other newspapers with an international reputation, and *Der Spiegel*. In this second case, Enzensberger attacks the magazine's technique of turning items of news into the form of a story and its personalisation of events. To criticise *Der Spiegel* at a time when it seemed to provide the only effective opposition to the Adenauer government was particularly controversial. The point is made, however, that it remains required reading, given the timidity of other sections of the press. Enzensberger is at his most critical on the subject of cinema newsreels. He analyses the various types of report shown and comes to depressing conclusions: 'Informational value and topicality of the newsreel are minimal.'[9] He goes on to suggest that it is the private interests behind the newsreels, rather than the medium as such, that are to blame. The point is similar to the one made about the 'consciousness industry' as a whole: Enzensberger rejects atavistic objections to modern technical developments, preferring rather to see such developments put to a more positive use.

The term consciousness industry is not restricted by Enzensberger to the mass media. He extends it, in two particularly critical essays, to include tourism and mail-order catalogues. On the subject of tourism, he again criticises reactionaries who stuffily object to the growth of the industry. At the same time, he sees the whole phenomenon of mass tourism as preventing what it ostensibly seeks to make possible, namely an escape from the pressures of everyday life. He goes so far as to compare the herds of tourists being shepherded by guides with transports to concentration camps — a comparison that cannot be seen as valid, even by those who would never set foot in a holiday camp. The conclusion reached amounts to a variation of the Marxist argument of 'false consciousness'. Tourism reflects a genuine desire for freedom but one which cannot be fulfilled in the form such tourism takes. The freedom promised is a fraud, but the client 'does not admit to himself the fraud to which he falls victim'.[10] Maybe he actually enjoys himself!

On the subject of mail-order, Enzensberger is at his most scathing. He begins by pointing out that the catalogue of a certain mail-order company is a bigger bestseller than any other publication. The goods it advertises are seen, in the words of the essay's title, as the material manifestation of the 'plebiscite of the consumers', a view at odds with the New Left standpoint that would regard them as examples of 'consumption terror' imposed by manufacturers on hapless victims. Be that as it may, Enzensberger sees no reason to rejoice in the results of this process of choice: 'The majority among us has decided for a petty-bourgeois hell.'[11] He goes on to regret the lack of concern shown by government, trade unions and intellectuals about this state of affairs, without suggesting what they might do.

This first period of Enzensberger's writing shows him as a trenchant critic of society and an intellectual analyst of considerable perception, whose discussion of the media especially represented a radical new departure. As for specific political issues, he can be seen as a sceptical observer generally unwilling, despite his reluctant endorsement of the SPD in 1961, to identify with particular causes. A collection of essays, many of which again originated as radio broadcasts that appeared in 1964, underlines why this should be the case. Once more, the title *Politik und Verbrechen* (Politics and Crime) is significant. Enzensberger sees an intimate connection between the two, as he makes clear in his comments on the Eichmann trial: 'The original political act then, if we wish to listen to Freud, coincides with the original crime. There exists an old, close and dark connection between murder and politics.'[12] The remainder of the book concentrates on manifestations of violence, for example the Chicago of Al Capone or the regime of Trujillo in the Dominican Republic, which is seen as having a wider political significance. The interest in the Third World revealed in the essay on Trujillo prefigures the next perceived stage of Enzensberger's political development, in which the Cuba of Fidel Castro plays a significant role.

This second stage can be said to begin with Enzensberger's move to Berlin in 1965. Many of its features have already been hinted at, particularly in Chapter 4: the apparent espousal of revolutionary politics, the feeling that Europe and Germany were peripheral to the main developments in world politics, the rejection of literature and the foundation of a new kind of critical periodical with *Kursbuch*. The first two points are closely connected and will now be discussed in more detail.

By 1965 Enzensberger was in no mood to contemplate a further endorsement of the SPD. He appeared, in fact, to be becoming totally at odds with the direction the Federal Republic was taking. Equally, he seemed to be losing interest in the German question as a major issue in international politics. The mood of this time in Berlin is caught in the essay, which originally appeared in two parts in *Kursbuch*, appropriately entitled 'Berliner Gemeinplätze' (Berlin commonplaces). It begins with an echo of Marx, but the spectre said to be haunting Europe at this time is revolution. He begins by admitting that it may seem somewhat insubstantial, as there is no working class with a developed political consciousness to lead any revolution. Equally, there is no revolutionary mood among established intellectuals. He is particularly critical of his fellow-writers for their failure to develop political alternatives, despite their supposed oppositional stance in such bodies as the Gruppe 47. He says of this oppositional intelligentsia:

> Morality was more important to it than politics . . . Decently modest and sentimental, always concerned with preventing the worst or at least delaying it, these exemplary scholars of reformism have provided for twenty years suggestions for improvements within the system but no radical counter proposals . . . They have not produced a political theory worthy of the name.[13]

In as far as Enzensberger is referring to writers of literary fiction, detractors have not surprisingly asked whether the production of such theories should be regarded as part of the writer's task. The group with which Enzensberger does show sympathy, however, is the students, whose opposition to the existing parliamentary system he endorses. He specifically praises the SDS for being the only grouping to have put forward a theory 'free of deluded features',[14] a view that at the very least ignores the incomprehensibility of this theory for the majority of the population.

This period in the second half of the 1960s was also the time when Enzensberger was most active within the political life of the Federal Republic. He played a prominent part in the campaign against the emergency laws, making what can only be described as particularly fiery interventions. In a speech in 1966 at a Frankfurt congress against the proposed legislation, he began with a series of rhetorical questions which asked if the Federal Republic was a banana republic comparable to Haiti or Portugal. His main point, however, was that the campaign against the new laws was necessary to prevent such a development. Indeed, his statement: 'The republic we have is still needed'[15] implies some degree of identification with existing institutions. Two years later, in another speech on the same subject, the emphasis was different. This time his remarks culminated in the demand that everyone go out on to the streets and emulate the events of May 1968 in France: 'Misgivings are not enough. Distrust is not enough. Protest is not enough. Our goal must be: Let us finally create, in Germany too, French conditions.'[16] That this plea has become almost a part of folk memory in accounts of the era of student unrest does not alter its essential inappropriateness in terms of the political situation of the day. Finally, to underline the nature of Enzensberger's political activity at this time, another incident is worthy of mention. In 1967 he donated the 6,000 DM given to him as the recipient of the Nuremberg Literature Prize to aid 'political prisoners' in the Federal Republic. At the same time, he wrote a highly critical letter to the Minister of Justice, an unusual target in that the incumbent of that post at the time was the liberally minded Gustav Heinemann.[17]

The other dimension to this 'revolutionary' period was, as already stated, the growing identification with the political struggles of the Third World. Once more, a gesture comparable to the demand for French conditions highlighted — in this case literally — the direction Enzensberger was taking. In early 1968 he resigned from a fellowship at the Center for Advanced Studies at the Wesleyan University of Middletown, Connecticut, clearly a town with an inappropriate name for Enzensberger. In a well-publicised open letter to the university's president, following criticism of the Vietnam War and imperialist exploitation of the Third World, he announced his intention of spending a long period in Cuba, where he felt he could be of use and also learn a lot.[18] In the event, he was there during parts of 1968 and 1969, the main product of his stay being the documentary drama *Das Verhör von Habana* (The Havana inquiry). Dedicated to the Cuban poet Herbert Padillo, whose subsequent arrest and imprisonment contributed to Enzensberger's later disillusionment with the Castro regime, this play reproduces parts of the hearings, in which participants in the abortive Bay of Pigs invasion were questioned about their political motives. That such an event took place at all was an exciting new development for Enzensberger, as he states in his introduction to the play entitled 'Ein Selbstbildnis der Konterrevolution' (A self-portrait of the counter-revolution): 'The imprisoned counter-revolutionaries are not isolated in the cellars of the political police or incarcerated in concentration camps but confronted with the people who have defeated them.'[19] In this introduction Enzensberger rejoices not only in the political victory of the revolution but also, as the above passage implies, in its moral superiority.

Enzensberger's abiding concern with the role of literature and with the media is reflected in this period in the 1960s and early 70s, as already seen, in his contribution to the debate on the 'death of literature' and in the development of *Kursbuch*. The harnessing of writing for social and political ends is now at the centre of his concerns. The change in emphasis is already visible in a 1962 essay 'Die Aporien der Avantgarde' (The Aporias of the Avant Garde). The old avant-garde, as represented, for instance, by the French surrealists, is no longer seen as relevant but simply as an 'anachronism'.[20] The scepticism towards literature as a whole visible in 'Gemeinplätze die neueste Literatur betreffend' is developed in the 1970 essay 'Baukästen zu einer Theorie der Medien' (Constituents to a Theory of the Media). In this essay the positive opportunities offered by the media to promote social change are stressed much more than in the earlier essay 'Bewusstseins-Industrie', a view that no doubt led him to form his own publishing company for *Kursbuch* from 1971. As for the writer or traditional 'artist', his job is now said to be that of making himself superfluous. In the period of transition he has an educative function as 'agent of the masses' until such time as they themselves 'become authors, authors of history'.[21] At this point of Enzensberger's development there is a merging of literary and political utopias.

The opening comments in this chapter have already made it clear that this kind of utopianism was not permanent. If once more a single indication of a change of direction, comparable to the letter of resignation in the USA, were to be sought, then it could be found most easily this time within a literary work, the long, quasi-epic poem described by Enzensberger himself as a comedy *Der Untergang der Titanic* (The Sinking of the Titanic) that appeared in 1978. The title itself refers not just to the loss of the ship but also to the loss of a previous vision. Three years earlier Enzensberger had published a collection of poems under the title *Mausoleum*, whose subjects were people connected, in the words of the sub-title, with the 'history of progress', for instance I. K. Brunel, Malthus and the French town-planner Haussmann. Whereas this earlier collection looks with general scepticism at the whole concept of progress, *Der Untergang der Titanic* has specifically to do with the loss of a previous belief in social and political progress. Since the poem was first conceived during the sojourn on Cuba, one must conclude that the fate of the luxury liner as a symbol of social and political developments was originally to be used to promote a different viewpoint. What in the final version is regarded as lost or as having sunk can be seen from lines in the third canto:

> Damals dachte kaum einer an den Untergang,
> nicht einmal in Berlin, das den seinigen
> längst hinter sich hatte. Es schwankte
> die Insel Cuba nicht unter unsern Füssen.
> Es schien uns, als stünde etwas bevor,
> etwas von uns zu Erfindendes.
> Wir wussten nicht, dass das Fest längst zu Ende, . . . war[22]

(At that time hardly anybody was thinking of decline, not even in Berlin, which long since had its behind it. The island of Cuba was not shifting beneath our feet. It seemed to us that something was imminent, something to be invented by us. We did not know that the party was long over . . .) The spectre of revolution invoked in 'Berliner Gemeinplätze' is here laid to rest. This is not a cause for despair; the poem ends with the words 'ich schwimme weiter' (I swim on), another sign of — dare one say — the fluidity that marks Enzensberger's intellectual development.

The direction in which he chose to swim away from the wreck of revolution can again be shown by reference to a new publication, this time the magazine *TransAtlantik*, which was started by him and the former student leader and nephew of Salvador Allende Gaston Salvatore in 1980. The title itself is amazing enough in view of the previous criticisms of America; that it was in no sense meant ironically is confirmed by the glossy covers and the kind of advertising attracted, in many cases very much that associated with up-market glossy magazines. The aim was to create a 'new style' of magazine, marked it would seem by wit and urbanity. One example from a regular feature headed 'Ventil' (safety-valve) will show the overall tone and the kind of political stance adopted, if the following comments on the working class can be said to have a political content at all: 'The history of the workers' movement is dreadfully boring — lots of workers and little movement for long stretches. Except for the highlights when time and again a few hundred workers were butchered.'[23] Individuals are free to decide if this is wit or superciliousness; what it is not is the kind of writing associated with the student movement. In the event, the 'new style' did not prove attractive enough. *TransAtlantik* was in a financial crisis at the end of 1982 and Enzensberger and Salvatore left the magazine, which, however, has managed to survive.

Enzensberger's own major contribution to *TransAtlantik* was a series of essays later collected, along with some contributions to *Kursbuch*, under the title *Politische Brosamen* (Political crumbs). Their general tone is one of ironic detachment, with the anger and passion of earlier years having given way to humour and whimsy. There are many passages which vouch for his own claim that he is no longer left-wing. In an essay on the petty-bourgeoisie, for instance, he stresses the continued existence of this class, although this fact may well embarrass 'the lovers of clean, nice, coherent world-views'.[24] How far he has dissociated himself from Marxist dialectical theory can be seen from the following statement, which could not be more categorical, namely 'that there is no world spirit; that we do not know the laws of history'.[25] By contrast, Enzensberger now speaks favourably about what he calls normality, that is to say everyday life and people. His essay defending normality concludes: 'As far as the species is capable of surviving, it will presumably owe its continued existence not to some outsiders or other but to quite normal people.'[26] The lambs are now being defended against the Marxist or intellectual wolves.

As for comments on specific political events, these too are marked by playful distance or one might say a tone that is the equivalent of the wise man shaking his head at human folly. He parodies a media discussion on housing, and suggests that the solution to the problems besetting education would be a return to a house tutor system. In this second case the tongue is very firmly in cheek, as it is in the essay on economics, playfully entitled 'Blindekuh-Ökonomie' (Blind man's buff economics). The point being made is that, despite all the talk, nobody knows anything for sure on the subject. The same tone is maintained in Enzensberger's most recent political writing following *Politische Brosamen*.

Following the Flick Affair — the discovery of payments by a major industrial concern to political parties in return for favours — he wrote a long commentary 'Ein Bonner Memorandum' (A Bonn memorandum) for *Der Spiegel* in late 1983. In it he directs his satire at the political parties not for financial corruption in any personal sense — he does not think that individuals are lining their own pockets — but for their profligacy in advertising and the like to prove their importance in the political system. He sees the world of the political party as being in fact as far removed from reality as that of the drug addict. In order to overcome any self-doubt, the parties are obliged to act according to the following maxim: 'I spend money therefore I am.'[27] After such a brilliant formulation it seems churlish to point out the constitutional role of the parties and, more specifically, that not all the parties behaved equally badly in the face of financial temptation.

To suggest that the above division of Enzensberger's political writing into three main phases could be more than an approximate generalisation would be a travesty of the truth. Not only are the frequent shifts from one phase to another bewildering, but it is also frequently possible to find statements within a phase that run counter to the general direction of his views at that particular time. There is a Marxist streak in his earlier work, whilst more significantly in the second, apparently revolutionary period, there is much that runs counter to the image of Enzensberger as the supporter of Third World liberation and of revolutionary German students. In contrast to *Das Verhör von Habana*, for instance, there is a very cool appraisal of Cuban politics in the 1970 essay 'Bildnis einer Partei' (Portrait of a Party), which deals with the Cuban Communist Party. In it he points out that since the revolution predated the party, it does not enjoy the status of other communist parties. Moreover, the traditional communists were far from supportive during the period of revolution. Finally, the party is seen as lacking a coherent ideology, as Castro is unwilling to lay down a consistent line. That the Cuban state is less than perfect is implied by the following comment on the question of inconsistency:

There is no programme of the PCC. Who inquires about its ideology is always referred to Fidel's speeches, whose contradictions are notorious; whoever uses them is well advised to quote the last one at any given time. To repeat what Fidel said a few years ago could have the most unpleasant consequences.[28]

Equally, in 'Berliner Gemeinplätze', despite the overall revolutionary stance, the point is made that revolutions in history have always taken over the inhumanity of their previous opponents, a point not dissimilar to that made by Grass to justify his rejection of revolution *per se*. Finally, it is worth mentioning that at approximately the same time as Europe was being reduced to a peripheral status and the German question regarded as an anachronism, there is the long 'Katechismus zur deutschen Frage' (Catechism on the German question), written by Enzensberger with three collaborators, consisting largely of eminently sensible suggestions, many of which were in fact implemented as part of Brandt's Ostpolitik.[29] As for the most recent period, leftist positions or at least terminology are not entirely lacking. In *Politische Brosamen* there is still reference to 'the state apparatus of surveillance'.[30] Nothing with Enzensberger is ever clear cut.

The conclusion that has to be drawn is that it is insufficient in any study of Enzensberger to restrict oneself to chronicling changes of attitude that are often less decisive than they appear. Such changes, interesting as they are, do not tell the whole story, unless one wishes simply to conclude that Enzensberger is a rolling stone entirely without moss, and therefore unworthy of much attention. Before such a conclusion could be reached, it would, however, be necessary at least to ask whether there are features in his writing that remain constant regardless of the standpoint he is espousing at a particular time. In fact, there is no shortage of possible explanations of the essential Enzensberger.

One is to define Enzensberger as someone who remains in tune with current intellectual fashion, as 'the precise seismographer of intellectual moods', as Hans-Thies Lehmann puts it.[31] It is clear that for a long time Enzensberger's thinking was roughly in line with that of many others, not least during the period of student unrest. More recently though, this has not been the case; for instance, he does not appear to have taken part in the whole peace discussion. Moreover, in earlier times he was rather in the vanguard of developments; his move to Berlin predated the rise of student activism. To sum up: one can perceive some correlation between Enzensberger's development and changes in the intellectual climate; to leave it there, however, would sidestep the question of whether there is any inherent continuity in his writing.

It might be more profitable to regard the very changes Enzensberger's thinking undergoes, almost paradoxically, as the factor that provides continuity. In other words, what remains constant is the element of doubt or scepticism towards fixed positions. The poem entitled 'Zweifel' (Doubt), which stylistically is punctuated by a series of interrogatives, is revealing of such an attitude:

Ich höre aufmerksam meinen Feinden zu.
Wer sind meine Feinde?
Die Schwarzen nennen mich weiss,
die Weissen nennen mich schwarz.
Das höre ich gern. Es könnte bedeuten:
Ich bin auf dem richtigen Weg.
(Gibt es einen richtigen Weg?)

(I listen to my enemies. Who are my enemies? The blacks call me white. The whites call me black. I like to hear that. It might mean: I am on the right path. (Is there a right path?))[32]

Doubt, as reflected in the refusal to take up fixed positions, is regarded positively; what is more, it provides the basis for experimentation, another essential element in Enzensberger's approach to politics. This can be seen from the suffix to *Politik und Verbrechen*, where he speaks of the whole project as an experiment, not as the last word on the subject: 'This book does not wish to be right. Its answers are provisional, they are disguised questions.'[33] The titles of many essays too, in which words like 'theory' and 'constituents' recur, are a sign of the same phenomenon. They show not only an academic desire to analyse but also a delight in trying out new positions. The obvious charge of inconsistency that can be levelled at such a method is disarmingly countered at the end of 'Berliner Gemeinplätze'. He happily admits to changing stances, pointing out himself occasions when he has said something different and claiming 'The truth is revolutionary'.[34] This of course was the lesson that had to be learned on *Animal Farm*.

The refusal to be tied to a fixed position so apparent in Enzensberger's development can also be connected with his proclaimed insistence on facts rather than confessions of faith, his position in the dispute with Weiss over Vietnam. The early, frequently anthologised poem 'Ins Lesebuch für die Oberstufe' (For the sixthformer's anthology) also expresses the same view in a more metaphorical form:

Lies keine Oden, mein Sohn, lies die Fahrpläne:
sie sind genauer. . .

(Do not read odes, my son, read timetables: they are more
precise. . .)[35] The permanence of this stance is further implied by
comments in *Politische Brosamen*, where he criticises left-wing
ideologues for ignoring or seeking to prevent discussion on any real
phenomenon whose occurrence does not fit in with their scheme of
beliefs: 'Our ideologues make themselves ridiculous when they try
to eradicate indestructible images like flood and fire, earthquake
and hurricane.'[36] The distinction being made is between sterile
theories that are clung to dogmatically in the face of contrary
evidence, and those that are put forward experimentally with the
aim of extending insight into a particular topic. A good example of
this experimental method is the 1973 essay 'Zur Kritik der politischen Ökologie' (Critique of political ecology).[37] Incidentally, the
title is yet another example of Enzensberger's delight in playing on
and modifying others' words and the year it was written, some time
before there was widespread concern over ecological issues, a sign
of how he has frequently been in the forefront of social developments. In the essay he neither accepts nor rejects the ecologists'
case, but treats it as a hypothesis from which certain conclusions
can be drawn. Hence, these conclusions are entitled 'Hypothesen
über eine Hypothese' (Hypotheses on a hypothesis). Whether such
a degree of conditionality makes it impossible to say anything of
substance is not a question that will be addressed at this point; it is
intended at present only to illustrate the method employed.

One question that has to be posed in connection with this method
is whether Enzensberger in his writing follows what might be called
its inner logic. An experimental framework would seem to demand
an overall experimental or flexible approach, but in reality he is
often surprisingly dogmatic in his statements. The impression
gained is that he is saying something akin to 'anybody who does not
agree with my view, even though it is a provisional one, is pretty
stupid.' The use of the word 'commonplaces' in essay titles, for
instance, is a rhetorical pistol inviting or even demanding acquiescence; elsewhere the reader is frequently reminded that something
is obvious or not even worthy of discussion. One example of this is
a few lines from the essay on ecology referred to above, in which
those who use the metaphor 'spaceship earth' are taken to task for
implying that all the world's inhabitants are in the same position

and therefore for ignoring social differences. Within seven lines the reader is told that the falsity of the metaphor is both obvious and crystal clear, and that it is a platitude not even worthy of the term idealism.[38] A key word used throughout his writing by Enzensberger is *Binsenwahrheit* (truism); it too insists on the reader's compliance. There is then clearly an unusual interplay between doubt and dogmatism that requires further investigation.

It will help at this point to mention another epithet frequently applied to Enzensberger: that he is 'anarchistic', a state or quality which at least partly explains his rapid adoption and abandonment of political positions. This term is not generally used to imply that he is a follower of the specific political ideology of anarchism, although there is one work, the documentary novel of 1972 *Der kurze Sommer der Anarchie* (The short summer of anarchy), which presents a sympathetic picture of Spanish anarchism. What is generally meant is a deliberate reluctance to be restricted for a long period by any position he has embraced, however wholeheartedly. As Reinhold Grimm puts it in a long essay on his social criticism: 'Enzensberger not only constantly entangles himself in a choking net but he also constantly seeks again and again to free himself from it.'[39] To some, this is betrayal. The poet Volker von Törne has said of him: 'when things got serious he always took to his heels.'[40] For Enzensberger himself though, betrayal does not appear to represent a particularly reprehensible action. His sixth-former in the poem already referred to is told to be ready to commit acts of treason.

What might also be seen as anarchistic is Enzensberger's tendency to equate different historical periods and different social systems, usually in a single gesture of criticism or condemnation. One point that helps to underline this is his generally negative attitude towards East Germany, incidentally something that has frequently been reciprocated by GDR critics except in relation to *Das Verhör von Habana*, which was produced almost simultaneously in both German states. It clearly does not follow that someone who is critical of the Federal Republic should embrace the political system of the GDR. What is unusual in Enzensberger's case, however, is the tendency to overlook the differences between the two systems, to see a mirror reflection of phenomena in one German state in the other. As already mentioned, he has nothing but scorn for anthems written for either state. Equally, the official terminology used in both countries is subjected to blanket criticism in a speech given in Darmstadt in 1963 on the occasion of his being awarded the Büchner prize. He takes various terms used in the two states and suggests that they mean in every case the opposite of what they seem to say. Thus the GDR term 'worker and peasant power' means power used against these groups, whereas in the West unconstitutional actions are called 'protection of the constitution'.[41] This equation of the two German states, however unusual, is, however, perhaps only a minor manifestation of the phenomenon. Grimm is able to quote one sentence where almost every ideology and every political system are lumped together.[42] In deference to the serious political ideology of anarchism, it is probably more appropriate to describe this feature of Enzensberger's writing as chaotic.

Yet another phenomenon within Enzensberger's work that reflects a similar mode of thinking is his tendency to draw sweeping conclusions from limited evidence or dubious premises. How permanent a feature this has been can be illustrated by reference to three essays written at different stages of his development. The first is part of *Politik und Verbrechen*, the portrait of the former dictator Rafael Trujillo referred to already. Enzensberger's thesis is that neither he nor his regime should be regarded as a unique deviation from civilised norms but that the world abounds with comparable systems. He claims that he can only think of eight countries which do not bear some resemblance to the kind of state generally disparagingly labelled a banana republic. (Incidentally, it might be an interesting game to guess which eight were meant.) Even without the aid of such tenuous concepts as 'imperfect democracy', one must still say that this claim is wildly exaggerated. Many countries may be ruled autocratically, but there is clearly a difference between such states and the arbitrary dictatorship of the kind practised after Trujillo by, for instance, Amin. Enzensberger is correct to claim that bestial regimes recur, but not to link them with the great mass of governments. In fact, he even goes so far, in keeping with his connection between politics and crime, to suggest that such regimes reflect the essence of politics:

> Trujillo's system was a parody. Like all parodies, it carried to the extremes the characteristic features of the original, showed them in ultimate purity and, in this way, revealed them. The original is nothing other than traditional politics, all traditional politics, as pre-historic statecraft.[43]

Besides once again lumping all ages and ideologies together, this statement also amounts to a variation of the dangerous cry from the depths of German history that politics is a dirty business. In many ways it is akin to a simplification such as saying that the internal combustion engine should be banned because of road accidents. Both internal combustion engine and political power can be dangerous; the issue is rather how the dangers can be limited and their potential, something Enzensberger does not seem to concede in the case of politics, harnessed. Habermas in his review of *Politik und Verbrechen* makes the point most succinctly: 'Crime as politics does not yet in itself expose politics as crime.'[44]

Exactly the same structure of argument is used in a more recent essay on the press 'Der Triumph der *Bild-Zeitung* oder die Katastrophe der Pressefreiheit' (The triumph of *Bild-Zeitung* or the catastrophe of press freedom). Here the point is that intellectual criticism of *Bild-Zeitung* ignores the common qualities of all newspapers, which, like Trujillo with politics, are most visible in this most extreme example. For Enzensberger, despite the differences in informational value between it and other publications, it remains the quintessential newspaper:

It already starts with the fact that no newspaper, no magazine, no television programme is conceivable which did not submit blindly to the demand of topicality. This has as its consequence that we find ourselves confronted day after day with non-events.[45]

Again, the question is whether the existence of *Bild-Zeitung* justifies talking about the catastrophe of press freedom. To paraphrase Habermas, press freedom as a catastrophe, in the case of the gutter press, may not be the same thing as the catastrophe of press freedom. As for the point about newspapers and topicality, it is, in Enzensberger's own terms, something of a truism.

The essay from *Politisch Brosamen* 'Das höchste Stadium der Unterentwicklung. Eine Hypothese über den Real Existierenden Sozialismus' (The highest stage of under-development. A hypothesis on Real Existing Socialism) provides the final example of this kind of argument. Before any detailed account of the essay is given, it should again be pointed out that Enzensberger is slightly varying well-known Marxist phraseology and that he is only affording his remarks the status of a hypothesis. He begins the essay by relating seven anecdotes about bizarre events in various countries, for example the production of Camembert cheese in a totally unsuitable climate, and the failure to do anything about a quagmire surrounding new flats. He then suggests that these and the other incidents could equally well occur in either communist or Third World countries, claiming: 'The Second and the Third World are dreadfully similar to one another.'[46] In the case of the examples just mentioned, the argument does break down, as it is not difficult to locate the two occurrences. Once again, it is a case of not having to let oneself be duped by the wit and elegance of Enzensberger's prose. That defects occur in both communist and developing countries does not mean that the two should be seen together; one might also ask whether there is any country where everything functions perfectly.

Another charge that has been levelled at Enzensberger throughout his literary career is that he is 'elitist'. This criticism can be linked with the tendency, already discussed, to be dogmatic and to insist on the support of all his readers with a modicum of intelligence. An essay written for *Der Spiegel* in 1976 and subsequently incurring the wrath of the Bavarian wing of the Christian Democrats, the CSU, in the election campaign of the same year, might well be seen as inviting this charge. It is Enzensberger's response to the changed climate of the 1970s, an expression of surprise that, in their reactions to terrorism, the Germans have allowed their excessive zeal to re-create abroad all the negative images associated with their country. The major hypothesis on this occasion is that his fellow countrymen are stupid, especially as the political system of the Federal Republic is not in danger:

Perhaps after all it was stupidity. There is much to suggest this, for example the incredulous amazement, the injured sense of dignity, with which official Germany notes the comments abroad. The so-called *Tendenzwende* would then be nothing more than the unconscious reflex action of a bourgeoisie which always tended to be politically backward.[47]

It is no wonder the CSU felt aggrieved. There are many other examples of apparent elitism, the attacks on mass tourism and the world of mail-order in *Enzelheiten*, for instance. The essay on mail-order contains the claim that the majority are living in a state nearer 'idiocy' than ever before, idiocy in fact being a word that recurs quite frequently in Enzensberger's essays. Yet it would not be Enzensberger if there were not conflicting evidence. Despite such an attack on the material goods offered to the majority, there are a number of occasions when he claims that there is nothing wrong with a high material standard of living, for instance in an interview with a Cuban magazine in 1969.[48] There is also the point, as already seen, that he is keen to defend himself against the charge of reactionary elitism in some of the essays in *Einzelheiten*. Despite these professions, there is at least a prima facie case, not least because of the tone he frequently adopts. Along with the cult of change and experiment, which can be said to subsume some of the features labelled as 'anarchistic', a detached arrogance can be said to be a recurring feature of Enzensberger's social and political writing.

What is to be said in conclusion about Enzensberger as a political writer? First, it seems impossible to see him as the kind of committed writer exemplified by Grass or Böll, who have both wrestled earnestly with the problems they have seen besetting their country and indeed the world. Reinhold Grimm's claim that there is a basic paradox within Enzensberger's social criticism — a desire for commitment yet simultaneously a desire not to be hamstrung by commitment — no longer provides an adequate explanation in the light of what has happened since his essay was written. One must rather wonder whether any apparent commitment, for instance to student revolution, was ever very deep. Certainly, Enzensberger himself now wishes to maintain that he was less than totally involved:

> It's true I let myself be led astray at that time but it was of my own will. I wanted to be there. How often does one have the good fortune to experience a revolution in Germany? Agreed the student movement was only the parody of a revolution, but nevertheless: it was great. As a writer I had to be there.[49]

This can of course be interpreted as a *post facto* rationalisation. Nevertheless, such factors as the manneristic linguistic variations on Marx in 'Berliner Gemeinplätze' and the theatricality of the demand for French conditions imply a certain dominance of posture over substance. What he writes about the eighteenth-century writer Diderot in the dramatic prologue to a recent radio play might well be applied, in spirit rather than literally, to himself:

I: Agent, doctor, confidence trickster, usurer, credit swindler, in a word: an artist.

He: Do you mean by that that there is only a small step between the artist and the criminal?[50]

The final line from a poem entitled 'Das Übliche' (The usual) also seems to sum up Enzensberger's essential standpoint. It follows a number of historical facts and a brief mention of the shortage of shoelaces in Cuba and consists of opposing conclusions:

Das macht nichts. Das ist schlimm. Das macht nichts.

(That doesn't matter. That's bad. That doesn't matter.)[51] Why cry if you can laugh?

A final question that has to be faced is the morality of Enzensberger's shifting stances. In absolute terms it is clearly ridiculous to demand total consistency, as he himself points out in the essay 'Das Ende der Konsequenz' (The end of consistency).[52] In it he describes the incongruity of the veteran SPD politician Herbert Wehner being confronted by an earnest ideologue with remarks made in 1926. Equally, in the field of intellectual discussion, shifts in opinion cannot be held against a person; it would be a strange individual who never changed his or her mind. Where Enzensberger's moral position can be doubted is over the question of the possible misleading of other, more vulnerable people. Again, the period at issue is that of the student rebellion. If, as he himself has subsequently claimed, he wished 'to try out what could be done with it',[53] the point arises how far he should have led others into the experiment. In this case the experimenting was not solely taking place on a personal or intellectual level. It is not now suddenly being claimed that an intellectual has great power to stir otherwise apathetic people into reprehensible actions; the question is rather how Enzensberger used any potential influence within an existing movement. He appears to have attached himself to what might be called the bandwagon of student rebellion merely to see if it would go any faster, whilst reserving the option of jumping off. Others denied themselves this chance. Again, this is not to blame Enzensberger for terrorism or other acts of violence, but to question his lack of concern about where student activism might lead — dangers that Grass, on the other hand, was well aware of — and about what might become of those whose misplaced revolutionary resolve was possibly stiffened by the call for a German version of May 1968 in Paris. Despite these reservations, it would be wrong to end on a sour note. There are many highly positive aspects within Enzensberger's political writing. The many changes of view, the product of a never satisfied intellect, are thought-provoking in that they invariably touch on highly pertinent questions, whilst the literary skills displayed are a frequent delight. Boredom is the last emotion to be felt on reading Enzensberger. It should be possible to show a little of the quality of his writing by citing one recent essay, whose subject is Hungary and which appeared in *Die Zeit* in May 1985 as part of an irregular series of travel impressions. He begins by saying that everybody likes Hungary before confessing his own fascination with what he calls this 'demi-semi paradise',[54] another example of a well-coined phrase. Nevertheless, the essay does not lack bite, as the withering portrait of a party hack shows. A series of sentences consisting almost entirely of main clauses and punctuated by the occasional simile or metaphor — the exact opposite of the prolix party style he criticises — cuts through the target like a rapier:

> Now he has been sitting on this chair for twenty-seven years already. You can see it by looking at him. He is tired, as tired as the doorman downstairs at the entrance of the press house, in his glass compartment, as tired as the grinding paternoster lift. There are the old desks, the old coffee pots, the old typewriters. A grey film lies over the office of the boss as over the columns of the party newspaper he edits. Other lines, other programmes, but the sentences have remained as they were, long, complicated, without images.[55]

The remainder of the essay covers such topics as the economic system, aspects of life in town and country, the position of gipsies and elements of Hungarian history. The particular writing skill that is most noticeable and, along with the documentary technique of recounting events that is so visible in *Politik und Verbrechen*, is a hallmark of Enzensberger's genius is an ability to convey an impression, as in the following passage describing the crowds in Budapest and reflecting his changed attitude to the people:

> A half-forgotten category is remembered as a result of this grey idyll: the people. Here it still exists 'as it used to be', undemon-

strative, shrewd, modest, without illusions. It is prepared for everything and has forgotten nothing. What with us has become dissolved in the mishmash of adaptation, in the melting-pot of some fictitious middle class, here it confronts one everywhere, as in the photographs of August Sander, peasant faces, proletarian faces, criminal faces, the physiognomies of professions and of the old classes. They are weathered but not destroyed.[56]

The balance between long and short sentences and within the sentences reveal the style as that of a poet. At such moments, it is a joy to read Enzensberger's work.

Notes

1. L. Ritter-Santini, 'Ein Paar geflügelter Schuhe' in R. Grimm (ed.), *Hans Magnus Enzensberger* (Suhrkamp, Frankfurt am Main, 1984), pp. 232–6.
2. H. M. Enzensberger, 'Armes Schweden', *Stern* no. 13, 24 Mar. 83.
3. H. M. Enzensberger, *Selected Poems* (Penguin, Harmondsworth, 1968), p. 23.
4. H. M. Enzensberger, *The Consciousness Industry* (The Seabury Press, New York, 1974), p. 78.
5. Ibid., p. 82.
6. H. M. Enzensberger, 'Schimpfend unter Palmen' in Weyrauch, *Ich lebe in der Bundesrepublik*, p. 25.
7. Ibid., p. 30.
8. Enzensberger, *Consciousness Industry*, p. 15.
9. H. M. Enzensberger, *Einzelheiten I* (Suhrkamp, Frankfurt am Main, 1964), p. 122.
10. Ibid., p. 204.
11. Ibid., p. 168.
12. H. M. Enzensberger, *Politik und Verbrechen* (Suhrkamp Verlag, Frankfurt am Main, 1964), p. 13.
13. H. M. Enzensberger, *Palaver* (Suhrkamp Verlag, Frankfurt am Main, 1974), p. 15f.
14. Ibid., p. 39.
15. H. M. Enzensberger, 'Was da im Bunker sitzt, das schlottert ja', *Der Spiegel*, no. 46, 14 Nov. 66, 78.
16. H. M. Enzensberger, 'Notstand' in *Tintenfisch 2* (Verlag Klaus Wagenbach, Berlin, 1969), p. 20.
17. This affair can be followed in H. M. Enzensberger, *Staatsgefährdende Umtriebe* (Voltaire Flugschrift 11, Berlin, 1968). It is interesting to note that Heinemann sensibly sought to play down the affair when questioned in parliament.
18. H. M. Enzensberger, 'Warum ich nicht in den USA bleibe', *Tagebuch*, März/April 1968, 12–13.
19. H, M. Enzensberger, *Das Verhör von Habana* (Suhrkamp, Frankfurt am Main, 1970), p. 24.
20. Enzensberger, *Consciousness Industry*, p. 41.
21. Ibid., p. 128.
22. H. M. Enzensberger, *Der Untergang der Titanic* (Suhrkamp, Frankfurt am

Main, 1981), p. 15.
23. A. Petersen, 'Nichts gegen die Arbeiterklasse', *TransAtlantik*, 2/1982, 77.
24. H. M. Enzensberger, *Politische Brosamen* (Suhrkamp, Frankfurt am Main, 1982), p. 197.
25. Ibid., p. 234.
26. Ibid., p. 224.
27. H. M. Enzensberger, 'Ein Bonner Memorandum', *Der Spiegel*, no. 48, 28 Nov. 83, 46.
28. Enzensberger, *Palaver*, p. 81f.
29. H. M. Enzensberger *et al.*, 'Katechismus zur deutschen Frage', *Kursbuch 4* (1966), 1–55.
30. Enzensberger, *Politische Brosamen*, p. 170.
31. H-T. Lehmann, 'Eisberg und Spiegelkunst' in Grimm, *Enzensberger*, p. 322.
32. H. M. Enzensberger, *Gedichte 1955–1970* (Suhrkamp, Frankfurt am Main, 1971), p. 81.
33. Enzensberger, *Politik und Verbrechen*, p. 398.
34. Enzensberger, *Palaver*, p. 40.
35. Enzensberger, *Gedichte*, p. 13.
36. Enzensberger, *Politische Brosamen*, p. 234.
37. Enzensberger, *Palaver*, pp. 169–232.
38. Ibid., p. 196.
39. R. Grimm, 'Bildnis Hans Magnus Enzensberger' in Grimm, *Enzensberger*, p. 176.
40. Quoted by U. Greiner, 'Der Risiko-Spieler', *Die Zeit*, no. 9, 25 Feb. 83.
41. H. M. Enzensberger, *Deutschland, Deutschland unter anderem* (Suhrkamp, Frankfurt am Main, 1967), p. 19.
42. Grimm, 'Bildnis' in Grimm, *Enzensberger*, p. 160.
43. Enzensberger, *Politik und Verbrechen*, p. 92f.
44. J. Habermas, 'Vom Ende der Politik' in Grimm, *Enzensberger*, p. 69.
45. H. M. Enzensberger, 'Der Triumph der *Bild-Zeitung* oder Die Katastrophe der Pressefreiheit', *Merkur*, vol. 37, no. 6 (1983), 658f.
46. Enzensberger, *Politische Brosamen*, p. 60.
47. H. M. Enzensberger, 'Traktat vom Trampeln', *Der Spiegel*, no. 25, 14 Jun. 76, 141.
48. 'Entrevista con Hans Magnus Enzensberger' in Grimm, *Enzensberger*, pp. 106–16.
49. Quoted by Greiner, 'Der Risiko-Spieler'.
50. H. M. Enzensberger, 'Das unheilvolle Porträt' in Grimm, *Enzensberger*, p. 22.
51. Enzensberger, *Gedichte*, p. 150.
52. Enzensberger, *Politische Brosamen*, pp. 7–30.
53. 'Gespräch mit Hans Magnus Enzensberger (1979)' in Grimm, *Enzensberger*, p. 125.
54. H. M. Enzensberger, 'Ungarische Wirrungen', *Die Zeit*, no. 19, 3 May 85.
55. Ibid.
56. Ibid.

MARTIN WALSER — THE VIEW FROM THE
LAKE

With his reproaches of his colleagues for preferring to remain at the periphery of society and his subsequent editing of the volume *Die Alternative oder Brauchen wir eine neue Regierung?*, Martin Walser can claim to have set in motion the development in the Federal Republic whereby intellectuals regularly express their political opinions, not least at election times. Without him there might not have been enough material for this book! This factor alone could justify his being chosen as one of the four authors to be studied in detail. It is, however, not just a question of gratitude. What is interesting in the case of Walser is that for all his involvement in politics, he does not conform to the stereotype of the committed author, either in his comments on politics or in his conception of the role of the writer. It is therefore proposed in this chapter to deal first with the development of his political views — the way they have changed is at a superficial level reminiscent of Enzensberger — before turning secondly to his view of the writer.

In an interview in 1985, Walser was prepared to speak somewhat disparagingly of *Die Alternative* as being characterised by the use of embarrassingly inadequate metaphors, something that reflected the contributors' lack of an appropriate style for political writing.[1] If this view is accepted, it must be said to apply to a large degree to his own contribution, which matches that of Grass for its literary style. Its title 'Das Fremdwort der Saison' (This season's foreign word), which refers to *Alternative*, is in itself a sign of this. Much of the essay consists of quasi-phonetic reproductions of political chit-chat, for example 'Soo wichtig ist Globke auch wieder nicht' (Globke isn't soo important after all),[2] whilst the choice offered by the election is one between 'puking up . . . and goose pimples'.[3] This latter metaphor almost sums up the volume's overall lack of enthusiasm for the Social Democrats; it is only the goose pimples engendered by the defence policy of Franz Josef Strauss that provide a reason for supporting them. Walser is also suspicious of any *rapprochement* between the two major parties, suggesting that if the SPD is not going to offer an alternative it would be more sensible to cancel the electoral contest and hold a special football

match between Hamburg SV and Barcelona. Revulsion at the sacri-
fice of principle for consensus was already visible in his first novel
Ehen in Philippsburg (The Gadarene Club) that appeared in 1957.
It has as one of its characters a Dr Alwin, whose intention is to
found a 'Christian-Social-Liberal Party of Germany'. The aim of
this grotesquely named hybrid is to abolish political conflict. Given
Walser's attitude, it is small wonder that the approach of the Grand
Coalition alienated him from the SPD.

Whatever stylistic problems there may have been in his contribution to *Die Alternative*, the early 1960s were the time when Walser
began to turn his attentions to politics. His interest in politics had
been aroused, he told the present writer, by evening discussions
that took place during meetings of the Gruppe 47. During this same
period he also began to concentrate on writing plays with a political
content. His essay of 1962 'Vom erwarteten Theater' (Expectations
of the theatre) directly states the ideal he was aiming for at that
time:

> A German author today has to operate exclusively with figures
> who either suppress the time from 33 to 45 or bring it into the
> open. Who suppress the German East-West situation or express
> it. Every sentence of a German author which is silent about this
> historical reality suppresses something.[4]

In the event, the plays inspired by this conception were not entirely
satisfactory theatrically. Only two of the three that were to form a
'German chronicle' were completed. To say this is not to question
the validity of the intention. Discussion of the Nazi past, frequently
a taboo subject in the 1950s, was overdue in the following decade.
Walser's contribution to this process was of considerable significance, as his essays of the time show.

That the official terminology that spoke vaguely of 'overcoming
the past' was totally unsatisfactory in the light of the enormity of
what had occurred, is the point Walser makes in the introduction to
the 1963 German edition of Elie Wiesel's account of his experiences
as a Jewish prisoner of the Nazis. He dismisses 'the whole socio-
hygienic vocabulary of a society only intent on quickly and cleanly
moving on to the next business' as grotesque.[5] His major essay on
the legacy of the past 'Unser Auschwitz' (Our Auschwitz), which
appeared two years later and is based on observations occasioned
by the trial of former Auschwitz guards, also seeks to examine the

responsibility of society as a whole in relation to Nazi atrocities. In the face of these horrors, German writers have tended to regard their perpetrators either as inhuman monsters or as mediocre non-entities, whose banality is akin to that of many other members of society. An example of the first conception is 'The Doctor' in Hochhuth's *Der Stellvertreter*, a Mengele-type figure who is more or less an embodiment of evil. Walser inclines much more to the second view. 'Unser Auschwitz' is an attack on the standpoint that views the Auschwitz murderers as diabolic. According to Walser, this only makes it easier for other members of society to evade any responsibility for what occurred by insisting on their own decency and hence their distance from any crimes. Walser, on the other hand, is not willing to dismiss the idea of collective guilt or at least the significance of the collective that is the German nation:

> If . . . nation and state are still at all sensible names for a politi-
> cal entity, that is to say for a collective that appears in history
> and in whose name justice is spoken or laws broken, then every-
> thing that occurs is conditioned by the collective, then the cause
> for everything is to be sought in this collective.[6]

What Walser also wants is for the events of Auschwitz to be seen not in isolation but in their wider historical context. Equally, their lasting significance is not just an individual moral problem, how-ever important it is to realise that the murderers were ordinary people 'like you and I'.[7] There are also political lessons to be learned; after Auschwitz it is inappropriate for a German state to pursue aggressive policies towards its eastern neighbours or to indulge in virulent anti-communism. 'Unser Auschwitz' still remains a challenging essay whose standpoint is more convincing than Grass's attempt to see the Auschwitz guards to a large extent as representatives of the recurring historical phenomenon of the great criminal.

Walser's estrangement from the SPD at the time of the Grand Coalition was referred to in Chapter 3. A major reason for his dis-content with the party at this time is to be found in his view of the economic system of the Federal Republic, which after Godesberg was increasingly endorsed by the Social Democrats. His first two novels *Ehen in Philippsburg* and *Halbzeit* (Half-Time) concentrate on the struggles of individuals forced to make their way in the com-petitive society of the 'economic miracle'. In both cases material success is accompanied by moral and physical decline. His third novel *Das Einhorn*, that appeared in 1966 shortly before the formation of the Grand Coalition, seems to prefigure events in its picture of a world where the privileged of both parties enjoy the luxuries of the affluent society to the extent that supposed differences of opinion become meaningless. In the terms used of the novel it is irrelevant whether first-class passengers belong to the CDU or the SPD; what is important is the fact of travelling first class.

Walser's moral objections to the principles of the social market economy were underlined in a speech to young people in Friedrichshafen in 1967. Here too he was concerned with the effects of the competitive struggle:

> Kant said that the best constitution is one which would force even a society of devils to do good to one another. It would be possible to say of the rules of the market economy, by which our lives must be guided, that they would even force a society of angels to do ill to each other.[8]

This statement might be felt to be exaggerated and also a little simplistic in its implied determinism. Nevertheless, it does stress Walser's isolation from a political consensus based on an economic system he views entirely negatively.

Walser's second major reason for moving to the left of the Social Democrats was his reaction to the Vietnam War. On this point it is important to remember that he was not solely concerned with the actions of the United States. Of equal, if not greater importance for him, was the acquiescence of the German government in American policy, the refusal to question anything the Americans did. As he put it in a speech entitled 'Amerikanischer als die Amerikaner' (More American than the Americans), the Federal Republic, despite its economic strength, had 'made itself into a satellite'.[9] The title of the speech is also significant. Walser had no wish to indulge in crude anti-American polemics; he was in fact keen to point out how much opposition to the Vietnam War there was within the United States. It was only that the German government chose to ignore such expressions of dissent.

The frequent references to Walser in Chapter 4 of this book imply that in the late 1960s and early 70s he was a representative *par excellence* of certain tendencies in the developing pattern of literary commitment in the Federal Republic at that time. It is of course true that he was a keen supporter of the newly-formed VS, advocated the ADF in the 1969 election, and shared the general malaise about the role and nature of literature. Whilst acknowledging this, it is also necessary to note the distinctive nature of the positions he adopted, as already seen in Chapter 4 in his reactions to Enzensberger's apparent demand for revolutionary change. In other areas too, such as in his reactions to the student movement and in his contribution to the debate on literature, his comments were individual.

In general terms, Walser sympathised with the students. He saw them as a prospective force for extending democracy into more areas of society. Hence, in a speech at the University of Cologne in 1969, he urged the students not just to strive for minor reforms but for the ideal of a democratic university.[10] He had had a similar message for the young people of Friedrichshafen in 1967; democracy should not end at the factory gate but be extended into the field of the economy as well. Where he was more sceptical was over the chances of a solidarisation between students and workers. This comes over in the 1970 play *Ein Kinderspiel* (Child's play), which centres around a generation conflict between a brother and sister and their well-to-do father. Another interesting point about this play is the rapid modification of its ending made by Walser. In the first version it is suggested that the forces of youth do have the means to triumph over the existing order. The second conclusion, one has to say more realistically, is far less clear cut.

One development that can be associated with the student movement certainly did not meet with Walser's approval, the attempts to expand experience or consciousness through the use of drugs or other stimulants. This search is the subject of the 1980 essay 'Über die neueste Stimmung im Westen' (On the latest mood in the West). It criticises particularly the cult of the individual seen to be becoming more and more prevalent in both the United States and Germany. Walser contrasts social concern with the desire to explore the self with the aid of drugs, coming to the conclusion that little of value can be gained from such exploration: 'It still has to be shown that someone who returns from a trip can bring back anything that helps him here. Unless it is memory. Or a longing for the next trip.'[11] He also compares the political commitment of Günter Grass favourably with the activities of those who only look inwards. His comments show that despite his criticism of the SPD at this time, he was still able to differentiate. Although he concedes that his approval for Grass does not mean endorsement of the SPD, he still says that it is better to have it in power than the CDU. He is certainly far removed from the student view of the time that regarded Grass as the main intellectual adversary.

Walser's doubts about the validity of traditional literary forms became visible in *Das Einhorn*, which specifically calls into question the Proustain thesis that something of value can be achieved through the recall of the past in the form of literature. In the five years after its appearance, his work was marked by a search for new more appropriate forms of expression. In view of this and his social and political concerns, it is not surprising that he should respond to the call made by Enzensberger for the encouragement of new kinds of writing from new types of writers. What is important to note here, as with *Die Alternative*, is that Walser involved himself in a practical manner.

It was he, as already noted, who provided the introduction to *Bottroper Protokolle*. In it he again complains of a lack of democracy in the Federal Republic, differentiating between the privileged, including himself, who have democratic freedoms, and the workers whose lives are documented in the book and who are not generally able to enjoy the right of free expression. In his view this is because all literature in the Federal Republic is 'bourgeois', although, in contrast to Enzensberger, he does not necessarily accept that it is affirmative. It was to remedy this state of affairs that in 1968 Walser introduced and had published the autobiography of a young murderess, whom he had visited in prison.[12] In the appendix he states his view that the woman herself rather than a professional biographer is the best person to show the background to the deed. The following year he had published the biography of a young man whose early years in an orphanage are seen as inevitably leading to a life of crime. This time, in his appendix, Walser is more specific about his reasons for becoming involved with the project. He claims that the book shows that such unhappy biographies are an inevitable part of the society of the Federal Republic: 'what happens to this home inmate and prisoner is and has system.'[13] Because of this, it would be wrong to speak of individual failure or chance, even less is it a case of the misuse of free will. Walser is also at pains to explain in literary terms why he became involved in such ventures. He states the view that all literature should be informative, and that it is only such books that can throw light on previously ignored social phenomena.

The late 1960s and early 1970s were, of course, the epoch of 'documentary literature', whose aim, as has been seen, was to use authentic material for a social or political purpose. That Walser was not just following the fashion of the day in promoting writing less based on traditional concepts of artistic creativity can be seen by his continuing involvement in such projects. In 1974 he was involved in a third autobiography, and introduced a volume from the *Werkkreis Literatur der Arbeitswelt* in 1980.[14] At the same time, his involvement with this kind of writing was never exclusive; in the late 1960s and early 70s his own writing was marked by literary experiment, particularly with 'stream of consciousness' techniques, as he sought to move beyond traditional literary forms.

Following the failure of the ADF in 1969, Walser began to look more favourably on the DKP, now operating as a separate party. He never became a member of the party, nor did he fully identify with it. Even less did he immerse himself in Marxist or Leninist theory, abstract theorising being generally anathema to him. This incidentally is an interesting difference from Enzensberger, despite the shared academic background. What Walser saw in the DKP was a potential force for greater democracy and a better society in the Federal Republic. Something of his hopes can be seen in his most overtly political novel *Die Gallistl'sche Krankheit* (The Gallistl syndrome) that appeared in 1972. Gallistl is initially an archetypal Walserian hero in that he suffers under the constraints of West German society and, because of his difficulties, cannot achieve his potential as a human being:

> I am Josef Georg Gallistl. I should like to be Josef Georg Gallistl. I work in order to earn the money which I need in order to be Josef Georg Gallistl. Up until now I have always only been he who works for Josef Georg Gallistl who does not yet exist.[15]

In other words, economic survival is only achieved at the expense of personality. Equally, Gallistl's relationships with 'friends' suffer from the feelings of competition engendered by society. Unusually for a Walser novel, where the main characters generally only manage to survive and little else, the final part of *Die Gallistl'sche Krankheit* does suggest a solution. That it is headed 'Es wird einmal' — 'once upon a time' projected into the future — emphasises its utopian dimension. What is projected is Gallistl sharing his life with a group of true friends who are also communists. This final section also shows something of Walser's attitude to the DKP. His hero too has no time for ideological debates; the quarrel between Moscow and Peking reminds him only of 'quasi-theological altercations'.[16] The ideal put forward is of individual party members expressing their experiences and aspirations in a personal manner. By listening to its members, the party can become their democratic voice.

This view is also expressed in an essay written in the same year as *Die Gallistl'sche Krankheit* for the Federal election and entitled 'Wahlgedanken' (Election thoughts). It originally appeared in *Die Zeit*, but only with an accompanying article from the paper's editor, Countess Dönhoff, who took issue with Walser's views on the DKP and the political climate of the Federal Republic. That this should have been thought necessary shows that even the most liberal newspaper in the Federal Republic will tend to put anything that smacks of communism into a kind of quarantine. To the paper's credit, however, it must be pointed out that following the two contributions, it printed several readers' letters which agreed with Walser's stance. What is more, *Der Spiegel* had refused the original manuscript.

To return to the essay itself, it is in no sense an electoral endorsement of the DKP. Walser states that it is not his intention to tell people which party to vote for, a practice he criticises; he even admits to not knowing himself whom he will eventually support. His major concern is with the form elections are increasingly taking, that is to say with the role played by advertising agencies and celebrities, including writers and intellectuals, in the campaigns. The danger of this is that the individual voter will not decide on the basis of personal experience or interest but be swayed by external forces. He asks: 'Does the majority recognise its interest or does it let itself be persuaded by the endless hoo-ha into taking the interest of a minority instead of its own?'[17] The implication of this is that his own actions in 1961 started a dangerous tradition.

Now, in 1972, his worry is that the agencies who seek to influence the citizen are essentially conservative, as they represent, even in the case of intellectuals, established forces that only stand to lose if fundamental changes in society occur. The hegemony they have achieved is seen by Walser as making all prospective reformers, including the Social Democrats, extremely timorous. He expresses this view by means of a highly original comparison: 'The SPD appears to me to resemble someone who constantly digs out the roses in his own garden because his neighbour shouts across that they are weeds.'[18] The flaw in Walser's argument is that he cannot prove that the experiences of the majority do lead them in a certain political direction, any more than the other side can claim a 'silent majority', when, for example, radical demonstrators take to the street. Nevertheless, in terms of Walser's political development, it is important to note his stress on the importance of personal experience.

Where does the DKP come in this? Walser's first point is that the party, although it is not banned as unconstitutional, is not allowed to be part of the mainstream political life of the Federal Republic. Its supporters are discriminated against, its advertising not accepted in large sections of the mass media. Walser's succinct description of the situation is: 'This party is indeed permitted but excluded.'[19] It is hard to disagree with this claim; nor has anything changed much in the intervening period.[20] Where Walser is on less firm ground is in basing his argument for giving the party a fair chance on the claim that its continuing existence proves its constitutionality, as it would otherwise be banned by the Constitutional Court. This ignores the possibility that it is tolerated for reasons of expediency by many who consider it to be unconstitutional. To refer the matter to the Constitutional Court would not improve relations with neighbouring countries! Equally, Walser's claim that the DKP's lack of success is due to its twilight existence cannot be proved. It may just be that its policies are unattractive.

Walser's second point consists of advice to the party. This is in line with what is implied in *Die Gallistl'sche Krankheit*. The DKP should concern itself primarily with the direct needs of citizens in the Federal Republic. He praises its efforts in community politics — it is true that in the 1970s it fulfilled functions now more associated with the Greens — but, at the same time, regrets that it has still not established itself as a truly national party. Whereas the fictional Gallistl is unhappy that being a communist seems to imply the requirement of always justifying the GDR, in 'Wahlgedanken' Walser is unhappy that the party over-identifies with the USSR and its allies to the extent that it never utters a word of criticism. Once more, Walser makes his point in an original manner:

Take a vote sometime in the DKP when there is a football match USSR v. FRG to see whether the members want the FRG or the

USSR to win. If it turns out that the majority is for the USSR, then that provides a clear example of what I mean by a lack of love of the homeland and such funny-sounding words.[21]

The implication behind this suggestion is not entirely fantastic. That cases of soccer-induced schizophrenia did occur when the two German national sides met in the 1974 World Cup was reported to the present writer by a reliable source at the University of Marburg, at that time a centre of support for the DKP.

More important than football is the question of affection for the homeland or *Heimat*, in German a term generally applied to a person's native region. Once again, it is possible here to point to a difference between Walser and Enzensberger. Since establishing himself as a writer, Walser has always preferred to live in his home area near Lake Constance, a choice that has only gradually become comprehensible to the followers of social and intellectual fashion as the cult of modernisation has given way to a championing of the small, the manageable and the ecologically defensible. The role in Walser's writing of the Lake Constance area, the setting for most of his recent fiction, is a subject in itself. His attachment to his native district is clearly deep; in wider political terms it leads to a distrust of any force that relies on theories and ideology at the expense of an awareness of local conditions.

It was in fact this attitude that was to lead Walser to become disillusioned with the DKP. This can be seen from an interview given in 1980 in which he takes issue with the questioner's suggestion that it is possible to assess developments in the Federal Republic from the vantage point of the GDR. For him it is impossible for there to be anyone 'who, outside a society, can better judge the developments in this society than the people who sustain, make and suffer it.'[22] Equally, he rejects the idea that there is a 'science, a theory with whose help one can judge something that is actually happening somewhere'.[23] In his view the DKP has remained an ideological party that has its base in another country, that is to say in the GDR.

Long before this interview, Walser's growing estrangement from the DKP and its backers in the GDR had been visible in his reaction to the resignation of Willy Brandt in 1974, brought on, it will be remembered, by the discovery of a GDR spy in his entourage. He composed an angry open letter to the East German leader Honecker suggesting that he should resign because of the damage done to a man who had been so active in the case of peace. In itself, the suggestion was totally unrealistic, as its author no doubt knew, but the political stance revealed in the letter shows how much at variance Walser now was with the view of the Federal Republic presented by the GDR and the DKP. Incidentally, it is interesting to note that from this point Walser ceased to be a regular contributor to *Kürbiskern*. In his open letter he again stresses that the Federal Republic must find its own road to socialism, and that involves the SPD which he is in no way willing to write off: 'The SPD is worth a bit of hope.'[24] This is not an opinion likely to find much favour with ideologues in either the DKP or the GDR government.

In conclusion, it has to be said of Walser's period of sympathy with the DKP that his hopes were misplaced in as far as that party has never shown the slightest sign of deviating from the highly orthodox positions of its East German partner. Nevertheless, it must be remembered that he stopped short of the total commitment shown by others in the 1970s, for examples Kroetz,[25] and that his ideal was something more akin to Western-oriented Euro-communism than Stalinist orthodoxy.

Since the mid-1970s Walser has been less prominent in writers' discussions of political and social issues. Instead, he has shown a remarkable productivity in fictional writing with first his novella *Ein fliehendes Pferd* (Runaway Horse) and then a series of novels establishing him as a major best-selling author. When he has commented on political issues his remarks have often been characterised by confidence in the Federal Republic. His contribution to *Briefe zur Verteidigung der Republik* praises the SPD government for standing firm against hysterical demands for the death penalty, or the curtailment of human rights in the face of terrorism. In 1981, in an essay written following a visit to France, besides expressing envy over that country's more felicitous historical development compared to Germany, he speaks favourably of his own country: 'At the moment, whoever works a lot in the Federal Republic is after all in my view supporting a state which is really worthy of support.'[26] He also criticises the behaviour of certain German intellectuals abroad who pander to their hosts' prejudices and repeat 'clichés about *Berufsverbot*, terrorism, capitalism'.[27]

Another feature of Walser's recent writing has been a growing concern with the German Question. In 1977 he spoke of his dissatisfaction with the present state of affairs, expressing his desire to be able to visit such German areas as Saxony and Thuringia, now parts of the GDR, in different circumstances from those prevailing at present. As for the whole German Question, he affirms: 'We must keep open the wound that is Germany.'[28] In 1979 he contributed an essay on the national question to Habermas's publication to mark the thirtieth anniversary of the Federal Republic. Here too there is a refusal to see the issue of German unity laid to rest. The title of his essay is particularly striking: 'Händedruck mit Gespenstern' (Shaking hands with ghosts); what is haunting him is the desire to move towards some kind of German unity: 'I have a need of historically overcoming the condition that is the Federal Republic.'[29] This kind of comment is somewhat surprising if remarks made in the 1960s in the essay 'Ein deutsches Mosaik' (A German Mosaic) are borne in mind. These appear at first sight to be a negation of German nationality. The essay begins with the bald statement: 'My grandfather did not yet know that he was a German'[30] and ends with the expression of the hope that the Germans might become more European. A closer reading of Walser's words, however, shows that he is not following the example of Enzensberger, who asked in 1964 in *Encounter* 'Am I a German?' and rejected the whole concept of nationhood.[31] The implication of Walser's comment is that his grandfather was a German even if he was unaware of it. The major development is that in the 1960s Walser was largely concerned with the German past, his more recent concern has been with a possible future for the German people as a whole.

Especially in the light of this apparent nationalism, the question that arises is whether Walser has moved to the right. The nationalism issue will be considered shortly; initially it must be stated that any proposition that a general endorsement of the Federal Republic as a state equals betrayal of left-wing principle would be entirely ludicrous. Moreover, the evidence of the recent novels, which concentrate on the unhappy consequences of subservience and competition, give the lie to such a suggestion. His major subject remains the threat to human dignity posed by the workings of a harsh economic system. What he says in his 1980 introduction to the collection of workers' writings applies to his own work as well: 'The infringement of human dignity through dependence is the course of pain from which and against which this writing arises.'[32] Walser's most sustained non-fictional writing in recent years has been a series of columns appearing once every three weeks in the Swiss weekly *Die Weltwoche*. These too confirm his continuing radicalism in economic matters, as the example of an article that appeared in June 1985 clearly shows. In it, he attacks the persistently held view that society still rewards merit, when, given the large number of unemployed, it is often a matter of pure chance who will be offered a particular job. His — in the words of the article's title — 'hopeless proposal' is that such matters should be left to a lottery system, which ultimately would be more honest. In reality, such a solution would be unthinkable, as it would rob the present state of affairs of its aura of legitimacy. This depends on those who fail in an application, in many cases 90 per cent of all candidates, accepting that they are themselves to blame. Walser's reaction could hardly be stronger: 'In the field of morality such falsifications are called a perversion.'[33] On the question of power too he retains the scepticism of many of his colleagues:

It is exercised in the interests of those who have it. There it's the party, here capital. Capital may appear . . . preferable to the party that enforces its doctrine of salvation, but here and there it's a question of the preservation of power. And the exercise of power cannot be legitimised, only transfigured.[34]

As on the question of ideology, this comment distinguishes Walser as a member of the generation scarred by the memory of National Socialism.

On the national question, Walser's renewed interest is part of a more widespread concern that has developed in recent years on the left of the political spectrum, reflected for instance in the publication in 1981 of a volume of texts entitled *Die Linke und die nationale Frage* (The Left and the national question) by Willy Brandt's son Peter, and Herbert Ammon.[35] The aim of this collection, which includes Walser's comments on Saxony and Thuringia, is to show that the Left has always been interested in the German Question. At the moment, it is the fear of a common German death in the event of nuclear war that has sharpened a sense of national identity among writers in both German states, as the Berlin discussions on questions relating to peace show. The question anxious outsiders are bound to ask is whether this might be a rebirth of German nationalism behind a leftist veneer. This is certainly not the way the writers themselves see it. The ideal of re-unification as propounded in the Adenauer era has not been adopted. It is universally accepted by writers that such a re-unification is impossible at the present moment. The major concerns have rather been the preservation of a single German culture and the denial of any right of self-determination to the German people. That these issues can also be important for a younger generation of writers with no personal memory of a single German state can be seen from a work like Peter Schneider's *Der Mauerspringer* (The Wall-leaper), in which the hero, who appears to be semi-autobiographical, describes and reflects on contacts with colleagues in the GDR. His conclusion is that the potential common factor between the two German states is the language, and that this factor can only be developed by a refusal 'to ape the Church Latin of East and West'.[36] This is some way away from plans for world domination. A point frequently made by Grass is also worthy of note: that the national question is too significant to be left to the Right.

Nevertheless, there are difficulties in any discussion of the national question. This can be seen in remarks made recently by Walser. Commenting on the May 1985 celebrations in *Die Weltwoche*, he speaks of his own inability to celebrate the division of his country, theoretically a reasonable point of view but one which ignores that 1945 was more than the beginning of the division of Germany. Equally, in the same article, his explanation of the rise of Nazism and the origins of its racial excesses is much too limited, coming very close to the nationalistic excuse that it was the victorious Allies of the Great War who were responsible for the success of National Socialism because of the harsh terms imposed at the Treaty of Versailles:

> It was not anti-Enlightenment Teutonic games but six million unemployed: reparations which were pillage. Misery and radicalisation were the consequence. German racism would never have attained the level of mania without the inferiority to which the victors condemned Germany.[37]

This is also an inadequate explanation of the racial aspect of National Socialism. For all the justified scepticism towards seeing history solely in terms of abstract 'national character', these comments are an over-simplification in that they reduce the complex issues of racism and anti-semitism to a simple question of economics. To criticise Walser in this way is not to accuse him of rabid nationalism. This same article retains an awareness of the horror of Auschwitz, whilst the gulf between him and the traditional proponents of re-unification is clear from comments made in

1977: 'who speaks of re-unification cements division.'[38] Clearly, like his colleagues, Walser is not propounding aggressive nationalism. Those who object to this degree of national awareness must explain why universal rights should not apply to the Germans.

To understand Walser as a political writer and specifically the developments and changes described above, it is necessary to look in some detail at his conception of the writer, since in his case it is impossible to talk of an element of experimentation with a series of political positions in the manner of Enzensberger. A most important initial point is that he is frequently critical of intellectuals, as has already been seen in the references to the essay 'Skizze zu einem Vorwurf'. Before this, in the literary magazine *Akzente* he had published a scathing portrait of would-be intellectuals whose pretentions are the result of their failings in normal areas of life. They number among their ranks, for instance, 'husbands whose wives turn round more and more frequently to look at well-made swimming instructors'.[39] In the trilogy of novels centred around the salesman turned writer Anselm Kristlein, that began with *Halbzeit*, there is a critical portrayal of the radical intellectual in the figure of Kristlein's friend Edmund Gabriel. In the final novel *Der Sturz* (The fall), he commits suicide with the aid of a self-designed machine whose conception reflects his sexual inadequacies. The general implication is that the intellectual is largely impotent in social terms.

This same view is expressed in the 1967 essay 'Engagement als Pflichtfach für Schriftsteller' (Commitment as a compulsory subject for writers), which was originally a radio talk. In it he dismisses the typical activities of committed writers, most especially the giving of support to political parties at elections, as largely futile:

> Solely the climate becomes more tolerable; the Victorian aspect of the Federal Republic becomes visible, the comic element of its claim to power. In this way a feeling of activity arises. Because in reality nothing changes one may say, a game develops. Charming, entertaining. An appearance of movement within actual lethargy.[40]

The word 'activity' (*Betrieb*) is interesting. The term *Literaturbetrieb* has become established in the Federal Republic to refer to certain peripheral activities of literary life; it is generally used to refer to methods by which writers and their works are promoted. What Walser is saying therefore is that 'literary commitment' has a promotional and therefore a commercial aspect. This view is also reflected in the novel *Das Einhorn*, in which Anselm Kristlein travels around the Federal Republic playing the part of the radical committed writer at public meetings and in this way providing entertainment for the citizenry.

There are more recent examples of Walser expressing similarly sceptical views about the role of intellectuals, including himself: 'We opinion-theologians transfigure the exercise of power, we create the aura of justice, decency, dignity, constitution, democracy, pluralism, freedom of opinion. Without us power would be unadorned and reprehensible.'[41] Before these somewhat remarkable, not to say contradictory statements by someone who, as has been seen, has appeared to be an archetypal committed writer for much of his career, are considered further, it is intended to contrast them with a very different viewpoint that suggests that intellectuals exercise not just influence but also considerable power.

Helmut Schelsky's *Die Arbeit tun die anderen* has already been referred to in Chapter 8, on Heinrich Böll. Its sub-title 'Klassenkampf und Priesterherrschaft der Intellektuellen' (Class warfare and theocracy of the intellectuals) is in itself pretty revealing of its author's attitude. Schelsky's thesis is that intellectuals as a social class, despite their peripheral position in society in some respects, wield power akin to that of the priesthood in the Middle Ages. He leaves no doubt that this power is pernicious, not least because intellectuals have no grasp of the realities of life. The sum of Schelsky's position is the claim, in italics in the original German: 'The meaning producers [i.e. intellectuals — KSP] represent the unproductive class, that is to say the class that exploits the producers of goods.'[42] Despite his claim to be analysing sociological developments, it is immediately clear on reading Schelsky that his attacks are directed exclusively at left-wing intellectuals. In other words, they are part of the reaction to the student movement that gathered pace in the mid-1970s. This can be seen from a passage like the following:

> Progress, what is 'progressive' is no longer allowed to be a question of individual or social interests arising from personal experience of life but is claimed for intellectual ideas of the future promising salvation that are interpreted by those who

transmit the new promises of salvation.[43]

Schelsky is perfectly free to attack left-wing models of progress; one only wonders how they manage to be so powerful whilst his own book, one assumes, despite its large circulation, had no impact at all. The simple question that must be asked is whether intellectuals have power, as Schelsky claims, or whether their influence is negligible, as Walser seems to be saying and many of his colleagues seemed to be saying at the time of the foundation of the VS. As has been stressed throughout this book, there is no clear answer to this question. Nevertheless, it has to be faced, even if the only conclusion that can be reached is that the truth lies between the two extremes, however uninspiring such a conclusion may be. If, as cannot be disputed, Hochhuth was influential in bringing about the downfall of a prominent politician, then it would seem absurd to claim that writers have never had any influence on other occasions. At the very least, the large circulations achieved by committed writers suggest that they, in the term used by the political scientist Richard Löwenthal, 'articulate' opinion, that is to say contribute to the dissemination and hence the potential influence of a particular opinion.[44] The social significance of writers was underlined at the time of Böll's death. That it was the front-page headline in the *Frankfurter Allgemeine Zeitung* suggests that they occupy more than a peripheral role. On the other hand, a decade after Schelsky's attacks and following the return of a conservative government, it must be clear that particularly left-wing intellectuals do not enjoy the kind of power Schelsky wishes to suggest they have. Enzensberger's view of the early 1960s that the media or rather the 'consciousness industry' offer limited opportunities for intellectuals to exert influence seems much nearer the mark.

To return specifically to Walser, it has to be admitted that he takes an excessively negative view of the role and influence of writers, incidentally also a very different one from Böll, who insists on the subversive influence of literature.[45] One can sympathise with Walser in that not everything that finds expression as 'committed writing' is of value, and may well reflect the need for publicity among writers, editors and others involved in the media. This does not alter the point, however, that his own stance is contradictory, as he was willing to admit when talking to the present writer. On the one hand, he denigrates commitment, but still indulges in activities that normally come under the heading of committed writing. His difficulties are even visible in the polemic 'Engagement als Pflichtfach für Schriftsteller', in which, following the attacks on commitment, he seeks to defend his own involvement in the campaign against the Vietnam War, saying that it is something that developed despite himself.

To understand how Walser's predicament arises, it is necessary to consider another aspect of his view of the writer. For Walser, a writer is essentially someone who experiences a feeling of pain in the widest sense of the word and then reacts to this pain by writing. The comparison made in the 1974 essay 'Wer ist ein Schriftsteller?' (Who is a writer?) underlines the point: 'If one has a painful spot in the mouth, one cannot prevent the tongue from seeking it out, probing it.'[46] Writing is hence a highly personal affair that is almost involuntary. Such a view does not allow for either the academic propagation of abstract theory or for a required fulfilment of the role of committed writer, so to speak, on demand. The only form of commitment Walser can respect, therefore, is one into which a writer is more or less forced; in his essay on commitment he speaks of himself experiencing such a feeling in respect of the Vietnam War despite all his misgivings: 'On the other hand, I do not feel myself free in the face of such a war.'[47] Walser echoed this view in his 1985 interview with the present writer. He said that he in no sense regretted his activities in the 1960s, and that he would react in a similar way again if he felt it to be necessary, but that he still rejected any outside demand on him for commitment. His comment in a 1985 *Weltwoche* article is a somewhat light-hearted expression of this standpoint: 'I admit that I am pleased when I find something in an appeal that is being circulated for signatures which makes it impossible for me to sign.'[48] Such an attitude could be open to the charge of arrogance, but so is any action that runs counter to the expectations of the group. A more serious objection to Walser's criticisms of commitment is that they imply unprovable assertions about less than honest motives among writers commenting on social and political questions. They too might feel as constrained to comment as he does.

Another reason for Walser's objecting to certain forms of commitment can be found in the importance he attaches to literary style. In this respect he is a pefectionist, and his skill as a literary artist has generally not been in doubt over recent years. This leads to a dislike of certain forms of expression he associates with commitment. These are what he sees as bald statements of a point of view in a style he described in his interview with the present writer as 'Meinungsfrequenz' (opinion frequency). For him it is an unrealistic way of writing that expresses more wishful thinking than the result of a productive struggle with language. Again, what he finds lacking is a personal element, as can once more be illustrated by comments made to the present writer. He spoke about a projected essay on Goethe where his aim was not to express yet another opinion on Goethe but to try to stress the significance of Goethe for him personally. Another example of this standpoint can be seen in his attitude to literary criticism. He has consistently attacked criticism that is marked by an all-knowing stance, and critics who act, in the term used in an essay on the subject, like 'popes'. This essay 'Über Päpste' presents Walser's ideal critic as someone who is consciously a writer as much as the author of the work being discussed is. He says of such ideal critics: 'They test their own experiences with reference to examples of literature and then they inform about how this literature appears to them compared with their own experiences.'[49] Because of this approach, the style of such criticism will be tentative rather than dogmatic. The same criteria apply to political writing. Where the aim is to express something personal, the bold style of the manifesto is not called for.

Walser's conception of the task of the writer helps to explain his attitude to political writing and his own work in that area. In many respects his approach is much closer to that of Böll than that of his fellow academic Enzensberger, particularly in his rejection of any suggestion that he should write on the basis of some kind of theory. One objection to Walser's scruples and uncertainties might be that he can never have much effect, and that the robustness of, for example, Grass is required if writers are to influence opinion. His own methods might even be said to explain why he is so sceptical about writers' influence. On the other hand, the sensitivity he displays is a useful antidote to any possible tendency to simplify among committed writers. His aim is a more differentiated view. The appeal previously referred to that he refused to sign had to do with Nicaragua. He was unwilling to indulge in blanket criticism of the United States because there are many Americans who reject their government's policy.

The ideal Walser postulates is that of the realistic essay which reflects the author's individual personality. That he himself achieves this aim can be seen by reference to certain — some might say eccentric — passages in his essays. It is different, to say the least, that the 1972 essay 'Wahlgedanken' should start with a reference to something his wife dreamed, whilst 'Händedruck mit Gespenstern' is remarkably frank where Walser admits that his feelings on the national question may not be shared by others. It would also be wrong to think that this personal approach must inevitably be superficial. An essay like 'Unser Auscnwitz' combines sensitivity and intellectual insight to a remarkable degree. Walser's way of contributing to political debate is as valid and worthy of respect as any other, unless adherence to a specific theory or dogma is to be deemed an essential component of political commitment.

Notes

1. I was able to speak to Walser at his home in August 1985.
2. M. Walser, 'Das Fremdwort der Saison' in Walser, *Die Alternative*, p. 124.
3. Ibid., p. 126.
4. M. Walser, *Erfahrungen und Leseerfahrungen* (Suhrkamp, Frankfurt am Main, 1965), p. 64.
5. M. Walser, 'Vorwort' in E. Wiesel, *Die Nacht zu begraben, Elischa* (Bechtle Verlag, München und Esslingen, 1963), p. 7.
6. M. Walser, *Heimatkunde* (Suhrkamp, Frankfurt am Main, 1968), p. 20f.
7. Ibid., p. 11.
8. Ibid., p. 65.
9. Ibid., p. 100.
10. M. Walser, 'Rede an eine Mehrheit', *Kürbiskern*, 2/1969, 335–9.
11. M. Walser, *Wie und wovon handelt Literatur* (Suhrkamp, Frankfurt am Main, 1973), p. 23.
12. U. Trauberg, *Vorleben* (Suhrkamp, Frankfurt am Main, 1968).
13. M. Walser, 'Nachwort' in W. Werner, *Vom Waisenhaus ins Zuchthaus* (Suhrkamp, Frankfurt am Main, 1969), p. 264.
14. The third autobiography is: H. Kessler, *Der Schock* (List, München, 1974). The collection is: M. Walser (ed.), *Die Würde am Werktag* (Fischer, Frankfurt am Main, 1980).
15. M. Walser, *Die Gallistlische Krankheit* (Suhrkamp, Frankfurt am Main, 1972), p. 22f.
16. Ibid., p. 101.
17. Walser, *Wie und wovon handelt Literatur*, p. 102.
18. Ibid., p. 109f.
19. Ibid., p. 103.
20. It is of course another question whether the DKP should be discriminated against because it represents a potential threat to democracy. It is not proposed to repeat the various arguments here.
21. Walser, *Wie und wovon handelt Literatur*, p. 112.
22. 'Wie tief sitzt der Tick gegen die Bank zu spielen?'. Interview with Martin Walser in K. Siblewski (ed.), *Martin Walser* (Suhrkamp, Frankfurt am Main, 1981), p. 48.
23. Ibid., p. 48.

24. M. Walser, 'Offener Brief an den Ersten Sekretär des ZK der SED Honecker' in *Vaterland, Muttersprache*, p. 289.

25. In an interview with Heinz Ludwig Arnold, for instance, Kroetz spoke of his inability to conceive that the DKP could evolve a literature programme without his giving it his blessing. He goes on to say that he believes the SED to be equally democratic. (H. L. Arnold, *Als Schriftsteller leben* (Rowohlt, Reinbek bei Hamburg, 1979), p. 61.)

26. M. Walser, 'Deutsche Gedanken über französisches Glück', *Neue Rundschau*, vol. 93, no. 1 (1981), 52.

27. Ibid., p. 55.

28. M. Walser, *Wer ist ein Schriftsteller?* (Suhrkamp, Frankfurt am Main, 1979), p. 101.

29. M. Walser, 'Händedruck mit Gespenstern' in Habermas, *Geistige Situation*, vol. 1, p. 50.

30. Walser, *Erfahrungen und Leseerfahrungen*, p. 7.

31. H. M. Enzensberger, 'Am I a German?', *Encounter*, vol. XXII, no. 4 (1964), 16–18.

32. Walser, *Die Würde am Werktag*, p. 7.

33. M. Walser, 'Hoffnungsloser Vorschlag', *Die Weltwoche*, no. 26, 27 Jun. 85.

34. M. Walser, 'In den April geschickt', *Die Weltwoche*, no. 14, 14 Apr. 85.

35. P. Brandt, H. Ammon, *Die Linke und die nationale Frage* (Rowohlt, Reinbek bei Hamburg, 1981).

36. P. Schneider, *Der Mauerspringer* (Luchterhand, Darmstadt und Neuwied, 1984), p. 109.

37. M. Walser, 'Tartuffe weiss, wer er ist', *Die Weltwoche*, no. 5, 31 Jan. 85.

38. Walser, *Wer ist ein Schriftsteller?*, p. 99.

39. M. Walser, 'Jener Intellektuelle', *Akzente*, vol 3, no. 2 (1965), 135.

40. Walser, *Heimatkunde*, p. 104.

41. M. Walser, 'Beweise aus dem Revier', *Die Weltwoche*, no. 6, 9 Feb. 84.

42. Schelsky, *Die Arbeit tun die anderen*, p. 342.

43. Ibid., p. 108.

44. R. Löwenthal, 'Die Intellektuellen zwischen Gesellschaftswandel und Kulturkrise' in H. Baier (ed.), *Freiheit und Sachzwang. Beiträge zu Ehren Helmut Schelskys* (Westdeutscher Verlag, Opladen, 1977), pp. 102–14.

45. Böll, *Vermintes Gelände*, pp. 9–15.

46. Walser, *Wer ist ein Schriftsteller?*, p. 38.

47. Walser, *Heimatkunde*, p. 114.

48. M. Walser, 'Amerikanisches Allerlei', *Die Weltwoche*, no. 17, 25 Apr. 85.

49. Walser, *Wer ist ein Schriftsteller?*, p. 47.

**PART THREE:
CONCLUSION**

CONCLUSION: FORTY YEARS ON

Besides allowing President Reagan and Chancellor Kohl the opportunity of occupying what in this case might literally be called the
centre of the political stage, the fortieth anniversary of the end of
the war on 8 May 1985 also provides an appropriate point of
conclusion to this study of writers and politics in Germany. Once
the — in historical terms generally unmemorable — figure of forty
had been given a special significance, it was inevitable that the anniversary would attract the interest of leading representatives of both
Geist and *Macht* in the Federal Republic. It therefore provides a
suitable point of focus in drawing conclusions about the relationships between the two spheres. Before the implications of this one
day are examined, it is proposed to look more generally at the
topic, particularly with regard to the current incumbents of power,
the Christian Democrats. Once again, the task has been aided by a
specific event, the first full-scale debate on cultural matters in the
history of the Federal Parliament that took place in late 1984.

A series of incidents referred to in the course of this book, most
noticeably the use of the epithet 'pincher' by Ludwig Erhard, has
no doubt given the impression that the relationship between the
Christian Democrats and the majority of intellectuals has been
generally disastrous. To say nothing more though would be something of a simplification. There have been a number of attempts by
CDU politicians, if not by their Bavarian partners, to improve
relations with writers, not least by the current chancellor Helmut
Kohl, in a 1972 essay which propounded the ideal of a productive
conflict between the two groups. Such a proposition has much to
recommend it and is certainly an advance on total animosity. At the
same time, some of the views expressed by Kohl are problematical.
He was critical of what he perceived as the harmony between intellectuals and the Brandt government of the time, even seeing it as
part of a dangerous German tradition: 'We meet here a new version
of the Romantic intellectual which has tradition in German
history.'[1] The subsequent alienation of many intellectuals from the
SPD — incidentally also seen as part of an unhappy German
tradition by some close to the party, Kurt Sontheimer, for instance
— proved these fears to be unjustified, even if it is accepted that

229

Kohl's proposition about the undesirability of harmonious relationships is correct. In fact, one wonders whether it was simply a rationalisation of feelings best described as sour grapes. The answer to Kohl (and Sontheimer) is surely that intellectuals should enjoy the right of approbation as well as of criticism.

Half a decade after Kohl's more conciliatory intervention, relationships were again very bad. Most writers refused to take part in a congress on literature organised by the CDU in 1977 at the height of the anti-terrorism campaign, blaming the party for having created an atmosphere of hysteria in the country. The effects of the candidature of Strauss in 1980 have already been discussed. The placing of 'culture' on the parliamentary agenda in 1984 affords the observer the chance of seeing whether the advent of a CDU government under the less abrasive Kohl has restored a healthier relationship or, given the nature of the event, what the politicians might be doing to create such a relationship.

Unfortunately, it is not possible to report an entirely satisfactory occasion. Like so many debates in the world's parliaments, this one too attracted a sparse attendance. Moreover, the divide between some politicians and the majority of intellectuals was again clearly visible. The main speaker for the CDU was the right-winger Alfred Dregger, who chose to be particularly controversial. Although he conceded that the pincher insult had been regrettable and that writers had the right to express political opinions, he resurrected the old conflict between the CDU and the Gruppe 47 over whether the latter had unfairly monopolised the world of literature and he stressed in an exceptionally direct way the fallibility of intellectuals in political matters. This point was illustrated by a reference to the final years of the Weimar Republic: 'At the 1932 *Reichstag* elections the National Socialists were supported by a large list of writers and artists, among them Nobel Prize winners.'[2] Hence, it followed that writers might be equally wrong today about such issues as peace. Fortunately, the main speaker for the SPD, Freimut Duve, a man with a background in publishing, was able to point out how many writers had suffered at the hands of the Nazis. In fact, Dregger's comparison is not only a smear but also a strange piece of logic. If all professional groups were to be regarded as disqualified because of their predecessors' succumbing to the Nazis, there would be little place for politicians.

That the CDU is on other occasions less than totally critical of those on the undemocratic Right during the Weimar period was apparent in the reaction to the ninetieth birthday of Ernst Jünger in March 1985. Although not a Nazi, Jünger showed an aristocratic contempt for democracy and glorified war in the period in question. To commemorate his birthday he was not only visited by Chancellor Kohl but was also given an official honour, the ceremony being performed by the CDU Prime Minister of Baden-Württemberg, Lothar Späth, who saw in Jünger 'the most recent German author of European rank'.[3] To name but two, Grass and Böll would have had the right to feel aggrieved. As for Jünger himself, his remarks revealed not only his continuing mental vigour but also his conservative philosophy which sees life in terms of recurring cycles of, in this case, somewhat protracted duration:

> We live in times in which, as at the end of every millenium, fear dominates. This time it presents itself to us, in accordance with the spirit of the age, as a large-scale technical catastrophe. We have to accept the atomic era. In any case, if I may be allowed to quote myself, hope helps us more than fear.[4]

To return to Späth and Dregger: it is clear from their remarks how much parts of the CDU remain out of sympathy with the mainstream of writers in the Federal Republic. Nevertheless, it should not be concluded from this that the present government of the Federal Republic, even if it had the power, would wish to impose some kind of authoritarian cultural pattern on the country. That the era of crude animosity characterised by the pincher insult seems at an end is something to be grateful for.[5]

A further aspect of Dregger's comments on politics and culture that appeared dubious to a number of commentators was his insistence on their being largely separate worlds. The anniversary of 8 May 1985 surely shows through its significance for both writers and politicians how justified such scepticism was. This was an occasion with a moral and a political dimension of concern to representatives of both *Geist* and *Macht*. How writers and intellectuals faced what *Die Zeit* called the 'awkward anniversary' will be illustrated by the reactions of Kogon, Grass and Böll, whilst the most significant contribution to the debate by a politician came from the Christian Democrat Federal President Richard von Weizsäcker, who succeeded Karl Carstens in 1984.

The major issue that was raised in connection with the

anniversary was whether it should be remembered as a day of liberation or one of capitulation, that is to say of national tragedy for the German people. For Böll, it was entirely one of liberation. In a long essay in *Die Zeit* under the rubric of the awkward anniversary written in the form of a letter to his sons, he describes with all his novelist's skill his experiences in the final days of the war. Besides once more showing how the experience of war conditioned his whole thinking — the subsequent distrust of all those wielding power and authority — the essay contains a most clear statement of his position. It is marked in the typical manner of Böll by a distinction between those with the correct attitude and those with a false one: 'You will always be able to know Germans by whether they describe the 8 May as a day of defeat or of liberation. *We* waited for our 'enemies' as our liberators.'[6] In a BBC radio discussion with the American writer Kurt Vonnegut later in the same year, he maintained exactly the same position.[7] Eugen Kogon's contribution to the same series in *Die Zeit* stresses the link between defeat and liberation, the one being the precondition of the other. His major point is that just remembering the past is not sufficient; it is more important that the correct lessons are learned from the defeat of Hitler's barbaric system, namely that politics should be based on morality and that war does not provide a suitable solution to political problems.[8] Despite all the setbacks from rearmament to Pershing missiles, the spirit of the early years of the *Frankfurter Hefte* lives on!

Grass's comments on the fortieth anniversary of the end of the war were made in his capacity as President of the Berlin Academy of Arts. He too speaks of liberation, but describes the freedom gained as 'donated' to the Germans since they were unable to rid themselves of tyranny through their own efforts. His speech concentrates first on his own experiences in the Third Reich before a survey of the post-war development of Germany is attempted. Like so many intellectuals at the time, he expresses dismay about the early years of the Federal Republic, stressing particularly the failure to confront the past.[9] Not surprisingly, there is recognition of the achievements of the Brandt government, but the general tone is not one of contentment. Culturally, he is unhappy that the literature written by the exiles from National Socialism has not had the influence that might have been hoped for. Politically, like Kogon, he regrets that the dangers of war and armaments have not been recognised. He finds it particularly sad that the West Germans, in their relative freedom, did not reject rearmament at the outset. He concludes with a vision of the Germans in both parts of the country as people 'who wish to spread fear no more and are therefore prepared to lay down their arms before all other peoples.'[10] Both the expression of regret about the past and this vision of the future, despite its rhetorical appeal, appear unrealistic in that they ignore the realities of world power-politics, in which the Germans have only limited influence. This is not to decry the desire for peace, which also found expression in an appeal by the VS to mark the anniversary.

The major domestic political commemoration of the end of the war was a special session of the Federal Parliament held on 8 May 1985. The main speaker was the Federal President von Weizsäcker. He made his position absolutely clear: 'The 8 May was a day of liberation. It freed us all from the violent rule of National Socialism and its contempt for humanity.'[11] Unfortunately, not all members of parliament were willing to hear this message, with some right-wing Christian Democrats preferring to boycott the occasion, whilst Alfred Dregger marked the anniversary by writing a letter to American politicians in which he stated his continuing pride in having fought communism right to the end of the war. Despite such aberrations, 8 May 1985 was not an occasion on which there was a general split between the views of writers and politicians, nor even between writers and all Christian Democrats. That those who spoke of liberation won the argument seems clear from the echo attained by Weizsäcker's speech, for which there was a demand of 650,000 copies.

One occasion when the vast majority of writers held the more tenable position against an incorrigible minority of politicians does not in itself provide sufficient grounds for proposing the thesis that in their conflicts with representatives of the world of politics, writers have invariably had right on their side. Besides Schelsky, there have been other commentators who have attacked the kind of influence wielded by writers and intellectuals in the Federal Republic, most notably over the last decade or so Professor Kurt Sontheimer, a founder-member, it will be remembered, of the Sozialdemokratische Wählerinitiative. His first major expression of his growing alienation from certain intellectual positions was his 1976 book *Das Elend unserer Intellektuellen* (Our sorry intellectuals). As in the case of Schelsky, this book too must be seen as a reaction against some of the intellectual currents prevalent at the time of the student movement. Sontheimer's major point is that political consensus in the Federal Republic is being undermined by leftist theory, and that the impact of this theory is to make those in responsible positions doubt the value of what they are doing. His other major criticism is that the theory produced by the Left is totally esoteric and couched in a language that the majority cannot understand. The immediate problem for the reader is how incomprehensible theory can have such an effect, a difficulty Sontheimer seeks to overcome as follows:

> The discredit or, to put it mildly, the variations of understanding, into which once relatively undisputed central values and concepts of the political consensus of the Federal Republic have fallen, proves quite clearly our thesis that even the non-dominating, in political terms insignificant seeming radical sector of political consciousness can have effects on the ruling sector which weaken it and plunge it into difficulties of self-justification.[12]

Clearly, Sontheimer does not go as far as Schelsky in his strictures, but he is surely over-estimating the influence of theory, especially that of largely peripheral and frequently foolish outpourings, whose existence at the time of the student movement cannot be denied. In a conversation with the present writer in 1984, Sontheimer again spoke of writers' lack of understanding of politics, their lack of tolerance and their tendency to claim a monopoly of morality. At the same time, he did acknowledge their right of political commitment and the duty of politicians to take their interventions seriously. Nevertheless, the metaphor used in *Das Elend unserer Intellektuellen* that intellectuals over the decade since the beginnings of student unrest have offered the population stones rather than bread, amounts to a view that they have failed to fulfil their social function.

Martin and Sylvia Greiffenhagen in their book on the political culture of the Federal Republic see Sontheimer's change of position in the 1970s as an example of an unhappy German tradition — the tendency to be frightened of the consequences of previously held radical views and to lapse into reaction.[13] It might also be possible to rejoin in a similar metaphorical manner that man does not live by bread alone. That though would be to evade the issue: whether writers are as much if not more to blame for any continuing alienation between them and the world of politics. Quite simply, do writers understand anything at all about the nature of politics? As the examples of Ende, Enzensberger and Walser, to name but three, show, there does often seem to exist among them a total suspicion of the whole fundamental political concept of power. J. P. Stern's point in his obituary of Böll that 'he never saw . . . the merits (as opposed to the unjust use) of power' might well be applied to many of his colleagues.[14] In reply to this, it should be pointed out that it is a major task of intellectuals to be aware, in the manner of Lord Acton, of the corrupting influence of power. Justice and morality should not be subservient to power in politics. Moreover, German intellectuals' distrust of power has to be seen in its historial context: the total misuse of power in the Third Reich. It is also important to remember that a degree of conflict between writers and politicians is to be expected and is to be viewed as positive, as Helmut Kohl realised in 1972. Nevertheless, where there appears to be no understanding or appreciation of the nature of politics, that is to say of the inevitability of power, however limited, criticism of individual authors is in order.

Another point on which writers have been criticised — and it was the one area in which in his interview with the present writer Walter Jens said he was prepared to accept criticism — is an apparent lack of identification with the Federal Republic as a state. What is certainly true is that the governmental world of Bonn has not attracted a great deal of attention from writers. Böll's posthumous *Frauen vor Flausslandschaft* is the first novel since those of Koeppen and Weisenborn in the 1950s to be set in the world of Bonn politics. One major critic, however, Reinhard Baumgart, still does not regard it as a political novel at all.[15] The same point has frequently been made about Koeppen's *Das Treibhaus*, which, it is true, often appears to be a repudiation of political activity. Particularly the use of imagery taken from nature suggests a view of human life as cyclical and unchanging, in other words incapable of improvement through politics. This is less the case with *Auf Sand gebaut* in that, despite all its criticisms of the world of Bonn, it does postulate the possibility of effective political action within the institutions of the Federal Republic.

There are a number of possible explanations of this neglect of the world of government. Baumgart in the review mentioned above suggests that the bizarre events that take place in Bonn make emulation by writers impossible. It is an interesting point, but comparable phenomena do not seem to deter writers in other countries. A possibly more plausible reason can be deduced from the comments by Martin and Sylvia Greiffenhagen on the aridity of life in Bonn, where politics dominates to the exclusion of everything else: 'Bonn society is not a cross-section of the West German elite. Whoever is invited is politically useful. There is no place for charm, *esprit* or witty conviviality. The female element is missing to a lamentable degree.'[16] It is clearly no place for artists. Only in most recent years has thought been given into making it into a genuine capital rather than a stopgap for Berlin. Nevertheless, the time still seems some way off before writers will flock to Bonn for its cultural ambience, and through greater proximity concern themselves more immediately with its political life.

One other major reason for possible neglect of the Federal Republic is the national question, as referred to in Chapter 10 on Walser. As long as many writers think in terms of Germany as a whole, there will be less than total emotional identification with the Federal Republic. Dieter Wellershoff expresses the point neatly:

And when I speak of the other people who live with me in this state, I call them the Federal citizens. That sounds to me as if I were speaking of the members of a club, to which I belong without emotion and deeper involvement. I approve of the rules of the club, I pay my contribution.[17]

This is obviously anything but a total rejection of the Federal Republic. It is something of a tightrope walk but understandable in the strange circumstances in which the German nation finds itself. Moreover, an interest in the national question does not preclude support for the Federal Republic and its democratic system, as the example of Grass, most especially in *Kopfgeburten*, shows.

One writer to become directly involved with the politics of the Federal Republic was the first president of the VS Dieter Lattmann, who served as a Social Democrat member of parliament in Bonn for two legislative periods from 1972 to 1980. He has published two collections about his experiences in politics, partly in essay form and partly more in diary form. *Die Einsamkeit des Politikers* (The loneliness of the politician) appeared in 1977, and *Die lieblose Republik* (The cold republic) in 1981 after he had left parliament. Although Lattmann states that his departure from Bonn is not to be interpreted as resignation, but as stemming from a desire to return to writing and the belief that not all parliamentarians should consider themselves as permanent incumbents until their death or pension, he has been criticised by Sontheimer in his book *Zeitenwende?* for his attitudes. Sontheimer takes him to task for not confronting and trying to bridge the gap between *Geist* and *Macht*, but rather retreating into the idealistic moral isolationism of the critical intellectual.[18]

It is possible to find instances in Lattmann's books that appear to reflect a lack of aptitude for politics. His first collection begins with the passage to which it owes its title:

> Hardly anyone is more abandoned than a member of parliament, who, after an evening meeting in his constituency, drives home at night behind his headlights for a hundred or more kilometres. After his role at the centre of discussion which he has just performed, isolation follows abruptly.[19]

However much sympathy one might feel, this claim does smack a little of self-pity. Equally, a proposition he makes about the workings of the economy of the Federal Republic is open to criticism both for over-simplification and for a lack of reality:

> Our economic system only functions so well because most of us constantly buy things of which we have no need at all to live. The republic has become cold. Nothing counts more than money. More and more often, we freeze in heated rooms.[20]

Even if the literary language is discounted, this passage reflects the unhealthy view sometimes found among some intellectuals that one individual is capable of determining another's needs. Lattmann is on firmer ground when he stresses the need for sensitivity and morality in politics. He also champions the individual parliamentarian frequently caught in crises of conscience, for instance between his own views and the overall requirement to support the party. In his own case, he was faced with this dilemma over the Schmidt government's anti-terrorist legislation. In the event, he became one of the four SPD members to vote against certain of the measures taken. He is justified in pointing out in *Die lieblose Republik* how well founded his scepticism was; the law introduced to prevent the glorification of violence, which could have threatened artistic freedom, was repealed in 1980, as it had proved futile.[21]

The acid test of Sontheimer's criticism is whether Lattmann goes beyond criticism of specific manifestations of the political system to reject the whole political process, in other words becomes non-political. If this is taken as a yardstick, then it must be concluded that Sontheimer exaggerates, even in the case of the more radical collection *Die lieblose Republik*. Lattmann remains aware of the realities of politics, for instance the need for a government to retain a majority in order to pursue its programme, whilst his portrait of the arch-pragmatist Helmut Schmidt is quite sympathetic. Furthermore, he is critical of those intellectuals whose comments reveal a naïve ignorance of economic matters.[22] In *Die Einsamkeit des Politikers* there is considerable awareness of the difficulties of politics, as expressed by Max Weber in his distinction between the ethic of the politician and that of the intellectual and in his celebrated image of politics as being 'boring down strongly and slowly through thick boards' — that is to say requiring infinite patience. It would therefore be inappropriate to accuse Lattmann of a total lack of realism.

In general terms, Lattmann's accounts of his experiences confirm the difficult relationships between the world of politics and that of writers. Herbert Wehner apparently greeted Lattmann on his entry to parliament by saying that the place had no need of poets. He himself speaks about 'a fundamentally damaged relationship' between writers and politicians.[23] In view of the long-standing difficulties, it is harsh of Sontheimer to blame Lattmann for not doing more to remedy the situation. It has to be concluded that writers' problems with the world of Bonn are a microcosm of the overall tensions between *Geist* and *Macht*.

Any attempt at a final assessment of the role of writers in the Federal Republic will inevitably involve a degree of generalisation. As was said in Chapter 7 on Grass, it is impossible to compute the number of times they have been right or the number of times they have erred, not least because it is impossible to reduce political issues in this way. Coupled with this difficulty there is the insoluble problem of the extent of their influence, if any. Nevertheless, even if scientific precision is impossible, it would be akin to cowardice to leave the matter there. Some attempt at a final assessment must be made; the subjectivity inherent in generalisation will, it is hoped, be accepted.

In contrast to Sontheimer, the present writer is led to the view that the political commitment of writers in the Federal Republic has been beneficial to the development of that country.[24] There may have been mistakes and excesses in some of the views expressed and in the manner of their expression, but these failings are outweighed by the major positive factor that the central issues have generally been identified and discussed: the need to confront the past, the establishment of democracy and the need to preserve peace, to name but three. Even the fact of commitment which has lasted far beyond the turmoil of the post-war years can be seen as valuable in itself, given the previous intellectual history of Germany.

Finally, it is important to point out that the Federal Republic, despite crises like the Spiegel Affair and the wave of terrorism in the 1970s, has remained a democratic state. What is more, it has advanced beyond the authoritarian democracy of the Adenauer era. Such achievements cannot be said to be simply the result of writers' efforts, but still less do they run counter to them. The democracy inherent in the country's Basic Law has remained a point of focus in many writers' commitment. An example of this is Walter Jens's statement in 1985 that the Basic Law must be the basis of political action, this despite the — possibly excessive — disappointment he expresses about the developments of the previous forty years.[25] It is also possible to see Grass's political activities as an attempt at sustaining the democratic state. If Peter Rühmkorf is to be believed, Grass suppressed his natural anarchistic temperament in his eulogies of tolerance and moderation.[26] Böll too seems to have been led to make sacrifices for his democratic conscience. It would in fact be hard to imagine the political life of the Federal Republic without the participation of intellectuals. Without doubt, such a state of affairs would impoverish the country's life and render its democracy less pluralistic.

For those to whom the idea of committed writers in a pluralistic society conjures up visions of moralising busybodies interfering with the efficient functioning of the state, it is worth quoting the frequently imprisoned Polish dissident Adam Michnik, whose experiences in a different kind of society lead him to a revealing conclusion: 'Where the power of morality no longer counts, the morality of strength begins to rule.'[27] I agree. If this view is misguided, I only ask, like Enzensberger, that others come and improve upon it.

240   *Conclusion*

Notes

1. H. Kohl, 'Für einen produktiven Konflikt. Die Intellektuellen und die CDU', *Die Zeit*, no. 19, 4 May 73.
2. *Das Parlament*, 1 Dec. 84.
3. *Stuttgarter Zeitung*, 4 Apr. 85.
4. Ibid.
5. The one incident since the advent of the Kohl government that has created a major stir was the refusal of the Interior Ministry to fund a film *Das Gespenst* (The spectre) by the Bavarian writer Herbert Achternbusch. Interior Minister Zimmermann considered the film blasphemous. Films, radio and television are the areas where political intervention in artistic freedom is potentially most likely. It must not be forgotten, however, that radio and television are largely under the control of the individual states.
6. H. Böll, 'Briefe an meine Söhne', *Die Zeit*, no. 12, 15 Mar. 85.
7. Reprinted in *The Listener*, 4 Jul. 85.
8. E. Kogon, 'Tag der Niederlage, Tag der Befreiung', *Die Zeit*, no. 17, 19 Apr. 85.
9. By contrast, in 1979 Enzensberger spoke somewhat disparagingly of those who demanded collective regret after the war. He says that the majority of people could not permit themselves psychologically 'really to understand what had happened' (Grimm, *Enzensberger*, p. 120). The point against facile moralising can be taken but some awareness of the past remains a moral imperative.
10. G. Grass, 'Die geschenkte Freiheit', *Die Zeit*, no. 20, 10 May 85.
11. *Das Parlament*, 11 May 85.
12. K. Sontheimer, *Das Elend unserer Intellektuellen* (Hoffmann und Campe, Hamburg, 1976), p. 63.
13. M./S. Greiffenhagen, *Ein schwieriges Vaterland* (Fischer, Frankfurt am Main, 1981), p. 182.
14. *Sunday Times*, 21. Jul. 85.
15. R. Baumgart, 'Götzendämmerung mit Nornen', *Der Spiegel*, no. 36, 2 Sep. 85, 188–92.
Baumgart's comment appears correct in that Böll's novel shows very little of the public aspects of political life. It concentrates on what goes on behind the scenes in one political party. The picture imparted is of endless extremely sordid intrigues and manoeuvres. As in most of Böll's novels there are those who manipulate — here too in many cases former National Socialists — and the sympathetic people who suffer. Among the latter group are the female characters alluded to in the title.
16. Greiffenhagen, *Ein schwieriges Vaterland*, p. 195.
17. D. Wellershoff, 'Deutschland — ein Schwebezustand' in Habermas, *Geistige Situation*, vol. 1, p. 78.
18. Sontheimer, *Zeitenwende?*, pp. 155–9.
19. D. Lattmann, *Die Einsamkeit des Politikers* (Fischer, Frankfurt am Main, 1981), p. 7.
20. D. Lattmann, *Die lieblose Republik* (Fischer, Frankfurt am Main, 1984), p. 146.
21. Ibid., p. 163f.
22. Ibid., p. 248.
23. Ibid., p. 45.
24. That both sides are equally to blame is the conclusion of Helmut M. Müller, whose survey of writers and politics is introduced by Sontheimer (see bibliography).
25. Quoted in *Media revue* (undated book catalogue for 8 May 1985), p. 4.
In his last major interview, Böll too affirmed his faith in a parliamentary system: H. Böll, 'Es stirbt täglich Freiheit weg', *Die Zeit*, no. 31, 26 Jul. 85.

26. Rühmkorf, *Die Jahre*, p. 134.
27. A. Michnik, 'Totalitäre Ruhe ist kein Frieden', *Der Spiegel*, no. 35, 26 Aug. 85, 110.

BIBLIOGRAPHY

Abromeit, H. and Burkhardt, K. 'Die Wählerinitiativen im Wahlkampf 1972', *Das Parlament*, 15 Sep. 73
Albertz, H. (ed.) *Warum ich Pazifist wurde* (Kindler, München, 1983)
Alt, F. *Frieden ist möglich* (Piper, München, Zürich, 1983)
Althammer, W. *Gegen den Terror* (Verlag Bonn Aktuell, Stuttgart, 1978)
Andersch, A. *Deutsche Literatur in der Entscheidung* (Verlag Volk und Zeit, Karlsruhe [1947])
Andres, S. 'Um die Freiheit unseres Handelns', *Die Kultur*, vol. 6, no. 113 (1958), 1–2
Arblaster, A. 'Ideology and Intellectuals' in R. Benewick, R. N. Berki and B. Parekh (eds) *Knowledge and Belief in Politics* (George Allen & Unwin, London, 1973), pp. 115–29
Arnold, H. L. (ed.) *Günter Grass — Dokumente zur politischen Wirkung* (Richard Boorberg Verlag, München, 1971)
—— *Als Schriftsteller leben* (Rowohlt, Reinbek bei Hamburg, 1979)
—— (ed.) *Die Gruppe 47* (Text und Kritik, München, 1980)
Baumann, M. *Wie alles anfing* (Anabas Verlag etc., Frankfurt am Main, 1977)
Baumgart, R. *Die verdrängte Phantasie* (Luchterhand, Darmstadt und Neuwied, 1973)
—— 'Götzendämmerung mit Nornen', *Der Spiegel*, no. 36, 2 Sep. 85, 188–92
Beloff, M. *The Intellectual in Politics and Other Essays* (Weidenfeld & Nicolson, London, 1970)
Benda, J. *La Trahison des clercs* (Bernard Grasset, Paris, 1928)
Bergsdorf, W. (ed.) *Die Intellektuellen* (Neske, Pfüllingen, 1982)
Berliner Begegnung zur Friedensförderung (Luchterhand, Darmstadt und Neuwied, 1982)
Bingel, H. (ed.) *Phantasie und Verantwortung* (Fischer, Frankfurt am Main, 1975)
Boehncke, H. and Richter, D. (eds) *Nicht heimlich und nicht kühl* (Ästhetik und Kommunikation Verlag, Berlin, 1977)
Böll, H. *Die verlorene Ehre der Katharina Blum* (DTV, München, 1976)
—— and Riese, H-P. 'Schriftsteller in dieser Republik', *L76*, no. 6 (1977), 5–37
—— *Essayistische Schriften und Reden* (3 vols., Kiepenhauer und Witsch, Köln, 1979)
—— *Vermintes Gelände* (Kiepenhauer und Witsch, Köln, 1982)
—— 'Keine Angst vor Systemveränderern', *die Tageszeitung*, 4 Mar. 83
—— *Bild Bonn Boenisch* (Lamuv Verlag, Bornheim-Merten, 1984)
—— 'Tausend Asylbewerber im Palais', *Der Spiegel*, no. 21, 2 Apr. 84, 40–1
—— 'Für Peter-Jürgen Boock', *Die Zeit*, no. 29, 13 Jul. 84
—— 'Briefe an meine Söhne', *Die Zeit*, no. 12, 15 Mar. 85
—— *Frauen vor Flusslandschaft* (Kiepenhauer und Witsch, Köln, 1985)
—— 'Es stirbt täglich Freiheit weg', *Die Zeit*, no. 31, 26 Jul. 85
Born, N. *Die erdabgewandte Seite der Geschichte* (Rowohlt, Reinbek bei Hamburg, 1979)
—— *Die Welt der Maschine* (Rowohlt, Reinbek bei Hamburg, 1980)
Bortkenhagen, F. H. U. (ed.) *Wehrkraftzersetzung* (Rowohlt, Reinbek bei Hamburg, 1984)
Brandt, P. and Ammon, H. (eds) *Die Linke und die nationale Frage* (Rowohlt, Reinbek bei Hamburg, 1981)

Brode, H. *Günter Grass* (Verlag C. H. Beck, München, 1979)
Buch, H. C. 'Von der möglichen Funktion der Literatur', *Kursbuch 20* (1970),
42–52
────── 'Deutschland — eine Winterreise', *Der Spiegel*, no. 11, 13 Mar.
78, 138–43
────── 'Herdentiere oder Einzelgänger'. Über die Krise des VS und die Möglich-
keiten ihrer Überwindung', *Vorwärts*, no. 13, 26 Mar. 83
Cepl-Kaufmann, G. *Günter Grass* (Scriptor Verlag, Kronberg/Ts., 1975)
Chomsky, N. *American Power and the New Mandarins* (Chatto & Windus,
London, 1969)
Coser, L. A. *Men of Ideas* (The Free Press, New York and London, 1961)
Dahrendorf, R. 'Der Intellektuelle und die Gesellschaft', *Die Zeit*, no. 13, 29 Mar.
63
Delius, F. C. *Kerbholz* (Rowohlt, Reinbek bei Hamburg, 1983)
Dutschke, R., Enzensberger, H. M. *et al.* 'Gespräch über die Zukunft', *Kursbuch
14* (1968), 146–74
Duve, F., Böll, H. and Staeck, K. (eds) *Briefe zur Verteidigung der Republik*
(Rowohlt, Reinbek bei Hamburg, 1977)
────── *Briefe zur Verteidigung der bürgerlichen Freiheit* (Rowohlt, Reinbek bei
Hamburg, 1978)
────── *Kämpfen für die Sanfte Republik* (Rowohlt, Reinbek bei Hamburg, 1980)
Eggebrecht, A. (ed.) *Die zornigen alten Männer* (Rowohlt, Reinbek bei Hamburg,
1979)
Ende, M. *The Neverending Story* (Penguin, Harmondsworth, 1984)
Enzensberger, H. M. *Einzelheiten I* (Suhrkamp, Frankfurt am Main, 1964)
────── *Politik und Verbrechen* (Suhrkamp, Frankfurt am Main, 1964)
────── 'Am I a German?', *Encounter*, vol. XXII, no. 4 (1964), 16–19
────── 'Europäische Peripherie', *Kursbuch 2* (1965), 154–73
────── *et al.* 'Katechismus zur deutschen Frage', *Kursbuch 4* (1966), 1–55
────── 'Was da im Bunker sitzt, das schlottert ja', *Der Spiegel*, no. 46, 14 Nov. 66,
78
────── *Deutschland, Deutschland unter anderem* (Suhrkamp, Frankfurt am Main,
1967)
────── *Staatsgefährdende Umtriebe* (Voltaire Flugschrift 11, Berlin, 1968)
────── 'Gemeinplätze, die Neueste Literatur betreffend', *Kursbuch 15* (1968),
187–97
────── 'Warum ich nicht in den USA bleibe', *Tagebuch*, März/April 1968, 12–13
────── *Selected Poems* (Penguin, Harmondsworth, 1968)
────── 'Notstand' in *Tintenfisch 2* (Verlag Klaus Wagenbach, Berlin, 1969),
pp. 19–20
────── *Das Verhör von Habana* (Suhrkamp, Frankfurt am Main, 1970)
────── *Gedichte 1955–1970* (Suhrkamp, Frankfurt am Main, 1971)
────── *The Consciousness Industry* (Seabury Press, New York, 1974)
────── *Palaver* (Suhrkamp, Frankfurt am Main, 1974)
────── 'Traktat vom Trampeln', *Der Spiegel*, no. 25, 14 Jun. 76, 40–1
────── *Der Untergang der Titanic* (Suhrkamp, Frankfurt am Main, 1982)
────── *Politische Brosamen* (Suhrkamp, Frankfurt am Main, 1982)
────── 'Der Triumph der *Bild-Zeitung* oder Die Katastrophe der Pressefreiheit',
Merkur, vol. 37, no. 6 (1983), 651–9
────── 'Armes Schweden', *Stern*, no. 13, 24 Apr. 83
────── 'Ein Bonner Memorandum', *Der Spiegel*, no. 48, 28 Nov. 83, 31–51
────── 'Ungarische Wirrungen', *Die Zeit*, no. 19, 3 May 85
────── 'Der arme Heinrich', *Der Spiegel*, no. 30, 22 Jul. 85, 137–8
Eppler, E., Ende, M. and Tächl, H. *Phantasie, Kultur, Politik* (Thienemanns
Verlag, Stuttgart, 1982)

Forbeck, K. and Wiesand, A. J. *Der Autorenreport* (Rowohlt, Reinbek bei Hamburg, 1972)

Frankfurter Hefte, vols 1–39 (1946–84)

Fuchs, J. *Einmischung in eigene Angelegenheiten* (Rowholt, Reinbek bei Hamburg, 1984)

Gegenwart, Die, vols 1–4 (1946–9)

Geiger, T. *Aufgaben und Stellung der Intelligenz in der Gesellschaft* (Ferdinand Enke Verlag, Stuttgart, 1949)

Girnus, W. 'Wer baute das siebentorige Theben', *Linkskurve*, no. 1/1984, 20–4

Grass, G. *Speak Out!* (Secker & Warburg, London, 1969)

—— *Über das Selbstverständliche* (DTV, München, 1969)

—— *Der Bürger und seine Stimme* (Luchterhand, Darmstadt und Neuwied, 1974)

—— *From the Diary of a Snail* (Secker & Warburg, London, 1974)

—— *Denkzettel* (Luchterhand, Darmstadt und Neuwied, 1978)

—— *Headbirths or the Germans are Dying Out* (Secker & Warburg, London, 1982)

—— 'Wir müssen lernen zu verzichten', *Der Spiegel*, no. 41, 11 Oct. 82, 252–63

—— *Widerstand lernen* (Luchterhand, Darmstadt und Neuwied, 1984)

—— 'Wir sind die Verfassungsschützer', *Die Zeit*, no. 9, 24 Feb. 84

—— 'Die geschenkte Freiheit', *Die Zeit*, no. 20, 10 May 85

Greiffenhagen, M./S. *Ein schwieriges Vaterland* (Fischer, Frankfurt am Main, 1981)

Greiner, U. 'Der Risiko-Spieler', *Die Zeit*, no. 9, 25 Feb. 83

—— 'Mut ohne Macht', *Die Zeit*, no. 39, 23 Sep. 83

Grimm, R. (ed.) *Hans Magnus Enzensberger* (Suhrkamp, Frankfurt am Main, 1984)

Grützbach, F. (ed.) *Freies Geleit für Ulrike Meinhof: Ein Artikel und seine Folgen* (Kiepenhauer und Witsch, Köln, 1972)

Haase, H. 'Ein Moralist und Meister des Wortes', *Neues Deutschland*, 18 Jul. 85

Habe, H. 'Leben für den Journalismus' (3 vols, Knaur, München, Zürich, 1976)

Habermas, J. (ed.) *Stichworte zur 'Geistigen Situation der Zeit'* (2 vols, Suhrkamp, Frankfurt am Main, 1979)

Hagelstange, R. 'Endstation Kühlschrank. Mass und Vernunft frieren ein', *Die Kultur*, vol. 6, no. 112 (1958), 2

Hochhuth, R. *Spitze des Eisbergs. Ein Reader* (Rowohlt, Reinbek bei Hamburg, 1982)

Hollington, M. *Günter Grass* (Marion Boyars, London, 1980)

Jacobsen, H-A. 'Vom Vergleich des Unvergleichbaren', *Die Zeit*, no. 50, 9 Dec. 83

Jens, W. *Deutsche Literatur der Gegenwart* (DTV, München, 1964)

—— *Republikanische Reden* (Kindler, München, 1976)

—— *Ort der Handlung ist Deutschland* (Kindler, München, 1981)

Karasek, H. 'Der unermüdliche Querkopf e.V.', *Der Spiegel*, no. 20, 14 May 84, 215

Karsunke, Y. 'Anachronistische Polemik', *Kursbuch 15* (1968), 165–8

Kogon, E. 'Tag der Niederlage, Tag der Befreiung', *Die Zeit*, no. 17, 19 Apr. 85

Kohl, H. 'Für einen produktiven Konflikt. Die Intellektuellen und die CDU', *Die Zeit*, no. 19, 4 May 73

Koopmann, H. 'Die Bundesrepublik Deutschland in der Literatur', *Zeitschrift für Politik*, vol. 26, no. 2 (1979), 161–78

Krueger, M. C. *Authors and Opposition* (Akademischer Verlag Hans-Dieter Heinz, Stuttgart, 1982)

Krüger, H. (ed.) *Was ist heute links?* (List, München, 1963)

—— 'Was bleiben sollte', *Die Zeit*, no. 33, 13 Aug. 71

Krüger, I. (ed.) *Mut zur Angst* (Luchterhand, Darmstadt und Neuwied, 1982)

Kuttenkeuler, W. (ed.) *Poesie und Politik* (Kohlhammer, Stuttgart, 1973)
Lattmann, D. (ed.) *Einigkeit der Einzelgänger* (Kindler, München, 1971)
—— (ed.) *Entwicklungsland Kultur* (Kindler, München, 1973)
—— *Die Einsamkeit des Politikers* (Fischer, Frankfurt am Main, 1982)
—— *Die lieblose Republik* (Fischer, Frankfurt am Main, 1984)
Leicht, R. (ed.) *Im Lauf des Jahres. Deutsche Texte und Dokumente 1981* (DTV, München, 1982)
Lipset, S. M. *Political Man* (Mercury Books, London, 1963)
Löwenthal, R. 'Die Intellektuellen zwischen Gesellschaftswandel und Kulturkrise' in H. Baier (ed.) *Freiheit und Sachzwang. Beiträge zu Ehren Helmut Schelskys* (Westdeutscher Verlag, Opladen, 1977), pp. 102–14
Mann, H. *Essays* (Claasen, Hamburg, 1960)
Mannheim, K. *Ideology and Utopia* (Routledge & Kegan Paul, London, 1968)
Michel, K. M. 'Ein Kranz für die Literatur', *Kursbuch 15* (1968), 169–86
Michnik, A. 'Totalitäre Ruhe ist kein Frieden', *Der Spiegel*, no. 35, 26 Aug. 85, 110–11
Mölling, H. *Heinrich Böll — eine christliche Position?* (Juris Druck und Verlag, Zürich, 1974)
Mülder, B. M. 'Nichts gegen die CDU', *Freibeuter 18* (1983), 76–83
Müller, H. M. *Die literarische Republik* (Beltz Verlag, Weinheim und Basel, 1982)
Neunzig, H. A. (ed.) *Der Ruf. Unabhängige Blätter für die junge Generation. Eine Auswahl* (Nymphenburger Verlagshandlung, München, 1976)
Nevermann, K. 'Die Linken und die Linke', *Die Zeit*, no. 41, 3 Oct. 80
Orwell, G. *Collected Essays* (Secker & Warburg, London, 1961)
Ost und West, vols 1–3 (1947–9)
Petersen, A. 'Nichts gegen die Arbeiterklasse', *TransAtlantik*, 2/1982, 77–80
Raddatz, F. J. 'Warum ich Pazifist bin', *Die Zeit*, no. 42, 9 Oct. 81
Richter, H. W. (ed.) *Die Mauer oder Der 13. August* (Rowohlt, Reinbek bei Hamburg, 1961)
—— (ed.) *Almanach der Gruppe 47* (Rowohlt, Reinbek bei Hamburg, 1962)
—— (ed.) *Bestandsaufnahme* (Kurt Desch, München, Wien, Basel, 1962)
—— (ed.) *Plädoyer für eine neue Regierung oder Keine Alternative* (Rowohlt, Reinbek bei Hamburg, 1965)
—— *Briefe an einen jungen Sozialisten* (Hoffmann und Campe, Hamburg, 1974)
Rühmkorf, P. *Die Jahre die Ihr kennt* (Rowohlt, Reinbek bei Hamburg, 1972)
Runge, E. (ed.) *Bottroper Protokolle* (Suhrkamp, Frankfurt am Main, 1968)
Schallück, P. *Zum Beispiel* (Europäische Verlagsanstalt, Frankfurt am Main, 1962)
Schelsky, H. *Die Arbeit tun die anderen* (DTV, München, 1977)
Scheuch, E. K. 'Die Arroganz der Ängstlichkeit', *Die Zeit*, no. 47, 13 Nov. 81
Schirmacher, W. 'Post-Moderne — Ein Einspruch', *Konkursbuch 11* (1984), 9–13
Schmidt, B. and Schwenger, H. (eds) *Die Stunde Eins* (DTV, München, 1982)
Schmidt, H. 'Fürchtet Euch nicht', *Die Zeit*, no. 52, 23 Dec. 83
Schneider, P. *Lenz* (Rotbuch Verlag, Berlin, 1973)
—— *. . . schon bist du ein Verfassungsfeind* (Rotbuch Verlag, Berlin, 1975)
—— *Atempause* (Rowohlt, Reinbek bei Hamburg, 1977)
—— 'Keine Lust aufs grüne Paradies', *Kursbuch 74* (1983), 80–8
—— 'Plädoyer für einen Verräter', *Der Spiegel*, no. 7, 13 Feb. 84, 66–9
—— *Der Mauerspringer* (Luchterhand, Darmstadt und Neuwied, 1984)
—— and Boock, P.-J. 'Gespräche eines Schiffbrüchigen mit einem Bewohner des Festlandes', *Die Zeit*, no. 15, 5 Apr. 85
Schreiber, H. 'Dabei sein ist out', *Der Spiegel*, no. 37, 6 Sep. 76, 46–52
'Schriftsteller und SPD', *Die neue Gesellschaft*, vol. 25, no. 11 (1978), 864–76
Schumpeter, J. A. *Capitalism, Socialism and Democracy* (Unwin University Books, London, 1970)

Schütte, W. 'Entfernung von der Truppe', *Frankfurter Rundschau*, 18 Jul. 85

Schwab-Felisch, H. (ed.) *Der Ruf. Eine deutsche Nachkriegszeitschrift* (DTV, München, 1962)

Siblewski, D. (ed.) *Martin Walser* (Suhrkamp, Frankfurt am Main, 1981)

Sieburg, F. 'Frieden mit Thomas Mann', *Die Gegenwart*, vol. 4, no. 14 (1949), 14–16

Sontheimer, K. *Das Elend unserer Intellektuellen* (Hoffmann und Campe, Hamburg, 1976)

⸻ *Zeitenwende?* (Hoffmann und Campe, Hamburg, 1983)

⸻ 'Brauchen wir eine Vision der Zukunft', *Neue Rundschau*, vol. 95, nos. 1/2 (1984), 155–62

Stein, P. (ed.) *Theorie der politischen Dichtung* (Nymphenburger Verlagshandlung, München, 1973)

Strauss, B. *Paare Passanten* (Carl Hanser Verlag, München und Wien, 1981)

Vaterland, Muttersprache. Deutsche Schriftsteller und ihr Staat (Verlag Klaus Wagenbach, Berlin, 1979)

Wagenbach, K. 'Über das geistige Befinden der Republikaner angesichts eines Landesfürsten', *Freibeuter 3* (1980), 18–24

Wallraff, G. *Der Aufmacher* (Kiepenhauer und Witsch, Köln, 1977)

Walser, M. 'Jener Intellektuelle', *Akzente*, vol. 3, no. 2 (1956), 134–7

⸻ (ed.) *Die Alternative oder Brauchen wir eine neue Regierung* (Rowohlt, Reinbek bei Hamburg, 1961)

⸻ 'Vorwort' in E. Wiesel, *Die Nacht zu begraben, Elischa* (Bechtle Verlag, München und Esslingen, 1963), pp. 5–9

⸻ *Erfahrungen und Leseerfahrungen* (Suhrkamp, Frankfurt am Main, 1965)

⸻ 'Praktiker, Weltfremde und Vietnam', *Kursbuch 9* (1967), 168–76

⸻ *Heimatkunde* (Suhrkamp, Frankfurt am Main, 1968)

⸻ 'Rede an eine Mehrheit', *Kürbiskern*, 2/1969, pp. 335–9

⸻ *Die Gallistl'sche Krankheit* (Suhrkamp, Frankfurt am Main, 1972)

⸻ *Wie und wovon handelt Literatur* (Suhrkamp, Frankfurt am Main, 1973)

⸻ *Wer ist ein Schriftsteller?* (Suhrkamp, Frankfurt am Main, 1979)

⸻ (ed.) *Die Würde am Werktag* (Fischer, Frankfurt am Main, 1980)

⸻ 'Beweise aus dem Revier', *Die Weltwoche*, no. 6, 9 Feb. 84

⸻ 'Tartuffe weiss, wer er ist', *Die Weltwoche*, no. 5, 31 Jan. 85

⸻ 'In den April geschickt', *Die Weltwoche*, no. 14, 4 Apr. 85

⸻ 'Amerikanisches Allerlei', *Die Weltwoche*, no. 17, 25 Apr. 85

⸻ 'Hoffnungsloser Vorschlag', *Die Weltwoche*, no. 26, 27 Jun. 85

Weiss, P. and Enzensberger, H. M. 'Eine Kontroverse', *Kursbuch 6* (1966), 165–76

' "Wenn ich so dächte wie Kunert, möchte ich lieber tot sein." Ein Zeit-Gespräch zwischen Wolf Biermann, Günter Kunert und Fritz J. Raddatz', *Die Zeit*, no. 47, 14 Nov. 80

Werner, W. *Vom Waisenhaus ins Zuchthaus* (Suhrkamp, Frankfurt am Main, 1969)

Weyrauch, W. (ed.) *Ich lebe in der Bundesrepublik. Fünfzehn Deutsche über Deutschland* (List, München, 1961)

Wildermuth, R. (ed.) *Heute und die 30 Jahre davor* (Ellermann Verlag, München, 3. Auflage, 1979)

Wolf, C. *Kassandra* (Luchterhand, Darmstadt und Neuwied, 1983)

Zensuren nach 20 Jahren Bundesrepublik (Verlag Wissenschaft und Politik, Köln, 1969)

Zimmer, D. E. 'Ein Kapitel Geist und Macht', *Die Zeit*, no. 21, 17 May 74

⸻ 'Deine Angst und meine Angst', *Die Zeit*, no. 47, 13 Nov. 81

Zweite Berliner Begegnung. Den Frieden fördern (Luchterhand, Darmstadt und Neuwied, 1983)

Zwerenz, G. 'Deutschland, automatisiertes Schlachtfeld', *die Tageszeitung*, 22 Apr. 83

INDEX

247